# Approaches to Teaching Pynchon's *The Crying of Lot 49* and Other Works

# Approaches to Teaching Pynchon's *The Crying of Lot 49* and Other Works

Edited by

*Thomas H. Schaub*

The Modern Language Association of America
New York 2008

Library of Congress Cataloging-in-Publication Data

Approaches to teaching Pynchon's The crying of lot 49 and other works / edited by Thomas H. Schaub.
p. cm.—(Approaches to teaching world literature series ; 99)
Includes bibliographical references and index.
ISBN: 978-0-87352-813-9 (hardcover)
ISBN: 978-0-87352-814-6 (pbk.)
1. Pynchon, Thomas—Study and teaching. 2. Pynchon, Thomas—Criticism and interpretation. 3. Pynchon, Thomas. Crying of lot 49. I. Schaub, Thomas H., 1947–
PS3566.Y55Z55 2008 813'.54—dc22 2007044729

ISSN 1059-1133

Cover illustration: *Bordando el manto terrestre* (1961), by Remedios Varo (1908–63). Oil on masonite

POD 2021 (first printing)

Published by The Modern Language Association of America
85 Broad Street, Suite 500, New York, New York 10004-2434
www.mla.org

# CONTENTS

**Preface to the Series** vii

**Preface to the Volume** ix

**PART ONE: MATERIALS**
*Thomas H. Schaub*

Novels and Short Fiction 3
Miscellaneous Writing 4
Biographical Materials 4
Pynchon's Reception 5
Book-Length Studies 6
Essay Collections 7
Uncollected Essays: Women, Gender, and Other Topics 8
Background Studies 8
Science and Literature 9
Literary Traditions 9
Handbooks, Reference Guides, and Web Sites 10
Bibliography 10

**PART TWO: APPROACHES**

**Literary Heritage, Influence, and Context**

Teaching *Crying*: General Education, the 1960s, and *Lot 49* 13
*Robert N. Watson*

Pynchon's Quest Narratives and the Tradition of American Romance 25
*Deborah L. Madsen*

Pynchon's Library 31
*Thomas H. Schaub*

Reading the Value System of *Gravity's Rainbow* with Marcuse, Freud, and the Yippies 39
*Molly Hite*

"Feeling Totally Familied Out": Teaching Pynchon through Families 46
*Mark Rohland*

**Teaching *The Crying of Lot 49***

Reading Race: *The Crying of Lot 49* and Early Pynchon 52
*Steven Weisenburger*

Teaching the Epochal Oedipa: *The Crying of Lot 49* as Political Dialogue 59
*Jerry Varsava*

*Lot 49*: Science and the Novel of Systems 66
*Stacey Olster*

Humor and Decentered Meaning in *Lot 49* 76
*Alison T. J. Preston*

Tragic Satire: Chasing Nazi Symbols in *The Crying of Lot 49* 83
*Inger H. Dalsgaard*

**Empire, History, and Postmodern Space**

Teaching Pynchon's V. 88
*David Cowart*

To Historicize Is to Colonize: Colonialism in V. and *Gravity's Rainbow* 99
*Michael Harris*

Antwerp and the Representation of the Holocaust in *Gravity's Rainbow* 106
*Luc Herman*

Mediating the Past: Narrative, History, and Teaching *Vineland* 114
*Robert L. McLaughlin*

Historiographic Metafiction / Metafictional Historiography: The *Mason & Dixon* Project 121
*Hanjo Berressem and Norbert Finzsch*

Postmodern Territories: Teaching *Mason & Dixon* and the Ideologies of Space 130
*Amy J. Elias*

**Reading Practices**

Pynchon's Polyvocality 141
*Gary Thompson*

Hypertextualizing *The Crying of Lot 49* 148
*Todd Rohman*

Teaching *Gravity's Rainbow*: Correlation in Life and Reading 155
*Alan Nadel*

Pynchon, Kant, Lyotard, and the Sublime 163
*Zofia Kolbuszewska*

**Notes on Contributors** 169

**Survey Participants** 173

**Works Cited** 175

**Index** 191

## PREFACE TO THE SERIES

In *The Art of Teaching* Gilbert Highet wrote, "Bad teaching wastes a great deal of effort, and spoils many lives which might have been full of energy and happiness." All too many teachers have failed in their work, Highet argued, simply "because they have not thought about it." We hope that the Approaches to Teaching World Literature series, sponsored by the Modern Language Association's Publications Committee, will not only improve the craft—as well as the art—of teaching but also encourage serious and continuing discussion of the aims and methods of teaching literature.

The principal objective of the series is to collect within each volume different points of view on teaching a specific literary work, a literary tradition, or a writer widely taught at the undergraduate level. The preparation of each volume begins with a wide-ranging survey of instructors, thus enabling us to include in the volume the philosophies and approaches, thoughts and methods of scores of experienced teachers. The result is a sourcebook of material, information, and ideas on teaching the subject of the volume to undergraduates.

The series is intended to serve nonspecialists as well as specialists, inexperienced as well as experienced teachers, graduate students who wish to learn effective ways of teaching as well as senior professors who wish to compare their own approaches with the approaches of colleagues in other schools. Of course, no volume in the series can ever substitute for erudition, intelligence, creativity, and sensitivity in teaching. We hope merely that each book will point readers in useful directions; at most each will offer only a first step in the long journey to successful teaching.

Joseph Gibaldi
Series Editor

# PREFACE TO THE VOLUME

From his first story, "Mortality and Mercy in Vienna," published in Cornell University's *Epoch* (1959), to the publication of *Against the Day* (2006), Thomas Pynchon's fiction composes one of the most important bodies of American fiction of the last fifty years. Emerging in the 1950s, Pynchon entered a literary world dominated by Ralph Ellison, Norman Mailer, James Jones, Jack Kerouac, J. D. Salinger, and Saul Bellow, to mention the most obvious, but with the publication of *V.* (1963), which won the PEN Faulkner award for best first novel, Pynchon inaugurated a new generation, his influence visible in the fictions of writers from Don DeLillo to David Foster Wallace, Richard Powers, and Neal Stephenson. At first, *V.* and then *The Crying of Lot 49* were sorted into the new categories of black humor, fabulation, and metafiction, but *Gravity's Rainbow* (1973), *Vineland* (1990), *Mason & Dixon* (1997), and *Against the Day* have taught readers to see his work as a prolonged meditation on the politics of modern social history—fundamentally that of the United States and "the West"—on an international canvas commensurate with the colonialist enterprises of First World nations.

This focus on the politics and economics of modern social history gives his writing a special relevance to our time, especially given the profession's current preoccupation with postcolonialism and the redefinition of American studies. It is worth bearing in mind that Pynchon came to maturity as a writer during the struggle for civil rights at home and the unseating of colonial powers around the globe. These developments apparently left their mark on Pynchon's imagination, for his work presages by many years the emergence of postcolonial studies and the postnational perspective of the new American studies.

Pynchon's entire oeuvre deploys unusually broad historical learning that constitutes a kind of quirky but substantive counterhistory of the modern world. The myriad pixels of this historical detail form a picture projected onto the screen of the reader's consciousness by the paranoid inquiries of characters and narrators. This "operational paranoia" (*Gravity's Rainbow* 25), to switch metaphors, serves as a survival device as well as a narrative search engine, the central analytic tool of the informing imagination of the early novels. For example, Stencil's search for "V" in Pynchon's first book allows the author to connect von Trotha's extermination of the Herero in South-West Africa with Eigenvalue's plastic surgery practice in New York City, the two apparently unrelated activities united by the paranoid suspicion that the twentieth century is witness to the progressive dehumanization of mankind. This dizzying paranoid history shares the antisystem Manichaeanism of the Vietnam era, present in such books as Ken Kesey's *One Flew over the Cuckoo's Nest*, Robert Coover's *The Public Burning*, and Marge Piercy's *Woman on the Edge of Time*, though unlike these novels Pynchon's are suspicious of their own systems of meaning and the reader's efforts to construct them.

Equally pertinent, the major political movements of the time—African nationalism, civil rights, feminism, and the antiwar movement of the Vietnam years—motivated a renewed understanding of the politics of writing history. Writers like John Barth, Truman Capote, and William Styron began to explore the boundary between fiction and history, but the underlying politics of historical narrative—who writes the history, using what materials, from what point of view, and with what narrative devices—came to the fore in experimental novels like Ishmael Reed's *Mumbo Jumbo* and in the appearance in American literature of formerly invisible histories and cultures, in such books as N. Scott Momaday's *House Made of Dawn*, Maxine Hong Kingston's *The Woman Warrior*, and Raymond Barrio's *The Plum Plum Pickers*. Sometimes categorized as the new journalism, works by Mailer, Capote, Joan Didion, Hunter Thompson, Tom Wolfe, and others featured a subjective viewpoint of historical accounts. Hayden White published *Metahistory* (which theorized the discursive, textual nature of history) the same year that *Gravity's Rainbow* appeared.

This recognition that narrative design and intention are shared by fiction and history alike—as well as its corollary that a fixed real or referential ground is always already textualized—is itself a fundamental feature of postmodern writing, one disparaged by Fredric Jameson as a "kind of flatness or depthlessness" of historical affect (*Postmodernism; or, The Cultural Logic* 9) but viewed more positively in Linda Hutcheon's "historiographic metafiction" concept (*Poetics* 5). At the same time, the picaresque quest narratives that mediate Pynchon's ambitious historicism enact a high degree of the stylistic pastiche characteristic of the postmodern aesthetic, mixing modes of popular culture—pop art, comics, limericks, musicals, and movies—with traditions of "high seriousness." *The Crying of Lot 49*, in particular, is frequently understood to dramatize the pivot between modernism and postmodernism, since the novel's heroine, Oedipa Maas, is a kind of noir modernist detective whose searches discover a postmodern textuality resistant to her best efforts to locate origin or connect signs to a freestanding truth.

Another feature of Pynchon's imagination, and another reason to teach his fiction, is that for him science and the humanities are not separate cultures but are fully integral in human experience and history. This isn't simply a matter of his drawing on a fairly elementary history of science for anecdotes and metaphors—such as his application of entropy to biological and social systems, an idea he borrows from *The Human Use of Human Beings*, Norbert Wiener's book on cybernetics for a lay audience (Wiener's original text was *Cybernetics*). Scientific ideas and their application through engineering are in Pynchon's synthesis vital elements in the lives of societies and as such are no less significant than political or aesthetic ideas and just as rich a source of understanding. Science and engineering are not other to the humanities but foundational, especially when harnessed by capital. As Richard Poirier writes in "The Importance of Thomas Pynchon," "Science, the analytical method, technology . . . are also a corporate expression of consciousness; they express us all as much as do [Wordsworth's] lyrical ballads" (25).

Among the reasons to read and teach Pynchon are his command of myriad stylistic registers, his masterful control of idiom and vernacular, his talent for creating literature from the debris of culture, and his sense of culture as the debris of discursive history. Teachers might help students recognize Pynchon's ability to generate historical atmosphere and to create sentences mesmerizing in their rhythm and sound, their design a complex architecture of connected images and ideas. Instead of merely teaching students to appreciate style for its own sake, one might point to the description of Mucho's car lot to show them how the eloquence expended on this lowly subject implies value, reminiscent of William Carlos Williams's "cinquefoil in the parched places" or Allen Ginsberg's "Sunflower Sutra." Alternatively, one may note in *Gravity's Rainbow* the narrator's reflections on the piles of lead toothpaste tubes saved to make bullets, while mouthwash bubbles in the Thames, connecting the bedtime brushing of teeth and reading of *Dumbo the Elephant* with World War II.

All these elements—historical learning and historicism, postmodernism and its integration of high and low cultures, science and literature, his control over prose—contribute to Pynchon's stature and make him worth reading and teaching, but many readers, including undergraduate and graduate students, find these aspects of his fiction more than a little daunting. To make matters worse, Pynchon's novels (like any number of modern novels) resist reading, thematize reading, and frustrate reader expectations. Pynchon has had little or nothing to say about these difficulties and more than most authors maintains an almost complete absence from public life. Among other goals, this collection aims to help teachers and students meet these challenges.

The resources gathered in part 1, "Materials," provide essential background on Pynchon's writing career and biography, secondary sources, guides, and bibliography. The essays collected in part 2 have been grouped into four sections. The first section, "Literary Heritage, Influence, and Context," begins with Robert Watson's essay about his experience of teaching *The Crying of Lot 49* to "aspiring scientists." For Watson, *Lot 49* not only provides a vehicle for teaching his students something about the 1960s but also offers them a picture of suffering and a "sense of the tragic" in human experience. Deborah Madsen situates Pynchon's quest narratives within conventions unique to American literature, from the Puritans and the writers of the American Renaissance to Pynchon himself. My own essay focuses on a small number of influential books of the 1950s and early 1960s that contributed to the ideas and structures of *Lot 49*. Molly Hite adds to this context an argument about the influence of Herbert Marcuse's *Eros and Civilization* on the underlying assumptions and values of *Gravity's Rainbow*. Mark Rohland suggests that asking students to read Pynchon's novels in "the context of something recognizable—families" helps them gain confidence in their ability to read these novels. Once their confidence is established, this point of access may be used to introduce other aspects of the fiction, including war, repression, and sadism. Written before publication of *Against the Day*, Rohland's essay finds confirmation in the expanded focus on family in Pynchon's most recent novel.

In the second section, "Teaching *The Crying of Lot 49*," are grouped essays that confront head-on the challenges of teaching *Lot 49*. While race has been a common topic in scholarship on *Gravity's Rainbow* and later work, Steven Weisenburger shows it to be a significant issue in *Lot 49* and Pynchon's early fiction as well. Jerry Varsava helps us see how Pynchon's novel can be understood as delineating a "site of liberal accommodation and compromise" between political positions on the left and right, while Stacey Olster situates Pynchon's novel in a course on the "systems novel" in contemporary fiction and suggests ways to deactivate student "science phobia." Alison Preston focuses on Pynchon's humor: off-putting to readers expecting high seriousness, this humor, Preston shows, establishes a kind of epistemological pivot between absurdity and meaningfulness. Inger Dalsgaard confronts the uneasiness students in her classroom often feel when they encounter Nazi references in apparently comic registers and uses this uneasiness as an opening into the recognition of the persistence of history in shaping the present.

The essays categorized in the third section, "Empire, History, and Postmodern Space," take up, from varying perspectives, the problematic relations among history, historiography, fiction, and empire. In the only essay in this volume devoted completely to Pynchon's first novel, David Cowart shows how to teach *V.* as a text about the pursuit of pattern and meaning in history, which, Cowart argues, Pynchon represents as a necessary though impossible enterprise. Michael Harris teaches the complicity of such efforts to structure history in *V.* and *Gravity's Rainbow* with colonialism. In an essay on representing the Holocaust, Luc Herman theorizes the presence of "laten[t]" or oblique historiography as part of Pynchon's narrative strategy in *Gravity's Rainbow*, and Robert McLaughlin shows concretely how he guides his students in their analysis of individual passages of *Vineland* to teach them ways that narrative mediates the past. The last two essays in this group, by Hanjo Berressem and Norbert Finzsch and by Amy Elias, demonstrate how to teach students to map *Mason & Dixon*. Berressem and Finzsch worked together as scholars of American literature and history to explain how the novel maps the discourses of historiography and fiction onto each other, in what they call a "twisted topology"; while Elias describes her experience teaching *Mason & Dixon* in a course titled Postmodern Territories.

Essays that focus on reading practices that the authors suggest to their students, as well as those practices that Pynchon's writing seems to require of the reader, are grouped in the last section, "Reading Practices." Gary Thompson shares his experience using Bakhtinian ideas to help students engage the multiplicity of voices in Pynchon's novels and to stress the social nature of reading. Todd Rohman suggests teaching *The Crying of Lot 49* as if the novel were a hypertext, which, he argues, helps students set aside their desire for convergence and coherence and learn to experience the novel as a text that opens out into multiple realms like a Web site does. In a related essay, Alan Nadel's approach to *Gravity's Rainbow* forces readers to confront the limitations of seeking comprehension through "acts of correlation." Finally, Zofia Kolbuszewska suggests reading *The Crying of Lot 49* from the vantage point of the sublime, as theorized by Immanuel Kant (*The Critique of Judgment*) and more recently by Jean-François Lyotard (*The Postmodern Condition*).

Though each of these essays offers a distinct approach to Thomas Pynchon's fiction, they have common and overlapping interests in narrative technique, in the representation of social justice (and its absence), in the ethics of representation, and in the interaction of character with global commerce and politics—in short, they display a shared conviction of the importance of Pynchon's work and its significance as a subject of teaching and study.

A number of people helped in the preparation of this volume: my thanks go to the contributors, for their willingness to share their ideas about teaching Pynchon and for their patience with my responses to their drafts; to Bernard Duyfhuizen and David Cowart, early readers of the project proposal, for their suggestions; to Margit Longbrake at the MLA, for the good humor and clear instructions with which she helped me through the stages of production; and especially to Eileen Ewing, a force for order and editorial expertise, who assisted me in all stages of compiling the book.

*Part One*

# MATERIALS

# Novels and Short Fiction

As of this writing, Thomas Pynchon has published six novels and one collection of his short fiction: *V.* (1963), *The Crying of Lot 49* (1966), *Gravity's Rainbow* (1973), *Slow Learner: Early Stories* (1984), *Vineland* (1990), *Mason & Dixon* (1997), and *Against the Day* (2006). Of this work, the most accessible and frequently anthologized are the short story "Entropy" and his second novel, *The Crying of Lot 49*. Often these are taught in combination because the story "Entropy" overtly, even schematically, introduces Pynchon's application of scientific concepts—as metaphors—to social and political situations. The idea of entropy, in thermodynamics and information theory, remains a central idea in Pynchon's novels of the 1960s and in *Gravity's Rainbow*, but is exploited to full effect in *The Crying of Lot 49*, whose heroine discovers an alternative relationship to her society, one she finds energizing even though it alienates her from the mainstream. Like *The Great Gatsby*, with which it has much in common, the concentrated brevity of *Lot 49* fits easily on a syllabus, offering instructor and students time to struggle with the novel's rich complexities.

*The Crying of Lot 49*, Pynchon's second novel, and *Vineland*, his fourth, form a pair: the first shows the consciousness-raising of a housewife in the 1960s, while the second serves as a coda to the 1960s from the standpoint of Reagan's America in the early 1980s. Moreover, in *Vineland* Pynchon depicts the 1960s counterculture as complicit in its own demise. This complicity seems already present in the fourth book of *Gravity's Rainbow* as the Counterforce loses interest in Slothrop and develops its own bureaucratic language.

In sharp contrast to *Lot 49* and *Vineland*, Pynchon's four major novels are lengthy, dense productions, employing a multitude of characters, depicting an international social and political tapestry, from the Fashoda incident (1898) to the Suez crisis (1956) in *V.*, from the Enlightenment in *Mason & Dixon* to the mid-1970s at the close of *Gravity's Rainbow*, and from the Chicago World's Fair to post–World War I Hollywood in *Against the Day*. These features shouldn't prevent instructors from teaching these novels—after all, we continue to teach *Moby Dick* and *Ulysses*—but they do require that special attention be given to approaching these novels and situating them in a course. A number of the essays in this volume suggest ways to do so. Of the three novels, *Gravity's Rainbow* is by most accounts Pynchon's tour de force, likely to remain his most remarkable, even charismatic achievement.

NOTE

Unless otherwise indicated, all textual references to Pynchon's fiction refer to the first-published editions of his novels and the short story collection.

## Miscellaneous Writing

In addition to numerous blurbs written for book jackets, Pynchon has published a few essays and book reviews. In "Is It O.K. to be a Luddite?" he writes about technology in literary history. One of his most important essays is "A Journey into the Mind of Watts," which appeared in 1966 and in which Pynchon meditated on the Watts riots and racial culture in the United States. Set beside his letter to Thomas F. Hirsch on the sources for chapter 9 of *V.* (reprinted in Seed 240–43) and the Herero of South-West Africa, these two essays give us some sense of Pynchon's thinking about race and colonial imperialism. Asked by the *New York Times Book Review* to write about one of the seven deadly sins, Pynchon wrote on sloth in "Nearer, My Couch, to Thee" (1993). Pynchon offers the most we have about his own development as a writer in the introduction he wrote to *Slow Learner: Early Stories*. The introductions to reissues of Richard Fariña's novel *Been Down So Long It Looks Like Up to Me* and Orwell's *1984* also offer valuable insight to Pynchon's ideas and values. Of his book reviews, the most notable is "The Heart's Eternal Vow," his review of *Autumn of the Patriarch*, by Gabriel García Márquez, for the *New York Times Book Review*.

## Biographical Materials

Pynchon biography is as much the stuff of legend as of fact, for one of its cardinal features is that we have had almost no access to Pynchon the author and thus know little about his personal life. Pynchon's determination to guard his privacy is respected by his family and friends, and as a result those interested in Pynchon the person have had to settle for rumor and "sightings." There exist but a few photographs: some yearbook pictures from high school and one photograph on the back of the dust jacket of David Cowart's *Thomas Pynchon: The Art of Allusion*—a mid-1950s shot of Pynchon as a young man dressed in navy uniform. (Unfortunately, many of the libraries holding copies of Cowart's book long ago discarded the jacket.)

One cannot help associating this avoidance of publicity with his fiction's celebration of the "preterite," those who are passed over by power and history, and of the discourse of "the underground" in a period of United States history marked by the New Left, civil rights workers in Mississippi, the Black Panthers, the Weathermen, feminism, and the antiwar and free speech movements. Nor can one help reading a biographical clue in Oedipa's discovery that many citizens are engaged in "a calculated withdrawal, from the life of the Republic" (*Lot 49* 124).

Several recitations of the facts about Pynchon's life are available. Matthew Winston's early essay "The Quest for Pynchon" (1975) reveals that we know more about the Pynchon family and its history than about Pynchon himself, but is still a very useful resource. Patrick O'Donnell's biographical summary, in his introduction to *New Essays on* The Crying of Lot 49 (1991) includes a bit more personal information or, as O'Donnell writes, "speculation concerning the lack of information," from Richard Fariña's memoir *Long Time Coming and a Long Time Gone*, Helen Dudar's "Pynchon: The Man Who Won't Come to Dinner," Brian McHale's "Thomas Pynchon: A Portrait of the Artist as a Missing Person," and Michael Hartnett's "Thomas Pynchon's Long Island Years," among other sources. Steven Weisenburger gives an account of an autobiographical sketch that Pynchon wrote in the summer of 1959 for a Ford Foundation Fellowship ("Thomas Pynchon"). Although Pynchon had the Ford Foundation close his file, several photocopies were made available to scholars, with the stipulation that they cannot be reproduced in any form. Apparently Weisenburger has one of these copies or has seen one, because his essay provides a detailed description of its contents and is well worth reading. Two long footnotes in Weisenburger's essay also list the extant biographical information on Pynchon's life (693nn3–4). Pynchon also makes cameo appearances in David Hajdu's *Positively 4th Street: The Lives and Times of Joan Baez, Bob Dylan, Mimi Baez Fariña, and Richard Fariña*.

## Pynchon's Reception

In *Marginal Forces / Cultural Centers*, Michael Bérubé comments on the curious fact that Pynchon enjoys a place among the canonized elite of postmodern writers yet retains a cult status, as if he were at the margins ignored by the cognoscenti. On the contrary, his first novel, *V.*, won the Faulkner First Novel Prize, *The Crying of Lot 49* won the Richard and Hilda Rosenthal Foundation Award of the National Institute of Arts and Letters, and *Gravity's Rainbow* was heralded as confirming Pynchon's place among the greatest writers of the twentieth century and, along with Isaac Bashevis Singer's *"A Crown of Feathers" and Other Stories*, won the 1974 National Book Award for fiction. In the same year, *Gravity's Rainbow* was nominated for the Pulitzer Prize. Pynchon also won the Howells Medal of the National Institute of Arts and Letters (1975) for all his work to date. Despite this public approbation, Pynchon continues to enjoy a cult status among his readers, perhaps in part because he spoofed the National Book Award by sending the comedian Irwin Corey to accept the award and rejected outright the Howells Medal. Adding to Pynchon's notoriety, the prize committee for the Pulitzer was overruled by the Pulitzer advisory board, partly on the grounds that *Gravity's Rainbow* is obscene.

# Book-Length Studies

Critical study of the stories and novels existed early in the 1970s, but when *Gravity's Rainbow* appeared, Pynchon scholarship and criticism began in earnest. Issues of *Critique* (J. Young) and *Twentieth Century Literature* (Levine and Leverenz, *Essays*) were devoted wholly or in part to his work, and in 1979 the journal *Pynchon Notes* was founded. At this writing there are over thirty-five full-length studies devoted to Pynchon's novels and short stories, including studies of single novels. A search of the MLA bibliography produces more than a thousand articles focused wholly or in part on his work. At this writing, no studies of Pynchon's most recent novel (save for book reviews) have appeared. A roundtable discussion on *Against the Day* took place at the International Narrative Conference in Washington (March 2007).

For analysis of central themes, narrative techniques, and research into Pynchon's allusions and knowledge base, respondents to the questionnaire sent out by the MLA to instructors most often cited Cowart's *Thomas Pynchon: The Art of Allusion*, Molly Hite's *Ideas of Order in the Novels of Thomas Pynchon*, Thomas Schaub's *Pynchon: The Voice of Ambiguity*, Joseph Slade's *Thomas Pynchon*, Deborah Madsen's *The Postmodernist Allegories of Thomas Pynchon*, and Peter Cooper's *Signs and Symptoms: Thomas Pynchon and the Contemporary World*. David Seed's *The Fictional Labyrinths of Thomas Pynchon*, another book frequently referenced, includes a valuable appendix: a letter Pynchon wrote in response to an inquiry from Thomas F. Hirsch about the research that went into the writing of *V.*'s chapter 9 (Pynchon, "Pynchon's Reading"). Tony Tanner's *Thomas Pynchon*, which provides a short introduction to Pynchon's oeuvre, was widely mentioned, especially as a study that may be assigned to undergraduates.

Several studies of single novels were noted by respondents, including Kathryn Hume's *Pynchon's Mythography: An Approach to* Gravity's Rainbow and Thomas Moore's *The Style of Connectedness:* Gravity's Rainbow. Recent studies of *Mason & Dixon* include Charles Clerc's *Mason & Dixon & Pynchon* and Joakim Sigvardson's *Immanence and Transcendence in Thomas Pynchon's* Mason & Dixon*: A Phenomenological Study*. A collection of essays on *Mason & Dixon* is described below.

The changes in interpretive paradigms occasioned by the influence of continental philosophy and the emergence of theory have yet to register a major effect on students and scholars of Pynchon's fiction. There are a few exceptions, including Hanjo Berressem's *Pynchon's Poetics: Interfacing Theory and Text*, Michael Bérubé's *Marginal Forces / Cultural Centers: Tolson, Pynchon, and the Politics of Canon*, Alec McHoul and David Wills's *Writing Pynchon: Strategies in Fictional Analysis*, and Brian McHale's discussions of Pynchon in his studies of postmodernism, *Postmodernist Fiction* and *Constructing Postmodernism*, especially part 2, "(Mis)Reading Pynchon." To these one should add Bernard

Duyfhuizen's essays "Hushing Sick Transmissions: Disrupting Story in *The Crying of Lot 49*" and " 'A Suspension Forever at the Hinge of Doubt': The Reader-Trap of Bianca in *Gravity's Rainbow*."

## Essay Collections

Special issues of *Critique* (1974) and *Twentieth Century Literature* (1975) and at least fourteen essay collections are devoted to essays on Thomas Pynchon. The first collection, *Essays on Thomas Pynchon* (republished as *Mindful Pleasures*), edited by George Levine and David Leverenz, continues to be a valued resource, especially for essays by Richard Poirier, "The Importance of Thomas Pynchon"; two influential essays on *V.*, Tony Tanner's "Caries and Cabals" and W. T. Lhamon, Jr.'s "Pentecost, Promiscuity, and Pynchon's *V.*"; Anne Mangel's exposition of science and metaphor in Pynchon's second novel, "Maxwell's Demon, Entropy, Information: *The Crying of Lot 49*"; and Edward Mendelson's foundational essay "Gravity's Encyclopedia." Mendelson's edited volume, *Pynchon: A Collection of Critical Essays*, includes Roger Henkle's important essay on *V.*, "Pynchon's Tapestries on the Western Wall"; "Decoding the Trystero" by Frank Kermode; and Mendelson's own oft-cited "The Sacred, the Profane, and *The Crying of Lot 49*." Richard Pearce's *Critical Essays on Thomas Pynchon* collects the essay "Science as Metaphor" by Alan J. Friedman and Manfred Puetz; Marcus Smith and Khachig Tölölyan's essay placing *Gravity's Rainbow* in the jeremiad tradition outlined by Sacvan Bercovitch in *The American Jeremiad*; and Lawrence Wolfley's important study, "Repression's Rainbow." Wolfley's essay, which may be paired with Molly Hite's essay in this volume, provides insights into the underlying psychoanalytic ideology of *Gravity's Rainbow* and situates the novel historically during the period when Norman O. Brown's *Life against Death* proved so compelling to the New Left and the anti–Vietnam War generation.

These collections were followed by volumes focused on particular novels: Charles Clerc's *Approaches to* Gravity's Rainbow; Harold Bloom's *Thomas Pynchon's* Gravity's Rainbow; *New Essays on* The Crying of Lot 49, edited by Patrick O'Donnell; *Pynchon and* Mason & Dixon, edited by Brooke Horvath and Irving Malin; and *The* Vineland *Papers*, edited by Geoffrey Green, Donald Greiner, and Larry McCaffery. The first International Pynchon Conference (1998) yielded a special issue of *Pynchon Notes*, *Approach and Avoid: Essays on* Gravity's Rainbow, edited by Luc Herman, and a volume edited by Niran Abbas, *Thomas Pynchon: Reading from the Margins*. More recently, Elizabeth Jane Wall Hinds has edited *The Multiple Worlds of Pynchon's* Mason & Dixon*: Eighteenth-Century Contexts, Postmodern Observations*, whose essays situate Pynchon's novel within the field of eighteenth-century literature and culture and thereby expand the relevance of Pynchon's writing to work in American studies.

## Uncollected Essays: Women, Gender, and Other Topics

Special attention should be given to those essays treating the subject of women and gender in Pynchon's writing. Though so much of his fiction constitutes a sustained critique of patriarchy, even that perspective seems to some students to leave women out of the mix. Pertinent essays include Cathy Davidson's early piece "Oedipa as Androgyne" and Marjorie Kaufman's "Brunnhilde and the Chemists," collected in the Leverenz and Levine volume. Later publications include Molly Hite's "Feminist Theory and the Politics of *Vineland*," Stacey Olster's "When You're a (Nin)Jette, You're a (Nin)Jette All the Way—or Are You? Female Filmmaking in *Vineland*," Patricia Bergh's "(De)Constructing the Image: Thomas Pynchon's Postmodern Woman," and Terry Caesar's "Motherhood and Postmodernism." See also Carmen Pérez-Llantada Auría's "Questing for Social Justice: The Role of Woman in Thomas Pynchon's Narrative."

In addition, three other uncollected essays deserve mention. Ronald Cooley's "The Hothouse or the Street: Imperialism and Narrative in Pynchon's *V.*" and two essays on *Lot 49*—Charles Baxter's wonderful discussion of Pynchon and F. Scott Fitzgerald, "De-faced America: *The Great Gatsby* and *The Crying of Lot 49*," and Jerry Varsava's political reading, "Thomas Pynchon and Postmodern Liberalism"—contribute substantial insights into Pynchon's first two novels.

## Background Studies

A number of essays in this volume suggest ways of teaching Pynchon's work in the context of the politics and social movements taking place during his lifetime. They join a larger body of scholarship that puts the fiction in dialogue with its time, especially the 1960s. Recommended reading among these includes David Cowart's essay in *Critique*, "Pynchon and the Sixties"; Frederick Ashe's "Anachronism Intended: *Gravity's Rainbow* in the Sociopolitical Sixties"; M. Keith Booker's "America and Its Discontents: The Failure of Leftist Politics in Pynchon's *Vineland*"; Matthew Guillen's "Pynchon's Social Aesthetics: Sixties Activism in Postmodern American Literature"; and Jeffrey S. Baker's "A Democratic Pynchon: Counterculture, Counterforce and Participatory Democracy."

Teachers and students may find useful readings in more-general historical and cultural backgrounds of the last sixty years: Philip Beidler's *Scriptures for a Generation: What We Were Reading in the '60s*; the collection by Alexander Bloom and Wini Breines, *"Takin' It to the Streets": A Sixties Reader*, which includes classic 1960s-era New Left manifestos from Students for a Democratic

Society, the Free Speech Movement, and so forth; and Todd Gitlin's *The Sixties: Years of Hope, Days of Rage*. For the broader perspective of the United States' culture during the cold war, readers may turn to Stephen Whitfield's *The Culture of the Cold War* and Alan Nadel's *Containment Culture*, among others.

## Science and Literature

Among the scholarship that studies the place of science in Pynchon's novels are Joel Black's "The Hermeneutics of Extinction: Denial and Discovery in Scientific Literature," Lance Schachterle's "Thomas Pynchon and the Civil Wars of Technology," Russell Blackford's "Physics and Fantasy: Scientific Mysticism, Kurt Vonnegut, and *Gravity's Rainbow*," Frank Palmeri's "Neither Literally nor as Metaphor: Pynchon's *The Crying of Lot 49* and the Structure of Scientific Revolutions," Robert Nadeau's *Readings from the New Book of Nature: Physics and Metaphysics in the Modern Novel* (135–48), and Lance Olsen's "Pynchon's New Nature: The Uncertainty Principle and Indeterminacy in *The Crying of Lot 49*." Special notice should be given to Anne Mangel's essay "Maxwell's Demon, Entropy, Information: *The Crying of Lot 49*" and Dale Carter's *The Final Frontier*, a study of the missile program and *Gravity's Rainbow*.

The last twenty-five years have witnessed the appearance of many writers for whose works science and technology are central, and literary scholarship has taken note. Further reading in science and literature might include Joseph Tabbi's *Postmodern Sublime*; two books by N. Katherine Hayles, *The Cosmic Web: Scientific Field Models and Literary Strategies in the Twentieth Century* and *Chaos Bound*; Tom LeClair's book about Don DeLillo and the novel of systems, *In the Loop*; and David Porush's *The Soft Machine*.

## Literary Traditions

Scholars have placed Pynchon's writing in various literary histories and genres: Tony Tanner's *The City of Words* finds Pynchon's desire to create order from language in keeping with a trend in American fiction since World War II. Edward Mendelson sees *Gravity's Rainbow* as an "encyclopedic narrative" with roots in Menippean satire ("Encyclopedic Narrative"). Deborah Madsen writes of Pynchon's allegories, and Michael Seidel focuses on satiric plots in *Gravity's Rainbow*.

By far the most common approach, however, has been to see Pynchon as a postmodern writer. The studies of postmodern literature frequently mentioned by respondents to the questionnaire for this volume include Fredric Jameson's

*Postmodernism; or, The Logic of Late Capitalism*; Brian McHale's *Postmodernist Fiction* and *Constructing Postmodernism*; and Linda Hutcheon's *A Poetics of Postmodernism*. *Postmodern American Fiction: A Norton Anthology*, edited by Paula Geyh, Fred G. Leebron, and Andrew Levy, is a useful collection of texts and essays and is widely available.

## Handbooks, Reference Guides, and Web Sites

J. Kerry Grant's companions to *V.* and *The Crying of Lot 49* were frequently mentioned by respondents. Nearly all identified Steven Weisenburger's *A* Gravity's Rainbow *Companion* as an indispensable guide to reading and teaching the novel, although some consider Douglas Fowler's *A Reader's Guide to* Gravity's Rainbow, now out of print, the best guide for undergraduate students.

Of Web sites maintained for scholars and students of Pynchon, particularly noteworthy are Tim Ware's *ThomasPynchon.com* and Penny Padgett's *San Narciso Community College Thomas Pynchon Home Page*, hosted by Pomona College (www.pynchon.pomona.edu). Both are interactive sites that include a vast array of links to pictures, bibliographic material, and more. Ware's site maintains ongoing and expanding concordances for each of Pynchon's first three novels. *Pynchon Notes*'s bibliography may be accessed at www.ham.muohio.edu/~krafftjm/pncumbib.html. Another useful site is Larry Daw and Allen Ruch's *Spermatikos Logos* (www.themodernword.com/pynchon/).

## Bibliography

*Pynchon Notes* has had an ongoing comprehensive bibliography since the journal's inception in 1979. Readers may also consult the *MLA International Bibliography*. The above Web sites, too, provide excellent bibliographic information. Published Pynchon bibliographies include Clifford Mead's *Thomas Pynchon: A Bibliography of Primary and Secondary Materials* (1989); Mead's "A *Vineland* Bibliography" in *The* Vineland *Papers: Critical Takes on Pynchon's Novel* (Green, Greiner, and McCaffery 179–88 [1994]); *Pynchon Notes*'s *The Index Issue* (1995–96), which contains indexes to all Pynchon's novels and shorter works preceding *Mason & Dixon* and a cumulative bibliography of *Pynchon Notes* through issue 34-35 (Krafft, Duyfhuizen, and Tölölyan); and Frank Osterhaus's "A Bibliography of Pynchon Scholarship in Japan," compiled for *Pynchon Notes* (1999).

*Part Two*

# APPROACHES

# LITERARY HERITAGE, INFLUENCE, AND CONTEXT

## Teaching *Crying*: General Education, the 1960s, and *Lot 49*

*Robert N. Watson*

The two hundred freshmen in my general education course on the United States in the 1960s are mostly aspiring scientists meeting distribution requirements. So Pynchon's engineering references intimidate them less than his wheeling, swooping syntax. *The Simpsons* and *The X Files* have inured them to scattershot pop-culture allusions and flirtations with dark paranoia on Sunday evenings, but they still come to class on Monday mornings expecting authors and professors to specify correct answers. So I begin with an intensive analysis of the opening sentence of *The Crying of Lot 49*, then address the appetite for resolution by focusing on the ending—and what may lie just beyond it.

The mission of these "cluster" courses at the University of California, Los Angeles, is to introduce students to several academic disciplines as well as to the subject material, and this short novel works beautifully: learning about classical and biblical allusions, about New Critical close reading, about old movies and older paintings, about social ethics, and about the political contexts of 1960s literature all become part of the same project. Using methods these students understand—especially the search for patterns in seemingly anomalous data, leading to a prediction—vindicates literary study for students reflexively dubious about its value, without any high-handed high-humanist dismissal of competing approaches. It also serves as a prophecy of the whole arc of the 1960s—the hopes for a revolution of spirit and justice, the terror those hopes provoked in people unready to cross over into any such future, and the difficult ending that left the revolutionaries unsure whether to weep privately at the intractable wrongs or to rise up publicly for a drastic last stand.

Halfway through the book, "Oedipa wondered whether, at the end of this (if it were supposed to end), she too might not be left with only compiled memories of clues, announcements, intimations, but never the central truth itself" (95). There are several ways to exploit pedagogically the predictable resentment of this inconclusion—by encouraging students to confront their own deterministic reflexes as consumers of genres, for example—but my less fashionable preference is to offer students a definitive hypothesis to test: that Oedipa is about to discover that she herself is the Tristero bidder who must stand up at the closing auction and begin claiming the legacy of the dispossessed.

This hypothesis—published more than twenty years ago, during what now seems the ancient prehistory of Pynchon scholarship (Watson)—proposes a familiar kind of novel here beneath the postmodern high jinks, a bildungsroman with anagnorisis and peripeteia toward the end. Not that I would risk invoking so much of the old Germanic and older classical models of literary criticism in that lecture hall; but it is worth suggesting that (for all its innovations) *Lot 49* still traces the protagonist's moral growth and education that builds toward crucial moments of recognition and reversal. So, after acknowledging the book's epistemological playfulness—and the mistrust of linear plots, ethical indoctrination, and "central truths" in contemporary fiction generally—I make the case for a delicious irony in Oedipa Maas's surveying the room, "trying to guess which one was her target, her enemy, perhaps her proof" (183), unaware of the imminent shock of self-recognition. Refreshing students' vague memories of ancient Greek drama and myth and providing them with a fifty-line passage from the Gospel according to Luke, some slides of Annunciation and pietá paintings, a few Hitchcock movie clips, and a continuing syllabus of political history allow *The Crying of Lot 49* to blossom into a truly multidisciplinary case study, one that demonstrates the value of intertextuality for articulating ethical questions too complex for more direct analysis.

The protagonist's name, prominent in the opening sentence, provides a ready way into the classical references. When Pynchon reports that Oedipa "left The Greek Way, and entered the city again, the infected city" (116–17), he signals an ominous allusion. Though students often look first for an easy Freudian joke, someone usually recalls that both the rise and the fall of King Oedipus came from solving riddles to which he himself was the surprising answer. From crawling as an abandoned infant to upright adulthood to staggering with a cane after blinding himself, Oedipus vividly embodies the human progression from four to two to three legs, which is the answer to the sphinx's question; and he proves to be the mystery patricide that the Delphic oracle warns has infected Thebes. Perhaps Pierce Inverarity's mystery functions like the sphinx's and the oracle's, leaving Oedipa Maas (like Oedipus's mother) "anxious that her revelation not . . . assume her to itself" (166). Oedipa guzzled "bourbon until the sun went down and it was as dark as it would ever get" and then "drove on the freeway for a while with her lights out, to see what would happen." The self-destructively extinguished headlights not only make Oedipa a de facto member of the Inamorati Anonymous network of failed suicides, they also allude to the guilt-racked Oedipus gouging out his eyes, an allusion reinforced two sentences later as she phones the Greek Way bar and her tears "build up pressure around her eyes" (176; cf. her eye-pressing guilt on 21).

The myth of Echo and Narcissus also permeates the story, corresponding to Oedipa's uncertainty whether the Tristero is a real entity whose calls we mistake for the rebound of our own voices or is merely the reflection of an overindulged self. Oedipa asks her "vanity mirror" whether she has "stumbled indeed, without the aid of LSD . . . onto a network by which X number of Americans are truly communicating . . . a real alternative to the exitlessness, to the absence of surprise to life, that harrows the head of every American you know, and you too, sweetie. Or you are hallucinating it" (170). Drawing students' attention to the situation and decoration of Oedipa's motel in San Narciso, where she shatters one mirror and dreams of others, is usually enough to make the point: "Echo Courts became impossible," partly "because of the stillness of the pool and the blank windows that faced on it" (47); a simulation of the mythic Echo stands in front of the motel, but "[t]he face of the nymph was much like Oedipa's" (26).

Students provided with the text of Luke 1.28–79 may notice that the Virgin Mary too was "greatly troubled" at the mysterious summons of a "grace" announcing that (though she now has "no husband") an impregnating power will penetrate and "overshadow" her. This language connects the passage to Pierce's last phone call to Oedipa, in the voice of a radio-serial character called the Shadow (11), as well as nine subsequent references to shadows and another nine to shades, all associated with Tristero. Oedipa's nascent promise to bring America's underclass back into its stolen inheritance and the dark Tristero back into the light resembles the promise in Luke (1.52, 79) that the power that once "put down the mighty from their thrones, and exalted those of low degree" will thus be reborn "to give light to those who sit in darkness." Under the suggestive pseudonym of Grace Bortz, Oedipa arranges for a pregnancy test but then decides to skip it (171)—perhaps unwilling to abort Grace. A few pages later, she dreams of "the soft dusk of mirrors out of which something was about to walk, and empty rooms that waited for her. Your gynecologist has no test for what she was pregnant with" (175). Students have heard Mary hailed as "full of grace" and can see from slides of medieval and Renaissance depictions of the Annunciation that Mary usually occupies empty, reflective rooms and that the impregnating Holy Spirit is represented by a dove, announced by a descending angel. Oedipa compares her own sensitivity to the Tristero to the "secular *announcement*" felt by an epileptic, the "pure *piercing grace* note *announcing* his seizure" (95; emphases mine). In the final few lines of the novel, the auctioneer Passerine, whose name refers to an order of doves, spreads "his arms in a gesture that seemed to belong to the priesthood of some remote culture; perhaps to a descending angel" (183).

When students are directed to the book's copyright page, they see that Pynchon first published portions of this novel under the title "The World (This One), the Flesh (Mrs. Oedipa Maas), and the Testament of Pierce Inverarity," and those with some Christian training quickly observe that, in handing down his last Testament, the (holy) ghost Pierce immaculately fathers a new dispensation within and through Oedipa, who has come from Kinneret—another name for Galilee—and will be the long-awaited "Word" made flesh. At Randolph Driblette's grave, Oedipa imagines Driblette's spirit as "a transient, winged shape, needing to settle at once in the warm host, or dissipate forever into the dark," then feels "briefly penetrated, as if the bright winged thing had actually made it to the sanctuary of her heart. . . . She waited for the winged brightness to announce its safe arrival" (162). Driblette says he directed *The Courier's Tragedy* so as "[t]o give the spirit flesh. The words, who cares?" (79). This manifesto evokes the Pauline triumph of the spirit over the letter, fulfilled when the reembodied Savior speaks again, in the form of the Last Judgment, announced by a trumpet. Oedipa must remove at long last the mute from the Tristero post horn and speak up at that Sunday crying of lot 49. Luke 1.64–70 says that God "hath raised up a horn of salvation" and that the Holy Ghost has opened the mouth of the dumb. The end of *Lot 49* gives way to an implicit day 50: Pentecost is the fiftieth day after Easter in the liturgical calendar, and on that day Pentecostal disciples find themselves speaking, as if possessed, in prophetic tongues. Oedipa may suspect (as the few scholars willing to posit a definite ending tend to suspect) that she is about to die; but if so, it is a redemptive death—reminiscent of Robert Browning's Childe Roland finally come to the dark tower, where, after "a click / As when a trap shuts . . . Dauntless the slughorn to my lips I set, / And blew" (lines 173–74, 203–04); Oedipa too, after hearing "a lock snap shut" (183), will boldly unmute the horn as she meets her dark fate.

When Oedipa holds the dying old sailor across her lap "as if he were her own child," she becomes instead the Mary of countless pietá paintings. Her first reaction to the sailor had reflected all the strategies of a person still possessed of a loving husband, a sane analyst, and an unbroken faith in the social system, which Pynchon encapsulates in terms that recall (and dismiss) all the liberal solutions to America's human problems—solutions epitomized by Lyndon Johnson's Great Society program—that emerged and collapsed during the 1960s:

> She ran through then a scene she might play. She might find the landlord of this place, and bring him to court, and buy the sailor a new suit at Roos/Atkins, and shirt, and shoes, and give him the bus fare to Fresno after all. But with a sigh he had released her hand, while she was so lost in the fantasy that she hadn't felt it go away, as if he'd known the best moment to let go.
>
> "Just mail the letter," he said, "the stamp is on it." She looked and saw

> the familiar carmine 8¢ airmail, with a jet flying by the Capitol dome. But at the top of the dome stood a tiny figure in deep black, with its arms outstretched. (127)

This passage allows me to combine two of my chief tasks in the course: describing the moral functions of literature and describing the struggles of 1960s idealism. Recognizing pain suspended in the fiber of historical narrative and recognizing the failure of the many facile, good-hearted palliatives and transcendences offered during those years, students trained in a culture of commercial success and social conformity confront the importance of simply bearing witness to human suffering—of listening to the story of the outcast. The implication that personal sympathy is finally more important—more realistic—than social policy may explain why Pynchon—who was twenty-eight when he wrote this book, the same age he gave Oedipa—hid out writing weird novels instead of, say, running for Congress.

Oedipa has crossed over to the side of the dispossessed without quite knowing it. The odd postmark on Mucho's letter suggests that it, too, traveled across California by Tristero courier; she and the sailor, whose letter is addressed to his estranged wife, are in the same sinking marital boat. She has walked the dreary route of a W.A.S.T.E. postman through the Oakland slums, lost all her heterosexual contacts, ridden the midnight buses, wept in a flophouse, even attempted suicide. Instead of actively pursuing hints of the Tristero, Oedipa, we are told, "now . . . kept a silence, waiting" (152), as if obeying the acronym: We Await Silent Tristero's Empire (169). She even imagines, as executor, fulfilling the Tristero executioners' claim to inheritance:

> What would the probate judge have to say about spreading some kind of a legacy among them all, all those nameless, maybe as a first installment? Oboy. He'd be on her ass in a microsecond, revoke her letters testamentary, they'd call her names, proclaim her through all Orange County as a redistributionist and pinko. . . . Perhaps she'd be hounded someday as far as joining Tristero itself, if it existed, in its twilight, its aloofness, its waiting. The waiting above all. . . . (181)

She is awaiting the apocalyptic moment when, according to the thirty-seventh Psalm, "those who wait for the Lord shall possess the land" and the meek shall inherit the earth, for which San Narciso and Inverarity Enterprises are metaphors and potential first installments. The conservative legal system and the right-wing community that narrowly defend property rights have become her enemies. Running away as a "fugitive" after the shoot-out at Hilarius's clinic (145), Oedipa is irreversibly on the road to becoming the force that her former comfortable "Young Republican" self (76) had perceived as the enemy, the other. After affairs with wealthy industrialists and corporate lawyers, she begins flirting with a man who looks as if he has been "[t]raining rebels up in the mountains" (167), and her life looks like a film of Sara Jane Olsen's (from Symbionese Liberation Army survivor to suburban housewife) run in reverse.

Teaching *Lot 49* in this cluster course has the wonderful effect of situating us all as Oedipa. Once we become—like the "sensitives" who can power the Nefastis machine with mental communication (104–07)—alert to what is on both sides of the shutter, we start noticing that binary function everywhere. It turns up so often in the readings assigned by my colleagues from other disciplines that we wonder, usefully, why we never noticed it before. Since the 1966 Los Angeles riots are local (and continuing) history for us, we read Pynchon's *New York Times Magazine* nonfiction piece "A Journey into the Mind of Watts," which makes an argument about American consumers' numbness to human suffering strikingly reminiscent of the one I am evoking from the novel:

> [T]he black culture is stuck pretty much with basic realities like disease, like failure, violence and death, which the whites have mostly chosen—and can afford—to ignore. The two cultures do not understand each other, though white values are displayed without let-up on black people's TV screens, and though the panoramic sense of black impoverishment is hard to miss from atop the Harbor Freeway, which so many whites must drive at least twice every working day. Somehow it occurs to very few of them to leave at the Imperial Highway exit for a change, go east instead of west only a few blocks, and take a look at Watts. A quick look. The simplest kind of beginning. But Watts is country which lies, psychologically, uncounted miles further than most whites seem at present willing to travel. (35, 78)

Oedipa eventually realizes that "she might have found The Tristero anywhere in her Republic, through any of a hundred lightly-concealed entranceways, a hundred alienations, if only she'd looked" (179). Students pursuing the literary comparison find themselves making the sociological connection as well, recognizing their own conveniently indirect roles in exploiting and thereby perpetuating the misery that a neatly vacuum-packed consumer culture helps them forget.

Another formative document of the early 1960s, Michael Harrington's great socioeconomic study *The Other America*, says something similar:

> The other America, the America of poverty, is hidden today in a way it never was before. Its millions are socially invisible to the rest of us. . . . The ordinary tourist never left the main highway, and today he rides interstate turnpikes. . . . Middle-class women coming in from Suburbia on a rare trip may catch the merest glimpse of the other America on the way to an evening at the theater. (3–4)

Oedipa's long, strange trip could hardly be better summarized—except that she finds herself, not a mere spectator at *The Courier's Tragedy*, but cast in the title role. And only a week before reading Pynchon, students were sensitized to this pattern by a 1966 *Ramparts* magazine piece about Chicago, assigned by the historian on our teaching team: "On the sidewalk on the west side of Ashland [Avenue] there was not one Negro. On the east side, not one white. No freeway, no park, no railroad tracks—just an invisible wall so familiar to the residents that no one even seemed to glance at it" (Marine 14).

In subsequent weeks, students keep seeing Oedipa Maas, not just behind the ambivalent activist heroine of Alice Walker's *Meridian*, but also behind the historical stories of women joining "the movement"—"[a]lmost a mystical term [that] implied an experience, a sense of community and common purpose" (Evans 102), as "the Tristero" does. Like Oedipa, these were educated women in the early 1960s trapped in "[t]he social isolation of modern housewives" (Evans 8): their husbands distracted by struggles at work, no other family nearby, and no real contact with other women beyond the shopping trips that punctuate their loneliness. Trying "to unravel the mystery of how a few young women stepped outside the assumptions on which they had been raised to articulate a radical critique of women's position in American society" (23), the historian Sara Evans, like Pynchon, describes women running across a vein of political energy and feeling simultaneously drawn to it and "scared to death" (Mimi Feingold, qtd. in Evans 62); "[t]here was no way to join; you simply announced or felt yourself to be a part of the movement" (Evans 102). They found—like Oedipa holding the dying sailor—that "finally it all boils down to . . . whether I shall go on living in isolation or whether there shall be a *we*. . . . It is a *I am going to sit beside you*" (Jane Stembridge, qtd. in Evans 65).

As Oedipa begins to look past the echo of "terror" in Tristero and to recognize the *tristesse*, the sadness, instead, students recall the political scientist on our teaching team describing his 1968 survey of postriot Detroit, where the fearful whites thought "Black Power" meant "black ruling over white" and "vengeance" and "disorder," and the educated blacks thought it meant "a fair share" and "black unity" (Aberbach and Walker 107–17). Thinking of this eerily ubiquitous network of figures in black even reminded one student of a 1967 pamphlet, *We Want Black Power*, advocating "oneness with a worldwide black brotherhood" (Student Nonviolent Coordinating Committee 146).

Now Oedipa finds herself a sister to that radical brotherhood, asking herself why she didn't bludgeon the Nazi skinhead Tremaine when she had the chance: "You're chicken, she told herself, snapping her seat belt. This is America, you live in it, you let it happen" (150)—almost exactly what James Baldwin tells our white students in *The Fire Next Time*. Baldwin helps the students link this cowardly evasion back to the cold war: "Behind what we think of as the Russian menace lies what we do not wish to face, and what white Americans do not face when they regard a Negro reality—the fact that life is tragic" (91). Tristero is not just about politics but about facing the darker facts of human existence. And it isn't just a black organization; W.A.S.T.E. is more inclusive than other groups we study, such as the SCLC (Southern Christian Leadership Conference) or CORE (Congress of Racial Equality) or the SNCC (Student Nonviolent

Coordinating Committee). It includes exiled Mexican anarchists, gay men, low-income Latinos in dirty dying old cars, American Indians, the hopelessly heart-broken, deaf-mutes, graveyard-shift black men, gambling addicts, alcoholic war veterans, late-night latchkey children, bored alienated engineers, the deserted spouse and fired executive, those who have failed at love and then even failed at suicide—all of them going postal in a seemingly new and ominous way.

Baldwin also explains our willful blindness toward this underclass: "the reason for this ignorance is that a knowledge of the role these people played—and play—in American life would reveal more about America to Americans than Americans wish to know"—including the threat of "a vengeance that does not really depend on, and cannot really be executed by, any person or organization, and that cannot be prevented by any police force or army: historical vengeance, a cosmic vengeance . . ." (101, 105). Baldwin also understood how Oedipa would be drawn from her isolated tower toward this dark force:

> The white man's unadmitted—and apparently, to him, unspeakable—private fears and longings are projected onto the Negro. The only way he can be released from the Negro's tyrannical power over him is to consent, in effect, to become black himself, to become a part of that suffering and dancing country that he now watches wistfully from the heights of his lonely power and, armed with spiritual traveller's checks, visits surreptitiously after dark. (96)

Tristero's inclusiveness does not extend to women, however. This omission initially reinforces Oedipa's sense of a threatening otherness, but it also prepares her to recognize that she is qualified for membership by forms of exclusion and exploitation that bourgeois comforts (as Betty Friedan's influential *The Feminine Mystique* argued in 1963) helped disguise. Students from relatively privileged backgrounds often see their mothers reflected in the comfortable but unfulfilled Oedipa of the book's opening passages—a perfect protoyuppie who shops upscale malls, cooks lasagna with home-grown herbs, reads *Scientific American* book reviews (10), and looks back on Mexican vacations with a wealthy industrialist, after the sort of college education that made her "unfit perhaps for marches and sit-ins, but just a whiz at pursuing strange words in Jacobean texts" (104). The end of the first chapter—like many of the chief sociocultural protests of the 1960s—describes this comfort as a trap, a closed and therefore maximally entropic system, as lifeless and neatly sealed as the Tupperware of the book's opening sentence. Pierce eventually penetrated the magic tower where the suburban princess languished (slipping the lock with a credit card, appropriately enough—the equivalent of Baldwin's "spiritual traveller's checks"):

> But all that had gone on between them had never really escaped the confinement of that tower. . . . Pierce had taken her away from nothing,

> there'd been no escape. What did she so desire escape from? . . . If the tower is everywhere and the knight of deliverance no proof against its magic, what else? (20–22)

What else is what follows—in the book and in the 1960s—and what Oedipa and the rest of us can learn from it: a process of critical unveiling that runs from the game of Strip Botticelli that exposes her body (36–43) to her repeated complaints that the conspiracy is "stripping away" the men who protect her (153) to the depiction of Tristero as a stripper who would "come back down the runway, its luminous stare locked to Oedipa's, smile gone malign and pitiless; bend to her alone among the desolate rows of seats and begin to speak words she never wanted to hear" (54) to that final auction where Oedipa will again be lurking in an audience of men, waiting for the big exposure, fearing the "smile practiced and relentless" of the person onstage (183), fearing especially that she will become the chief actor rather than the mere audience. As the opening chapter foresaw no way out of Oedipa's suburban insulation, the closing auction offers no way out of her Tristero conversion. If she bids for Pierce's stamp collection, then she speaks up for Tristero, wanting "to keep evidence that Tristero exists out of unauthorized hands" (176); if not, then she participates in Tristero's characteristic conspiracy of silence, declining to give evidence of her existence and membership and thus placing herself among the tragically disinherited in capitalist America.

Pynchon's love of movies produces clues for our film-savvy students. As Oedipa's journey into the oppressed shadow world of America threatens to become a one-way ride, a visit that becomes an identity, it rewards comparison with political films such as *Sullivan's Travels* and *Black Like Me*. The Tristero may remind students of the supremely mysterious, ubiquitous, and dangerous Keyser Söze in the campus favorite *The Usual Suspects*. The plot resembles a standard Alfred Hitchcock scenario: a comfortable innocent stumbles across an almost incredible conspiracy, becomes entangled in it and endangered by it, yet must struggle at times to decide whether the conspiracy is real or whether he or she has simply gone insane. When Oedipa has "some vague idea about causing a scene violent enough to bring the cops into it and find out that way who the man really was" at the final auction (183), the Hitchcock allusion becomes specific, and I use three brief film clips to support my argument that Oedipa will find herself rising as the Tristero bidder. The fugitive hero of *The Thirty-Nine Steps*, with a grim audience staring at him, unexpectedly finds himself obliged to give a speech and surprises himself with a rousing populist appeal; later he foils the villains by shouting from the audience exactly the question he fears the conspirators will soon be asking the man on stage. In *North by Northwest*, the character played by Cary Grant bids wildly for unwanted lots, hoping to gain enough attention from the public and the police to protect him from the men he believes are there to kill him as well as to bid themselves. All these parallels suggest that Oedipa will (however unwillingly and improvisationally) have to stand up and bid.

The last sentence tells us that "Oedipa settled back, to await"—that Tristero word—"the crying of lot 49." In our course on the 1960s, the key point is not whether Oedipa will ultimately bid; the point is that the auction confronts her with the same wonderful terrifying possibility that the bright, successful children of a conformist America were facing when the Free Speech Movement exploded in Berkeley, Freedom Summer began in Mississippi, and Students for a Democratic Society convened in Port Huron. She becomes a perfect exemplar of the way those children were drawn across a divide, into a world of which their parents had only repressed knowledge.

In tracing Oedipa's journey from safe suburban housewife to freakish underground warrior haunted by conspiracies and caught in shoot-outs, the novel prophesies America's journey from the Tupperware containment of 1950s suburban developments like Levittown to the weirdly beautiful mess of hippie centers like Haight-Ashbury in San Francisco in 1967 and to the military and police attacks on dissidents a few years later at Kent State University (and at Jackson State University, Columbia University, Berkeley, the Democratic convention in Chicago, various Black Panther residences, etc.). But Pynchon also offers an amazingly prescient vision of the division *between* Haight-Ashbury and Kent State, between absorption into a druggy sound-tracked voyage inward (like the psychedelic trip Dr. Hilarius offers Oedipa, with a "We want you" slogan that makes him a demonic Uncle Sam recruiting for a countercultural America [17]) and a program of explicitly political reforms. A persistent theme in our course is the emergent incompatibility of the hippie and the leftist aspects of the movement, neither of which (like inseparably conjoined twins) had the power to survive on its own. Pynchon foresees that problem and suggests an answer in the Oedipa whose psychic transformation and political indoctrination have progressed in tandem, ready to unite if she bids at the closing auction.

Faced with a diabolically resourceful system that (beyond its direct violence, as Herbert Marcuse's *One-Dimensional Man* warns our students) co-opted people with phony choices between corporate-owned politicians as leaders and among different styles of consumer goods through which to purchase an identity, many burnt-out activists retreated to farm communes and tried to conjure their own little gardens of Eden. Pynchon predicts this, too: "A calculated withdrawal, from the life of the Republic, from its machinery" (124). By the end of the 1960s, the Beatles' "Revolution" was warning that "carrying pictures of Chairman Mao" is counterproductive: "You say you'll change the Constitution? Well, you know, we all want to change your head. You tell me it's the institution. Well, you know, you'd better free your mind instead" (Lennon and McCartney).

The frustrations of organizing demonstrations and ballot initiatives bore little resemblance to the magic revolution, propelled by a shared absolute moral vision and youthful enthusiasm, that many people had thought was underway in the mid-1960s. Young people on the left awaited something miraculous, gathering in Woodstock like the children Oedipa (a few years earlier) finds playing in the park: "The night was empty of all terror for them, they had inside their circle an imaginary fire, and needed nothing but their own unpenetrated sense of community" (118). The Woodstock Nation imagined itself capable of dancing like those amazing deaf-mutes Oedipa sees, "a choreography in which each couple meshed easy, predestined. Something they all heard with an extra sense atrophied in herself" (131). With a rougher edge, it's what Pynchon's journalism says many people in Watts remember fondly: "through much of the rioting seemed to run, they say, a remarkable empathy: or whatever it is that jazz musicians feel on certain nights; everybody knowing what to do and when to do it without needing a signal" ("Journey" 84). It's what kept frustrated revolutionaries like Oedipa's friend Jesús Arrabal hanging on, waiting for a "miracle": "Where revolutions break out spontaneous and leaderless, and the soul's talent for consensus allows the masses to work together without effort, automatic as the body itself" (120).

In all the waste of the 1960s, I ask the students, was there a W.A.S.T.E.—some collective intuition of a society less insulated and more just? Certainly one "had to look closely to see the periods between the letters" (130). To pick up on another of Pynchon's scientific puns: when the 1960s produces d.t.'s, are they only the delirium tremens of drug abuse or the dt's of calculus—a meaningful difference of times, "a vanishingly small instant in which change had to be confronted at last for what it was" (129)? The book suggests that only information entropy can challenge physics entropy, as perhaps only literature (with its ability to "project a world" [82]) can challenge social deterioration; knowledge may be better than action for the preservation of possibilities. Maxwell's demon defeats the entropic tendency of a closed system just by recognizing the opposite particles. "Communication is the key," shouts John Nefastis (105)—and community (the other thing the materially comfortable Oedipa lacks at the beginning of this story) will follow. Otherwise labor becomes as alienated as at Yoyodyne, and America becomes a city like San Narciso, which Pynchon (in another prophecy, this one of the globalization that has roused the most 1960s-like activism among the current generation of students) describes in terms ominously evocative for Southern Californians: "less an identifiable city than a grouping of concepts—census tracts, special purpose bond-issue districts, shopping nuclei, all overlaid with access roads to its own freeway" (24).

Oedipa's husband Mucho—forced to confront the misery of Californian life on the margins, watching people trade their used cars under the illusion they can somehow change their hopeless lives—flees that recognition in familiar 1960s ways: he tries rock and roll (as a DJ) and free sex with teenagers, then disappears into the LSD universe, dreaming of "a couple hundred million" Americans speaking in unison. But Mucho is unable to come up with anything for them to say except "rich, chocolaty goodness"—an advertising line for cheap pleasure (142). The LSD experiment Dr. Hilarius called "the Bridge" is finally only a "bridge inward" (17), not anything that connects meaningfully to other people—or, as Mucho's fate warns, it connects you so indiscriminately that you have no self left to give (138–45). Good dope proved no more satisfactory an answer than the Great Society; and Pynchon somehow foresaw Charles Manson just around the next mind-bend (122).

Pynchon's novel suggests something that 1960s activists (from Zen-and-psychedelics figures like Baba Ram Dass to straight activists like Mario Savio) were just beginning to articulate, something I think it is crucial for our students to register deeply: however naive its methods, the counterculture recognized a need to rescue human individuality from the lifeless closed system of technocratic America. When his acid-intensified senses alert Mucho to a tiny flaw in the Muzak, he asks:

> Do you think somebody could do the dinosaur bone bit with that one string. . . . Figure out what his ear is like, and then the musculature of his hands and arms, and eventually the entire man. . . . He was real. That wasn't synthetic. They could dispense with live musicians if they wanted. Put together all the right overtones at the right power levels so it'd come out like a violin. (141–42)

Music synthesizers were rudimentary when Pynchon wrote this, I remind the students, but as an engineer he saw how it would be done, and as an artist he saw the hidden costs. That seems to be what brings the "too sensitive" Mucho to tears (12): "the human voice, you know, it's a flipping miracle" (143). It is a voice that students acknowledge is largely missing from the processed hits of the popular music charts (except sometimes in hip-hop, which many white youths value as their window into the universe of black America).

What students at a top California university now often lack is a sense of the tragic. I want them to read what is coded in that old mattress salted with the tears, urine, semen, and night sweats of the world's suffering and defeated citizens (126). When I teach *Lot 49*, I am also trying to teach crying; asking these often technocratic students, on their way from success to success, to read the sailor's letter—or at least to see that mailing it is not a waste of time, even if it solves nothing. Their growth as readers and citizens begins, as Oedipa's does, with reading some letters and then trying to think and feel. It may possibly end with somebody feeling compelled to stand up and demand a just redistribution of the legacy of America.

# Pynchon's Quest Narratives and the Tradition of American Romance

*Deborah L. Madsen*

One of the greatest challenges to students reading Thomas Pynchon for the first time is to understand the generic tradition out of which Pynchon's work emerges. This task is particularly difficult for students who do not have a firm grasp of American narrative forms and literary models. As a teacher of European students, many of whom have never studied American literature except as individual texts, divorced from the contexts provided by canon and tradition, I have found that introducing the American romance tradition is fundamental to teaching Pynchon's fiction. Familiarity with this context of key precursor texts enables students to perceive the generic nature of Pynchon's quest narratives and to evaluate his achievement within that tradition.

Students who have never studied American literature as a coherent body of knowledge evaluate Pynchon's achievement in terms of their familiarity with the canon of British literature. Consequently, their perception of what constitutes a novel in English is shaped by the classic nineteenth-century British novelists, such as Charles Dickens, George Eliot, and Thomas Hardy. Thus, these students anticipate that Pynchon's language will reflect the everyday quotidian world of his characters, who will conform loosely to E. M. Forster's prescription for "round" or "flat" characterization and who will inhabit fictional settings recognizably related to the world, the reality, in which the students live (65). The structure of the narrative, they expect, will then be based on the interaction of characters and the development of relationships among them that represent significant aspects of their culture and society.

Given these assumptions, students encounter difficulties with Pynchon's deployment of the quest structure, his use of language and symbolism, his types of characters, and their settings. Richard Chase, in his classic study *The American Novel and Its Tradition* (1957), observes that differences such as these mark American as opposed to English novelistic conventions. In his opening chapter, "The Broken Circuit" (1–28), Chase identifies what he calls the American "romance-novel," a generic classification that accounts for the distinctive features of the narratives that form much of the American literary canon: works by James Fenimore Cooper, Nathaniel Hawthorne, Herman Melville, and, I argue, Thomas Pynchon.

Chase stresses the importance of a shift in the attitude toward characterization: from the novelistic emphasis on comprehensive characterization to the romancer's interest in action and plot at the expense of detailed character portrayal. "Character itself," he writes, "becomes . . . somewhat abstract and ideal, so much so in some romances that it seems to be merely a function of plot" (13). By calling attention to this tendency, Chase highlights a feature of

Pynchon's narrative method that explains why critics have proposed a number of alternative generic classifications for his fiction, to account for his departures from the British novelistic tradition. Encyclopedic narrative (Mendelson, "Gravity's Encyclopedia"), Menippean satire (Kharpertian), allegory (Quilligan; D. Madsen), jeremiad (Smith and Tölölyan): all share this feature of abstraction and idealization.

The subject matter of the quest romance is abstract moral truth—good, evil, or what Hawthorne calls in the preface to *The House of the Seven Gables* (1851) "the truth of the human heart"(3)—as opposed to more particular sociological kinds of truth that arise from the ordinary or probable experiences in the novel. As a consequence, the romance is set not in the recognizable world of real life but in some neutral space where the marvelous and the ordinary, the imaginary events and actual locations may meet. The laws of possibility are suspended in this "Faery Land" (Hawthorne, Preface [*Blithedale*] 1) so that the abstract truths of human experience may be acted out in the narrative. This concept of "Faery Land" makes possible the famous metaphor in *The Crying of Lot 49* in which Oedipa abstracts the layout of San Narciso and compares it to a printed circuit. The metaphor permits her to reflect, "Though she knew even less about radios than about Southern Californians, there were to both outward patterns a hieroglyphic sense of concealed meaning, of an intent to communicate" (24). These metaphoric terms establish the abstract setting for Oedipa's quest—the highly stylized, fictional world of the romance; all is symbolic, but the symbolic meanings are not simple and obvious; rather, they are as ambiguous as the human situations being represented.

Hawthorne ends the preface to *The House of the Seven Gables* with a final instruction that his romance is not to be read historically, as a novel, but on its own terms, as "having a great deal more to do with the clouds overhead than with any portion of the soil of the County of Essex" (3).[1] Later, he warns his audience about the confusion that ensues when a romance is read too literally—as a novel—and describes in the preface to *The Blithedale Romance* a general American tendency toward literal-mindedness with which the European writer does not need to contend. (In Europe, Hawthorne asserts, fiction is not compared with reality in terms of the probability or plausibility of the things represented fictively.) When a romance is read as a novel, inevitably the romancer's attempt to dramatize the hidden truths of the human condition becomes but a weak "paint and pasteboard" representation of social reality. Pynchon, too, does not create rounded characters with fully developed interior lives or backstories; his characters bear disturbing names (such as Fallopian, Driblette, and Oedipa) that are profoundly evocative of—but do not reveal—substantive or determinate meaning. Like Hawthorne, Pynchon creates characters to represent moral ideas, just as he uses social history (especially in *Gravity's Rainbow*) as idea rather than as event.

In what follows, I offer a discussion focusing on *The Crying of Lot 49* and a set of literary influences on Pynchon that places his work in the romance tradition of American narrative, as distinct from the canon of British social realism. Emerson's "Nature," Cooper's *Leatherstocking Tales*, Hawthorne's *The Scarlet Letter*, and Melville's *Moby Dick* provide the generic context of American romance for a comparative exploration of Pynchon, an approach that helps teachers and students investigate the role of ambiguity in Pynchon's work, the nature of his narrative quest structure, and his treatment of such themes as nature, the relation between self and society, religion, and the search for the meaning of American experience.

Emerson's essay "Nature" provides a useful encapsulation of the Romantic themes that inform the genre of American romance narrative and the quest for meaning. The idea of nature as a symbolic text to be read, the transcendent meaning of which is the "living Unity" of the world, provides the foundation for Emerson's theory of "correspondences" (28). In "Nature," Emerson explains how individual subjectivity facilitates this unification through the interpretation of words as the signs of natural facts, which mediate between the human and natural worlds to represent a unified web of creation. Charles Feidelson's tracing of the Puritan legacy in the work of Emerson and his contemporaries is instructive here: the connections between romance symbolism and spirituality have been explored in a wider generic context by such scholars as Northrop Frye (*Secular Scripture*), but Feidelson's specifically American context is most relevant. In *Symbolism and American Literature* (1953), Feidelson argues that the Puritan reflex to read the landscape as a symbolic text of spirit was inherited by the Romantic writers of the American nineteenth century. He cites the Puritan interpretation of New England, not as a commercial enterprise but as a symbolic expression of "God's thought" (80) or of pure spirit, to explain the attitude toward the symbolic dimension that shaped the way later Americans (such as Emerson, Hawthorne, and Melville) would think about nature.

The concept of nature as a spiritual text and of language as a sacramental means of representation informs Pynchon's narrative through Oedipa's sacramental interpretative reflex. Like Stencil in *V.*, Slothrop in *Gravity's Rainbow*, and Mason and Dixon in the narrative named for them, Oedipa reads the landscapes that surround her in terms of patterns of connection. All of these characters seek in the connections they perceive a transcendent meaning that will unite them in a mystical unity. But while the central symbolism of *Lot 49*, focused on the Tristero, signifies many things, it never achieves a fixed reference. Oedipa searches for the significance of the Tristero, but even when she has uncovered the history of the organization, she is not satisfied and continues in an increasingly frustrated hunt. Pynchon's characters inhabit a stylized setting the significance of which refers directly back to Oedipa's quest: no detail enters the narrative that does not belong to her pursuit of the Tristero. If she is, as she suspects, "the dark machine in the centre of the planetarium, [seeking] to bring the estate into pulsing stelliferous Meaning" (82), then the characters around her are akin to the celestial bodies composing her patterns of significance.

Pynchon's style of writing is an aspect of this American quest for meaning and merits comparison with *Moby Dick*. The narrator, Ishmael, discovers that every word, every sign he encounters generates a plenitude of meanings that cannot necessarily be reconciled. Like Oedipa's quest for the meaning of the Tristero, his attempt to reach a complete definition of cetology is defeated by a continual proliferation of details, which produce an infinite complexity. Ahab confronts the spiritual consequences of this complexity: in particular the possibility that there is no transcendent unity such as Emerson envisioned. Ahab is compelled to his obsessive quest for the white whale both by the suspicion that in place of plenitude there is an ultimate absence at the heart of things and by fear of its discovery.

In Ahab's interpretation, the white whale is much like Stencil's Vheissu—a whiteness that represents not only the absence of color but the absence of all meaning as well. For Oedipa, the crowding in on her of clues to the meaning of Tristero culminates in a night spent at the hotel in Berkeley, where she "kept waking from a nightmare about something in the mirror, across from her bed. Nothing specific, only a possibility, nothing she could see. . . . When she woke in the morning, she was sitting bolt upright, staring into the mirror at her own exhausted face" (*Lot 49* 101). The prospect that she has somehow become the meaning of the Tristero by filling the interpretative void with her own subjectivity is anticipated in the quest romance tradition by such characters as Melville's Ahab.

For example, in the "Doubloon" chapter of *Moby Dick*, the narrative moves through multiple interpretations of a gold coin, and for Ahab (as for Oedipa) the interpreting subject becomes the meaning of its own interpretation. In this way the text resists the idea of a single unified truth, and a similar narrative refusal to admit an ultimate point of connection generates the ambiguity that characterizes Pynchon's work, particularly *V.* and *The Crying of Lot 49*. This ambiguity is an important feature of all American romances, which are all responding to the hermeneutic principles set out by Emerson. The romance narrative challenges Emerson's belief that the operation of human subjectivity on the symbolic language of nature will inevitably discover a transcendent unity in the multiplicity of natural experience.

The ambiguity that enters the structural and thematic dimensions of *The Crying of Lot 49* can be elucidated through comparison with the episode in *The Scarlet Letter* where the adulterous minister, Arthur Dimmesdale, perceives a celestial sign, which he interprets as God's personal message to him, an accusation, revealing God's knowledge of his guilt. He believes that a giant letter *A* is revealed in the night sky, as he stands in the dark with his illicit lover and their illegitimate child. Hawthorne suggests that Dimmesdale and his parishioners share a common delusion. If Dimmesdale is misled by the force of his egotism to interpret the comet as a personal sign of God's displeasure and accusation, then the entire community is misled by a mass egotism to interpret the comet as signifying "Angel" in token of Governor Winthrop's death (which occurs at the very moment the celestial sign appears). This instance is only one of many in Hawthorne's narrative in which signs are multiply interpreted, with the result that the semantic overburdening of the sign erodes its capacity to convey meaning.

Oedipa may "project a world" (82) by inserting her own subjectivity in the place of referent to the symbolic Tristero, but, like Hawthorne's Puritans, Pynchon's Californians are all engaged in projecting their egotism in the various forms of narcissism and paranoia that Oedipa encounters. Mucho's LSD-induced schizophrenia and accompanying delusion that he is at the center of "a walking assembly of man" (140); Driblette's narcissistic placing of himself at the center of his universe like "the projector at the planetarium" (79); Dr Hilarius's jealous embrace of the paranoid fantasy that he believes protects his unique selfhood; Metzger, Cohen, Nefastis—all deal in correspondences, the symbolic meaning of which returns them reflexively to themselves. The ambiguity of the Tristero, V, the rocket in *Gravity's Rainbow*, Mason and Dixon's Visto, Hawthorne's scarlet *A*, and Melville's white whale arises not from the absence of meaning but from the overdetermination of symbols that come finally to equate with the interpreting character's subjectivity.

The pursuit of transcendent meaning through repeated encounters with a given symbol shapes the narrative quest structure of the American romance, and the relentless pursuit of meaning gives rise to the episodic structure that characterizes *The Scarlet Letter* and *Moby Dick* as well as *V.*, *The Crying of Lot 49*, *Gravity's Rainbow*, and *Mason & Dixon*. The hermeneutic dimension of the romance episodes, the way in which the romance narrative seeks meaning in a sequence of hermeneutic encounters, distinguishes it from other episodic forms of narrative, such as the picaresque. In contrast to European quest narratives, the American emphasis on interpretation introduces complexities until the narrative proves incapable of making present any hermeneutic absolute—neither point of origin nor termination—and frustration takes the place of revelation. American romance narratives are structured in a series of hermeneutic moments, each of which introduces an iteration of the accumulation of symbolic meaning. Structure becomes inseparable from meaning, and both are inseparable from the themes that dominate the American quest romance.

These themes of nature, religion, self, and society are focused in the search for the meaning of American progress. In *Mason & Dixon* Pynchon questions the effect of the Visto on the wilderness of the New World; in *V.* he represents the self-conscious anxieties of the Whole Sick Crew, who wonder whatever happened in America to produce a generation such as theirs. In *The Crying of Lot 49* Oedipa discovers an underclass whose members are united in their sense of exclusion from the American mainstream. Such suspicions about the idea of progress have been an integral part of the American romance from the first of Cooper's *Leatherstocking Tales*, *The Pioneers* (1823), where Cooper's frontier hero leads the debate about the effect of encroaching civilization on the virgin wilderness of New England and beyond. The forces of conservative reaction play off those of innovation and generate the primary narrative dynamics, not unlike the conservative Oedipa, a child of the 1950s, reacting against the whole range of progressive characters she encounters. Waïl Hassan, in his 1993 essay "This Is Not a Novel: *The Crying of Lot 49*," observes that "Oedipa's dilemma is due to her being a character in the wrong novel: she is a logocentric human being in a decentered world" (96), but in fact, the clash of conservatism and innovation, old and new, the past and the present, is entirely characteristic of the kind of narrative world in which Oedipa moves. Indeed, several of the features that supposedly define *Lot 49* and other Pynchon works as postmodern are actually characteristics of the American quest romance: the self-conscious foregrounding of narrative, the infinite deferral of meaning, the self-reflexive concern with reading and textuality. By placing Pynchon's work within the tradition of American romance, teachers can guide students out of their confusion and use the texts' unfamiliar, challenging elements to enhance their awareness of the rich potential of narrative.

## NOTE

[1] When reading this warning, one must keep in mind that the narrative that follows features the real-life Pyncheon family residing in New England (of which Thomas Pynchon is a descendant) and that living members of the family believed that Hawthorne was (mis)representing them specifically. Hawthorne, therefore, had reasons for insisting on a sharp distinction between real and fictional histories.

# Pynchon's Library

*Thomas H. Schaub*

One way to engage student interest in *The Crying of Lot 49* is through the novel's debt to influential books of the 1950s and early 1960s. To be sure, Pynchon's fiction is known for intertextual quotation and parody, but students may find especially compelling the influence exerted by those essays which became part of the national discourse contemporary with Pynchon's development as a writer. Exploring these influences shows the writer engaged with the social and political issues of his time and reveals the ways his fiction responds to them.

The social context that underlies the novel's satiric portrait of United States culture in the mid-1960s is increasingly beyond the historical horizon for most students today. Having students read and study selected excerpts from such widely read books as Norbert Wiener's *The Human Use of Human Beings* (1950, 1954), Mircea Eliade's *The Sacred and the Profane* (1959), Betty Friedan's *The Feminine Mystique* (1963), Michael Harrington's *The Other America* (1962), and Marshall McLuhan's *Understanding Media* (1964) gives them some understanding of the ideas circulating in that social context and of the issues Pynchon's books sought to redress. Students may find even more intriguing the opportunity such reading offers to peek into the writer's workshop, to see how the writer's imagination transformed contemporary debates—about men and machines, the materialism of United States culture, gender and poverty—into image, character, plot, and setting.

## *Metaphors of Closed Systems in a Novel without Closure*

Because the scene in which Oedipa converses with John Nefastis and tries to operate the Nefastis Machine is so revelatory of the novel's wider purposes, I always begin my discussion of *Lot 49* there. With the Nefastis Machine, Pynchon has ingeniously adapted the discussion of the Scottish physicist Clerk Maxwell and his theoretical refutation of thermodynamics' second law, from Wiener's *The Human Use of Human Beings*: *Cybernetics and Society*. Wiener's book was familiar to many readers; its pertinence to Pynchon's fiction was first discussed by Joseph Slade in *Thomas Pynchon* and by Anne Mangel in "Maxwell's Demon, Entropy, Information: *The Crying of Lot 49*."

Wiener received his doctorate in mathematics from Harvard University at the age of eighteen and was professor of mathematics at the Massachusetts Institute of Technology from 1919 to 1964. In the afterword to *Human Use*, Walter Rosenblith writes of Wiener's lifelong concern with "the social implications of what he came to call the cybernetic or second industrial revolution" (272). In 1948, Wiener published his ideas in *Cybernetics: Control and Communication in the Animal and the Machine*, but colleagues prevailed on him to write a less technical book for the nonscientific audience. Published in 1954, *The Human Use of Human Beings* became widely read and quoted in the fields of sociology, psychology, and the natural sciences. (I myself was assigned the book in a college humanities class, in the fall of 1966.)

Asking students to compare Wiener's discussion of Maxwell's demon in chapter 2 of *Human Use* with Pynchon's account, presented through the words of Stanley Koteks (ch. 4; 85–86) and John Nefastis (ch. 5; 105–06), is a useful exercise: students quickly see how accessible is the science knowledge required of them for understanding Pynchon's novel and how Pynchon uses this episode from science history as a complex metaphor. Most important, however, Wiener's cogent discussion of entropy and information feedback provides students with a way to approach their most common questions: What is the Trystero? Does it exist in Oedipa's world? Why doesn't Oedipa find it? Especially because *Lot 49* parodies the detective mystery genre and seduces the reader into the search with Oedipa (or makes clear that reading for meaning is a kind of detection), the novel's indeterminacies, throughout as well as at the end, can provoke not only frustration but also resentment and disappointment. One should respect these as useful reactions, by asking students, "What is at stake in the status of the Trystero? What would result from finding an actual Trystero? What might be the virtue of not finding Trystero?" Such questions may lead students to focus on the role of Trystero in developing Oedipa's consciousness over the course of the novel, from that of the bored housewife to the curious detective, marked by a new attentiveness and sensitivity to the social world around her.

The novel represents Oedipa's (and the reader's) uncertain position as the demon in the Nefastis Machine, in chapter 5. The figure of this machine organizes the novel's conceptual motivation and is an allegorical representation of both Oedipa and the reader (both are sorting demons within possibly closed systems), but the feature of the Nefastis Machine most vital to Pynchon's design is the twentieth-century recognition that the demon will wear down, unless supplied with energy from outside his box. As Oedipa points out to Koteks, "Sorting isn't work?" (86; see Mangel).

Sorting is the key metaphoric activity, not only for Maxwell's theoretical demon but also for Oedipa's activity as executrix and the reader's activity as interpreter. Not incidentally, the sorting, as an antientropic activity, also ties the concept of organization to the United States postal system and the novel's themes of communication. As Wiener observes, the ability to sustain work inside the box depends on feedback—in some form—from outside the box. This inside-outside structure is the central problem of the novel and its nested analogies and is why the novel's uncertainties are necessary.

I usually draw these nested analogies—extensions of the central metaphor—on the board, encouraging the students to help label each successive enclosing box (see illus.). Students readily assent to the first of these nested boxes: the demon, which is or may be inside the Nefastis Machine, requires the energy of a

# “A Metaphor of God Knew How Many Parts”—Thomas Pynchon, *The Crying Lot of 49* (109)

The physical or thermodynamic level of the metaphor: for the demon on the inside to sustain the energy necessary to sort the fast and slow molecules—to maintain regions of difference necessary to perform the work of moving the pistons—the demon needs energy from the outside to be communicated to him. “Communication is the key” (105).

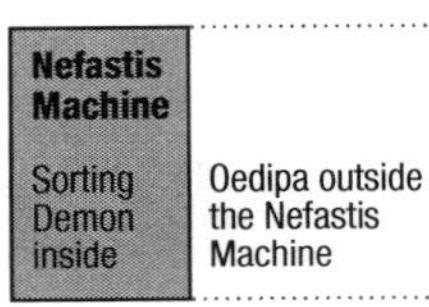


The social and political level of the metaphor, in which Oedipa is the demon inside the Republic but is unable to determine if she has come across an “underground” outside Pierce’s will—that is, a source of energy to counter the “the exitlessness” and “absence of surprise to life” (167, 170).

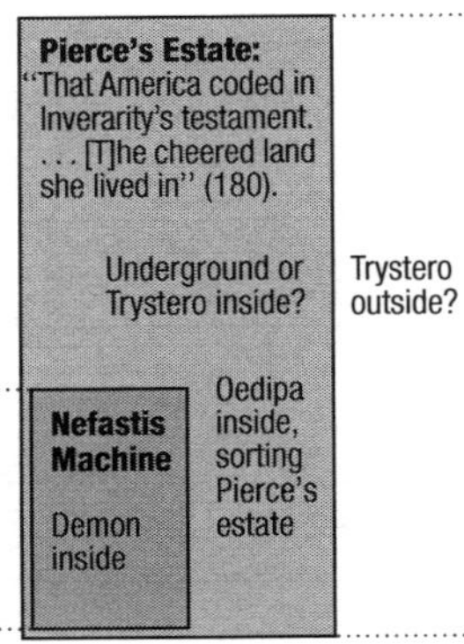


The hermeneutic level of the metaphor: reader as the sorting demon.

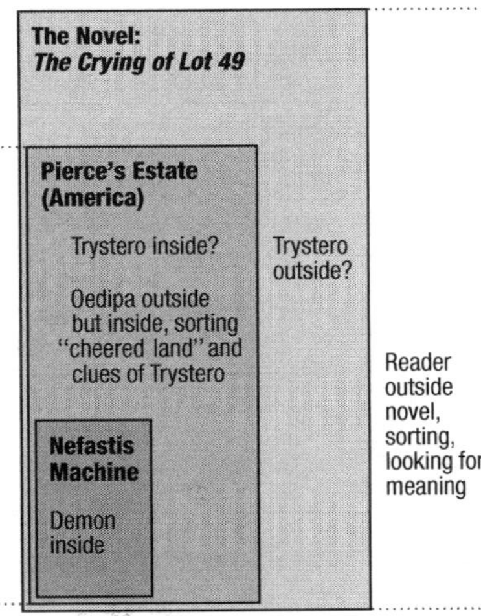


The religious or metaphysical level of the metaphor.

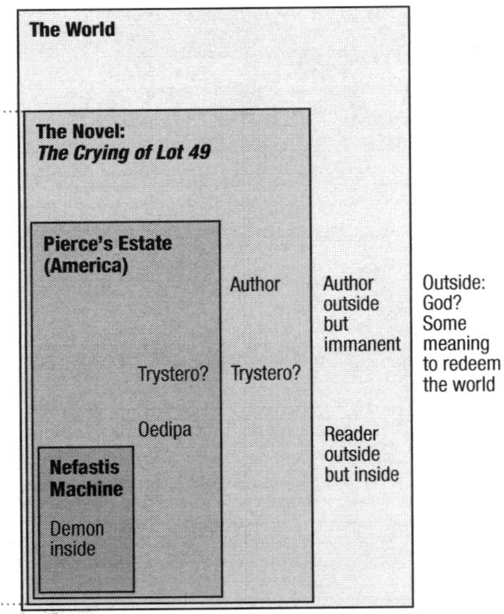

sensitive—Oedipa—on the outside. Analogously, Oedipa's position is an inside position: inside her projections and connection making, inside the environment of Pierce's estate holdings, and inside the "America coded in Inverarity's testament" (180). Just as for the demon, the question for Oedipa becomes whether or not there is an outside source of energy or information to sustain her flagging search, to make sense of Pierce's estate, or to redeem an otherwise profane and meaningless "America."

Since Pierce's estate, Oedipa discovers, is nothing less than America itself, another box may be drawn around the Nefastis Machine–box. In this Pierce's estate–America box, Oedipa is now a citizen of the Republic taking on the task of redeeming her society. Implicit within the structure of these nested analogies, is the position of the book, the reader, the author, the United States, this world and the next. (Part of the novel was first published in *Esquire*, with the title "The World (This One), the Flesh (Mrs. Oedipa Maas), and the Testament of Pierce Inverarity.")

Unfolding and diagramming the implicit logic of the Nefastis Machine metaphor also lays bare the three registers or realms the metaphor evokes: physical or thermodynamic (subject to entropy); social and political (subject to monopolistic control and exclusion); and religious or metaphysical (the world subject to meaninglessness). Only with some form of an outside can these realms persist: through feedback, diversity, or redemption. This exercise helps students trace the development of Oedipa's consciousness and clarifies the structural necessity of the novel's indeterminacy: within each nested box the possibility exists that there may or may not be an outside—a redemptive energy, information, or message—to keep the perpetual motion machine running, to give Oedipa's world meaning, and to redeem the profane materiality of American society.

Reinforcing the possibility of an inside without recourse, Pynchon introduces the motifs of incest and narcissism, metaphors of closed systems drawn from two other sources: the story of Oedipus's complicity in the famine of Thebes and McLuhan's *Understanding Media: The Extensions of Man*. From Sophocles come Oedipa's name and the motif of incest, mentioned explicitly in the description of Mucho's view of the used car lot: "To Mucho it was horrible. Endless, convoluted incest" (14). Students may be asked to identify the ways in which Oedipa's story parallels that of Oedipus Rex.

The publication of *Understanding Media* made McLuhan, a literature professor at the University of Toronto who had published on popular culture and advertising since the 1950s, into a widely read public intellectual. His ideas seemed in keeping with cultural change in the 1960s, especially with the development of the new electronic media and the view that print culture was in decline, and *Understanding Media* and the earlier *Gutenberg Galaxy* became especially influential. According to the back cover of the 1964 Mentor edition of *Understanding Media*, the *New York Herald Tribune* called him "[t]he most important thinker since Newton, Darwin, Freud, Einstein, and Pavlov." Pynchon mentions reading McLunhan in his letter to Thomas Hirsch ("Pynchon's Reading").

Among the uses Pynchon made of *Understanding Media*, perhaps none is as central as McLuhan's analogy between the closed system and the myth of Echo and Narcissus:

> The Greek myth of Narcissus is directly concerned with a fact of human experience, as the word *Narcissus* indicates. It is from the Greek word *narcosis*, or numbness. The youth Narcissus mistook his own reflection in the water for another person. This extension of himself by mirror numbed his perceptions until he became the servomechanism of his own extended or repeated image. The nymph Echo tried to win his love with fragments of his own speech, but in vain. He was numb. He had adapted to his extension of himself and had become a closed system. (51)

Of special interest here, McLuhan's admonition not only explicates the relation in Pynchon's novel between thermodynamics and narcissism—both describe closed systems—but also strongly suggests that McLuhan's analogy was the source of that relation in *Lot 49* and thus of the Echo Courts motel, the town of San Narciso in its Sunday "silence and paralysis" (26), and all the other references to narcissism in the novel.

These three metaphors—the closed system, narcissism, and incest—are triplicate figures for the state of Oedipa's culture and the predicament in which she finds herself. The scene in which Oedipa dodges a can of hair spray allegorizes this predicament. The hair spray and the mirror are instruments of vanity and of an identity formed through a structure of narcissism (perhaps a version of Lacan's mirror stage). The can itself is a closed system that literally runs out of gas, as the second law predicts, and falls to the floor, though not before breaking the bathroom mirror, which later causes Oedipa a "moment of nearly pure terror" when she can't find her(self) in a reflected image (41). The quandary presented by these mutually reinforcing metaphors might be restated by Ludwig Wittgenstein's aphorism in *Tractatus Logico-Philosophicus*—another book we know that Pynchon read: "For all that happens and is the case is accidental. What makes it non-accidental cannot lie *within* the world, since if it did it would itself be accidental. It must lie outside the world" (145; proposition 6.41).

## Alternative Sources of Energy

Just as Pynchon structures his novel with images of the closed system, he also supplies possibilities for alternative sources of energy to keep the system from running down—that is, to keep it "open." These possibilities are all gathered together and given unity by Oedipa through the term "Trystero," but the method by which Oedipa does this work of gathering and sorting clues also comes from one of McLuhan's most disseminated aphorisms, "The Medium Is the Message," the title of *Understanding Media*'s first chapter. Deploying the method of this aphorism, Oedipa discovers there is "revelation in progress all around her" (44). Here a source of meaning can be found in the medium of the culture, as against what the culture says about itself; think, for example, of the messages sent by way of the classroom versus the message sent by the medium—the room itself, with desks bolted to the floor. Oedipa first begins to shift her attention from the ostensible content of a message to the medium that conveys the message when she receives a letter from her husband Mucho: "It may have been an intuition that the letter would be newsless inside that made Oedipa look more closely at its outside" (46). This "sensitiz[ing]" (45) may be described as the beginning of Oedipa's education in alienation or estrangement from a mainstream point of view—as the moment she discovers a world of pain and disinheritance, an underside to the "affluent society" Kenneth Galbraith wrote about in 1958, of which she, Oedipa, had been a member. (Galbraith's book is another that students can be assigned to read and study, especially chapters 1 and 23 ["The Affluent Society" and "The New Position of Poverty"].)

Ironically, this troubled alternative world, which was given little visibility in the self-congratulatory culture of post–World War II America, serves as a renewing difference from the oppressive sameness of the majority culture. In the novel's eloquent last pages, Oedipa remembers Americans "in exile from somewhere else invisible yet congruent with the cheered land she lived in" (180).

Pynchon dovetails McLuhan's distinction between ostensible content and information latent in the medium with Eliade's argument in *The Sacred and the Profane* that the sacred may reside within or occupy the same space as the profane. As Edward Mendelson has shown, Pynchon borrowed the term *hierophany*, invented by Eliade, to describe those experiences when an object is both profane and sacred at the same time (Mendelson, "Sacred"). Eliade's introduction to the book gives students another look into Pynchon's workshop, for there they will find the origin of a metaphor Pynchon deploys in the wonderful description of Oedipa's entry into San Narciso, where the "vast sprawl of houses" reminds her of a radio's printed circuit: "there were to both outward patterns a hieroglyphic sense of concealed meaning, of an intent to communicate" (24), and a similar scene a few pages later in which she senses "some promise of hierophany" (31). Like the terms *closed system*, *narcissism*, and *incest* (elements of a profane world), the medium-as-message and hierophany are similar ideas in different registers, one secular and one religious. In both ideas, a shift of focus and consciousness creates the possibility of immanent meaning.

Students may be asked whether the novel's rhetoric reinforces either the inevitability of entropy or the possible alternative sources of information and meaning, and they should now be in a position to understand why Trystero cannot be found and why the novel's ending provides no resolution to Oedipa's quest. For, were Trystero to be found, it would then become simply or "just" Trystero, another element inside Oedipa's world and, like the other elements in that world, subject to its entropic forces. Trystero, then, as Mendelson puts it, is not community itself but rather a metaphor for community and as such is an example of the way that language can be a source of community. Certainly for Oedipa, "Trystero" is a figure for the meaning of the world, for the possibility that the Republic and the world have some meaning, "[a]nother mode of meaning behind the obvious," rather than "none" (182).

## *Closed System as Social Critique*

In *Lot 49*, the entropic forces that threaten Oedipa are not literally those of thermodynamic heat death or the hemophilia of incestuous offspring but the cultural, economic, class, and gender inequalities for which entropy, incest, and narcissism serve as metaphors. In many ways, this social and political dimension of the novel is easier for students to grasp (and care about) than the complexities of Oedipa's consciousness and the indeterminate results of her search, for while Trystero remains dispersed and disembodied, the nonsuburban underworld she discovers along the way is a much more concrete and still recognizable portrait of social illness in need of cure. Two widely read and influential books of the early 1960s seem to motivate central elements of Pynchon's social critique, Friedan's *The Feminine Mystique* and Harrington's *The Other America: Poverty in the United States.*

Friedan's landmark book alerted America's readers to the stagnating lives experienced by a sector of American women like Oedipa—college-educated middle-class women—and helped create the new feminism of the 1960s. Invariably, college-age students, especially women, are fascinated by the story Friedan tells of a national culture in which women were to be completely fulfilled by their femininity: as wife, mother, and homemaker. Like the women Friedan interviewed, Oedipa Maas is a bored housewife who attends Tupperware parties and prepares whiskey sours for her husband. She leads a "buffer[ed]" suburban existence (20), dependent on men and lacking a will of her own. All this changes in the course of her quest for Trystero. Cannily, Pynchon associates Trystero with such feminine iconography as the sea, the moon, and the graceful dancers of *The Courier's Tragedy*, "effeminate, dressed in black tights, leotards and gloves" (73), while the closed system is figured in masculine images of the sun, founding fathers, and the mail (male) system (the United States Postal Service). Significantly, Oedipa must lose her men—that is, she must cease being one of McLuhan's "extensions of man" (*Understanding*)—before she can see the America coded in Inverarity's testament.

The America Oedipa discovers is other and vulnerable: children, the aged, the dying, the out of work, citizens largely invisible to members of the affluent society. Bringing this world to the attention of United States readers and policy makers was the motive behind Harrington's *The Other America*. Hailed by *Time*, *Newsweek*, and the *New York Times*, *The Other America* "went on to inspire the most ambitious 'scheme of social reform' of the later twentieth century in the United States, the war on poverty launched during the administration of President Lyndon Johnson" (Isserman vii). Pynchon's phrase "invisible yet congruent" may well have derived from the title of Harrington's first chapter, "The Invisible Land." This influence, noted by Pierre-Yves Petillon, connects Pynchon's novel with the depression-era fiction of John Steinbeck and John Dos Passos. Pynchon's "drifters" and "walkers along the roads at night" are in a direct line of descent from Dos Passos's character Vag, hitchhiking at the close of *The Big Money* (1936). Indeed, the lineage is striking. In the famous peroration of Camera Eye 50 in *The Big Money*, the speaker echoes Benjamin Disraeli, "[A]ll right we are two nations"; Harrington in turn titles his final chapter, which discusses the chasm between the affluent and the poor, "The Two Nations." The failure of the affluent to eradicate poverty, Harrington writes, "is to a great extent one of vision. The nation of the well-off must be able to see through the wall of affluence and recognize the alien citizens on the other side" (156). Walking along the railroad tracks, Oedipa realizes she could have found Trystero "anywhere in her Republic . . . if only she'd looked" (179).

There are many ways to bring Pynchon's library into the classroom, but if the class size permits, my favorite method is to establish a kind of treasure hunt, on which students research one item—anything from "the Shadow knows" to Jay Gould, John Lothrop Motley's *History of the Dutch Republic*, Freud's Oedipus complex, Ovid's story of Narcissus and Echo, the exile painter Remedios Varo and her works, the Spanish dramatist Fernando Arrabal, and so forth. For the books discussed in this essay as influencing Pynchon, however, it makes more sense to assign each to one or more students, have them research the book, its issues, its timeliness, and its influence, and then ask them to use the book to advance class understanding of Pynchon's intriguing and inexhaustible novel.

# Reading the Value System of *Gravity's Rainbow* with Marcuse, Freud, and the Yippies

*Molly Hite*

What values inform *Gravity's Rainbow*? How do we discern whether scenes and passages describe activities and opinions that we ought to take seriously—that is, that seem authorially sanctioned? What tonal cues signal irony and, moreover, signal a *kind of* irony that points to an unlicensed sentiment, an authorially devalued character? How is it that readers can deal with narratological complexity and subtlety while remaining radically unclear about the moral and political views of a novel that seems passionately committed to both an ethics and a politics?

Like many critics, my graduate students appeal to Michel Foucault, Gilles Deleuze (with or without Felix Guattari—the duo later satirically invoked in *Vineland*'s reference to the "indispensable *Italian Wedding Fake Book*, by Deleuze & Guattari" [97; Hite, "Feminist Theory"]), Julia Kristeva, Jacques Derrida, and Jacques Lacan to find contexts for the critique of Western hegemony and the psychoanalytic schema that can somehow account for "The Penis He Thought Was His Own" (Pynchon, *Gravity's Rainbow* 216 [see Mattessich; McHoul and Wills]). But their analyses leave unilluminated some of the most characteristic tendencies of the novel. For instance, erotic descriptions titillate as well as represent titillation in many scenes of conventionally problematic sex—pedophilia, whipping, bondage (Bérubé). Furthermore, the narrator of *Gravity's Rainbow* is often oddly sympathetic to characters easily thematized as destructive and malevolent, like Ned Pointsman, Greta Erdmann, Thanatz, and especially the SS officer Blicero. Most of all, this narrator is frequently nostalgic in ways that embarrass today's antiessentialists: yearning for an apparently lost realm of connectedness with natural forces that is metaphorized by the myth of the Titans or the nineteenth-century hypothesis of "the Aether" (*Gravity's Rrainbow* 720, 726).

One reason the theorists most likely to be read in academic literary graduate programs of the 1980s and 1990s fall short of illuminating much of the value system of *Gravity's Rainbow* is that they are not the writers that United States academics—and, more important, activists—were reading in the late 1960s, the period during which Pynchon was writing the novel. Because theory first penetrated the academy in the United States and Britain through departments of French, English-language scholars are most familiar with writing that takes as its touchstone 1968 in Paris, rather than 1968 in the United States—when, along with many other spectacular protests, the Youth International Party (or Yippies) ran a pig for president. In 1967, the Yippy founder Abbie Hoffman, the poet Allen Ginsberg, and many others claimed that they had chanted so powerfully during a massive demonstration that they had levitated the Pentagon several inches to exorcise its demons. Two years earlier, Hoffman, Jerry Rubin, and several other activists had thrown hundreds of dollar bills from the visitors' gallery over the floor of the New York Stock Exchange, closing it down when brokers abandoned their megadeals to crawl around on the floor grabbing the free money (Hoffman, *Autobiography* 100–02).

Such actions seem as fabulous as Roger Mexico's lengthy piss on "Their" (628) board of directors or the gross-out session staged by Mexico and Seaman Bodine at the Krupp banquet (*Gravity's Rainbow* 636, 715–17). The Yippies' motivations were political but embodied a kind of politics that had almost disappeared from public consciousness during the decades when I first taught *Gravity's Rainbow*. A key element of this politics was play. During the 1969 trial of the Chicago Seven, young men indicted for disrupting the 1968 Democratic National Convention, Hoffman (who inevitably was one of them) testified that in contemporary America, having fun "was a direct rebuttal of the kind of ethics and morals that were being put forth in the country to keep people working in a rat race which didn't make any sense because in a few years machines would do all the work anyway. . . ." He went on to denounce "a whole system of values that people were taught to postpone their pleasure, to put all their money in the bank, to buy life insurance, a whole bunch of things that didn't make any sense to our generation at all. . . ." Hoffman concluded "that fun actually was becoming quite subversive" ("Testimony").

One method, then, to help students identify the value system of *Gravity's Rainbow* is to have them read selected excerpts from such works as Hoffman's *Autobiography* and *Steal This Book*, anthologized reprints of Paul Krassner's great magazine *The Realist*, transcripts of the Chicago Seven trial, and other documents of countercultural activitism. This subversive play by all sorts of 1960s radicals was often rooted in the sociocultural theorizing of Herbert Marcuse—a Frankfurt School critic and assistant to Martin Heidegger—who as a German Jew immigrated to the United States in 1934. Marcuse had a long career as a philosopher and professor. He was teacher and mentor to Abbie Hoffman, Kathy Acker, and Angela Davis. His enormously influential 1955 cultural synthesis, *Eros and Civilization: A Philosophical Inquiry into Freud* (reissued with an important political preface in 1966), provides a framework for exactly those elements of the novel that have proved most pressing and elusive. *Eros and Civilization* elaborates a radical analysis of postindustrial civilization and affirms a system of oppositional values, many of them strikingly offensive or "perverse" by the standards of the 1950s and 1960s dominant culture (and, to some extent, of the dominant culture today).

Along with Khachig Tölölyan's "War as Background in *Gravity's Rainbow*" (which we read with part 1 of *Gravity's Rainbow*, "Beyond the Zero"), I assign *Eros and Civilization* in its entirety to my graduate students for discussion the week before we begin Pynchon's novel. Because undergraduates require less reading and more guidance, I spend two classes of the senior-level seminar reading Marcuse and provide an initial short description of the general outline of his argument in *Eros and Civilization*. We read the first four chapters of part 1 and chapters 7 and 8 ("Phantasy and Utopia" and "The Images of Orpheus and Narcissus") in part 2. In what follows I offer some of the salient connections between Marcuse's text and Pynchon's epic novel, suggesting along the way strategies to engage students in making these connections for themselves.

Lawrence C. Wolfley has linked the values of *Gravity's Rainbow* to the revisionist psychoanalytic writings of Norman O. Brown, a more mainstream cultural critic of the 1950s and 1960s who was deeply influenced by Marcuse. But Brown's emphasis on the individual and on normative standards of sexual behavior fit poorly with the radical politics and polymorphous sexual exuberance of Pynchon's novel (Wolfley). There can be little question that Pynchon knew *Eros and Civilization*, however, and that it influenced his 1973 epic.

*Gravity's Rainbow* picks up specific motifs from Marcuse's study. Even more important, finding connections between *Gravity's Rainbow* and *Eros and Civilization* helps students study the historical situation of a text and the ways a writer can be influenced by contemporaneous ideas. For example, Marcuse's book presents a nontraditional characterization of Orpheus as a figure connected not only with music and memory but also with play, desire, "perverse" sexuality, receptivity, and nonproductivity. The study lays out an origin and theory of what Marcuse calls the "sublime administration" (*Eros* 91–92) and Pynchon calls Them. It bases part of its argument on the same two geometrical figures that *Gravity's Rainbow* associates with the Rocket—the ascending arc, a mapping of literal flight and metaphorical progress; and its counterfigure, the circle. Both Marcuse and Pynchon elaborate these figures as a commentary on transcendence—transcendence as the central value of Western culture and a *negative* value.

Most of all, Marcuse's argument supplies students with a context for Pynchon's novel indicating how the postwar decades both resemble and are an effect of the period from the 1930s through World War II. Marcuse claimed that the society in which Pynchon wrote *Gravity's Rainbow* existed in a privileged historical moment, when surplus production seemed likely to allow citizens to work much shorter hours. At this point, when a "leisure society" became for the first time economically feasible, Marcuse proposed that affluent societies might conceivably "regress," reversing their monomaniacal demand for increased productivity and consequent "progress" toward increasing armaments and nuclear "overkill."

Going backward, returning, or reversing direction all became in Marcuse's thinking positive values, ways of claiming a mode of life that would not be dedicated to the endless increase of productivity and domination over nature and other cultures. As Marcuse wrote in this political preface, "Historical backwardness may again become the historical chance of turning the wheel of progress to another direction" (*Eros* xvii). Many prominent sociologists and economists theorized that in the affluent society Abbie Hoffman had predicted, there would be less need for repressive structures of work, time, and competition

(Galbraith). In the unprecedented Zone of possibility anticipated for the postwar West, Marcuse could well have declared with the Argentine anarchist Squalidozzi, "[O]ur hope is limitless. . . . So is our danger" (*Gravity's Rainbow* 265). Squalidozzi explains that hope lies in a geographic area where "this War—this incredible War—just for the moment has wiped out the proliferation of little states that's prevailed in Germany for a thousand years." The postwar Zone is a brilliant spatial representation of a temporal condition no longer compartmentalized and regulated by the demands of productivity. For Squalidozzi this new zone recalls an apparently archaic object of desire, an ur-Argentina, "that first unscribbled serenity . . . that anarchic oneness of pampas and sky . . ." (264–65; ellipses in orig.). The new and in many respects unprecedented Zone signals possibility and thus futurity but takes the form of nostalgia for a mythic past: a golden age or prelapsarian Eden always described in terms of oneness or an absence of oppositions, distinctions, or binaries.

Students of psychoanalysis, especially those attuned to British object-relations theory or the matricentric writings of Julia Kristeva, will hear in this nostalgia regret for the dissolution of the pre-oedipal bond between mother and child. According to Freud and Lacan, as well as Melanie Klein, D. W. Winnicott, and Kristeva, the infant's primordial perception is of being the universe, of constituting a seamless unity with the mother and, through her, the world. This primitive certainty exists to be betrayed, however, by desires that cannot always or cannot immediately be fulfilled. Because the infant is not satiated on every occasion of want, she or he must eventually come to terms with a break between self and mother, self and other, and finally self and world: a break that violates an impression of originary wholeness but allows conceptualization and language to arise as means of bridging the gap.

Psychoanalysis thus takes an entire Western metaphysical and theological preoccupation with the longing to eradicate the distinction between subject and object and assimilates it to a story about individual psychic development. Freud was well aware how his narrative about the origins of the individual dealt with desires motivating Western disciplines from mysticism and gnosticism to the dialectical historicism of Hegel and Marx. In the essays generally called metapsychological, notably *Totem and Taboo*, *Beyond the Pleasure Principle*, and *Civilization and Its Discontents*, he drew from his theories of individual development a more speculative account of how present-day civilizations came into being and operate.

As a political philosopher, Marcuse was most directly concerned with these essays because they construct a narrative of Western history as ever-increasing repression. Freud postulated that human beings have learned to deny or defer more and more of their instinctive desires for pleasure (called variously Eros, the life instinct, or the pleasure principle) as societies have become more sophisticated and work has required more skill, training, and single-mindedness. In *Civilization and Its Discontents* he suggested that repression has so thwarted or attenuated the pleasure principle that advanced civilizations are in danger from a group of instinctive impulses striving for death (Thanatos, or the death drive). Directed outward, as aggression and destruction, these instincts clash with the "binding" or uniting power of the pleasure principle. Freud observed about the interwar period, "Men have gained control over the forces of nature to such an extent that with their help they would have no difficulty exterminating one another to the last man" (112). This situation of genocide gone global is dramatized at the conclusion of *Gravity's Rainbow*, where the last Rocket hangs an infinitesimal distance over the heads of "us, old fans who've always been at the movies (haven't we?)" (760). Pynchon's narrator seems cozily assured that "we" recognize the disaster and our collusion in it.

In *Eros and Civilization* Marcuse accepts much of Freud's melancholy story, emphasizing even further the intrinsic tendency of a civilization based on increasing repression to "progress" toward its own destruction. His project begins with bringing historical particularity to a story that Freud presented as universal. Marcuse argues that civilization in general need not take the form that Western civilization has taken. Indeed, there are many cultures in the Third World that have developed in strikingly different ways. (The key example in *Gravity's Rainbow* is Herero culture in what is now Namibia.) Most important, Western civilization relies on what Marcuse calls the performance principle, an impetus to detach from and dominate the natural order. The performance principle has its origin in the need for survival but cannot stop when survival is assured. The increased control of nature, entailing exploitation and technological transformation, becomes the definition of progress, to which human happiness is subordinated. The performance principle denies people's desire for what we might call, following Pynchon's original title for *Gravity's Rainbow*, mindless pleasures—sexual, playful, and nonproductive (or nonreproductive)—in order to promote labor that becomes ever more alienated from its products and purposes. As the society evolves to the point where it can satisfy basic human needs, the demand for more—and more complicated—goods and thus technologies of production entails more work, more alienation, and more repression.

In Marcuse's analysis, the industrial society that can provide for everyone (but of course does not) and that continues to raise its standards of productivity requires a "surplus-repression" from its members (35). The restrictions on pleasure, deferring or simply denying the gratification of many desires, which Freud saw as necessary to organize socially and to survive in a world of material necessity, grow more encompassing and more arbitrary. As the performance principle accelerates and exacerbates its own processes in the drive toward more power, functional knowledge, and transformation of the natural world, it serves increasingly aggressive and ultimately destructive ends. In the terms that Freud developed in *Beyond the Pleasure Principle*, productivity serves the death drive, rather than the life force that is Eros. The organization of Western societies under patriarchal capitalism, the monogamistic family, and the work ethic is for Marcuse always defined by the requirement of transcendence—that is, of exceeding the present moment and thrusting into the future in order to dominate and control further. And for Marcuse the most poignant symbol of such transcendence is the ascending curve, a visual representation of endless progress (*Eros* 118, 124).

This ascending curve is the central idea and the title figure of *Gravity's Rainbow*. The Rocket rises under human guidance and in response to a humanly defined demand to mount above natural processes, but ultimately it is "betrayed to Gravity" and descends uncontrolled and unguided (758). It is the major image in *Gravity's Rainbow* of the tendency of the performance principle to fall into service to the death drive. Another embodiment of this principle is Enzian's vision of a vampirish transnational economy that exceeds human controls and goes on to create and feed off human power struggles (521). Enzian's "paranoid" revelation concurs with Marcuse's observation that the human endeavor leading to advanced technologies has given these technologies a momentum that endows them with something akin to motivation (*One-Dimensional Man*). Technological development now has its own wants and needs. Although national and corporate leaders claim to be in control, they seem determined to go as far as they can in developing annihilating weapons, destroying resources necessary to sustain human life, and constraining the possibility that anyone can think differently—including ahead.

As Freud spells out in *Beyond the Pleasure Principle*, the goal of the death instinct is to return life to the state of the inorganic: life is always "a detour to death" (46–47). Marcuse adds that in postindustrial civilization this move toward the inorganic is economic and social and its reach is global. Pynchon dramatizes both observations by emphasizing how the productions of advanced industrial society attempt to transcend life by imitating it. His two main examples are key developments leading to World War II and the cold war era: chemical synthesis, especially polymerization, and the rise of intricate international corporate structures (as legal entities, corporations are inorganic persons). In a brilliant moment early in the story, Pynchon has the ghost of the assassinated industrialist and Weimar foreign minister Walther Rathenau explain to a séance of Nazi and German corporate elite that their ostensible "growing, organic Kartell" disguises a "real movement . . . from death to death-transfigured . . . just as the buried coal [the matter that is transformed by chemical polymerization] grows denser, and overlaid with more strata—epoch on top of epoch, city on top of ruined city" (166–67). In *Gravity's Rainbow*, societies driven by the performance principle create ersatz life. They permute and combine molecules to form polymers, culminating in the "*erectile*!" plastic (699) Imipolex G (which has some provocative connection to Tyrone Slothrop and his apparently death-dealing erections). They design, test, and use a supersonic Rocket that seems to draw charisma from the generations of leaders and scientists who dreamed of its potential for both literal and figurative transcendence. And they transcend visible human leaders by making the real power progressively less locatable. The logical extension of ungraspable boards of directors, vanishing CEOs, and heads of state in undisclosed locations is the shadowy superauthority called Them, controllers whose intentions are wholly self-interested, wholly unknowable, and finally inhuman.

*Eros and Civilization* also provides a positive framework for *Gravity's Rainbow*'s alternative communities, for nonproductive or "perverse" sexual pleasures—especially eroticized dominance and submission, for the value of chemically altered consciousness (Marcuse does not mention hallucinogenic substances, but *Eros and Civilization* was accepted by the 1960s counterculture as an argument in favor of drug-induced mental states), and for the overtly essentialist appeals to an unconscious *not* structured like a language and a correlative idyllic realm of the natural (*Eros* 143; Schaub, "Environmental Pynchon"). It also theorizes the botched oedipal politics whereby fathers kill their offspring and whereby the revolution is betrayed by "[t]he Man" who "has a branch office in each of our brains" (*Gravity's Rainbow* 712).

I have come to regard readings about countercultural worldviews of the 1960s as the most important keys I can offer to students beginning *Gravity's Rainbow*. Of all these readings, Marcuse's *Eros and Civilization* provides the indispensable background to a fictional universe no longer contemporary with its readers.

# “Feeling Totally Familied Out”: Teaching Pynchon through Families

*Mark Rohland*

It is difficult to stimulate discussion of Pynchon’s novels among undergraduates, especially those who are not English majors. They may approach a famously intriguing work like *The Crying of Lot 49* with interest, but the text rebuffs them. One reason students find these narratives hard to connect with is that their characters seem unfamiliar: a classroom focus on Pynchon’s characters in the context of something recognizable—families, especially parent-child relations—facilitates understanding of the novels and is a useful first step for approaching Pynchon’s challenges. To illustrate this teaching approach, I outline the role of families in Pynchon, discuss some helpful classroom strategies, and propose some benefits of the strategy.

## *Pynchon’s Families*

Pynchon’s novels require readers to figure out where to focus interpretive energy. One often overlooked aspect, even when readers focus on the author’s puzzling characters, is the pervasive and pedagogically useful characterization of families, particularly unhappy ones in which children are neglected or abused. At the heart of *V.*, *Gravity’s Rainbow*, and *Vineland* are children suffering from parental misconduct, sometimes, as in Slothrop’s case, into adulthood. Some adults who stand in parental positions—like V. for Mélanie or Weissmann for Gottfried—are portrayed, like fairy-tale stepparents, as lethal. Even in *Lot 49*, where a solitary figure is central, familial unhappiness, represented at different levels in Oedipa’s marriage and her name, is important. Action in the later novels, too, concerns families: the Wheelers’ problems are central to *Vineland*, and families in *Mason & Dixon* continue to haunt the explorers in the New World.

It is possible to finish a Pynchon novel feeling, like Prairie Wheeler at the family reunion, “totally familied out” (*Vineland* 374). Yet the major role of families in the novels is not extensively acknowledged in Pynchon criticism, where themes garner more attention than characterization. In forty years of Pynchon criticism, only a few articles, like Strother Purdy’s survey of the children of the Zone and N. Katherine Hayles’s analysis of kinship in *Vineland* (“ ‘Who’ ”), have made families their central concern. Roger B. Henkle’s early assessment of Pynchon’s “weakness [in] realizing character” represents a typical view that finds the author’s characters less achieved than his themes and narrative devices (“Pynchon’s Tapestries” 214).

Students, too, often complain that Pynchon’s characters are weakly realized, but examining the figures in a familial context can shift classroom responses from complaint to analysis. In making invidious comparisons between Pynchon's realization of character and, say, Saul Bellow's rich psychological portraits, critics risk overlooking the meaning of that difference, which can often be found by examining the interactions of Pynchon's characters. These interactions reveal zones of conflict in which character is conditioned by forces like war and abandonment that weaken families and fail to nurture strong character development. As Edward Mendelson notes in an early essay on *Gravity's Rainbow*, Pynchon works against "the modern prejudice that gives primacy to the affective aspects of personality," choosing instead to develop his characters' "relations to large social and economic systems" ("Gravity's Encyclopedia" 179–80). For example, significant characters like Paola in *V.* and Bianca and Gottfried in *Gravity's Rainbow* are in an abused child's relation to the social world around them—exposed to danger, searching for safety, and enmeshed with harmful parental figures—and therefore are weak (vulnerable) and characterized without much interiority. Thus the purported weakness of Pynchon's characterization may not be a flaw but may be an effect of failures of socialization (in families and the world) that leave adults childlike. In other words, what readers see as poor characterization can instead be understood as strong renderings of familial and social influence.

## Teaching Pynchon's Families

Fictional families may be useful to the instructor interested in having students consider history in Pynchon: the author noted for his difficult vision of history is also a family historian, and students often find concerns of the household more intelligible than those of international history. Indeed, it could be hypothesized that Pynchon views history as that which attacks the family and against which the family fights back. Undergraduates are generally more interested in family issues than historical trends, and Pynchon's work can show them how history influences problems like child abuse and divorce. Thematic insight arises from insight into relationships among characters, and if students are encouraged to examine the effects of history on families and given some textual examples—the effects of the events of the 1960s on marriage in *Lot 49* and *Vineland* or the effects of war on children in *V.* and *Gravity's Rainbow*—they may become more enthusiastic about the novels' historical themes than when such themes are presented abstractly.

In an undergraduate class, starting a discussion of a Pynchon novel with students' responses to the characters works well. Although students will want explication of the baffling immediately, it is helpful to let them find their own way for a bit before offering guidance. Once opinions and questions about characters are aired, teachers can prompt the class to focus on characters in the context of families. The extent to which familial troubles shape a character's actions—Stencil's impersonations in *V.*, Oedipa's flight in *Lot 49*—might be examined. It can also be helpful to relate the actions to students' experience. They usually remain silent about their own families but are able to connect parental misconduct they have witnessed (and its effects) to textual incidents. Such connections make the characters easier to talk and think about.

One might assign "The Secret Integration" as an introduction to Pynchon's play of allusions and ideas. In the story, adults like Tim's racist mother are clearly cast as villains, while children attempt—unsuccessfully—to create a world safe from dangerous adult intrusion. In discussion, students can easily connect the story's events to their own childhood relations with grownups and other children, reflections that can then be applied to less familiar instances of threatened children in the novels.

Though student responses are crucial, it is important for the instructors to stimulate and structure discussion of a Pynchon novel, especially at the beginning. For the first hour, I find it effective to assign a reaction sheet in which students explain what interests them about a character to which they respond strongly. In class, I ask some or all students to share their reactions so that we can find figures of common interest and focus attention on key passages. Often, much interest develops in characters to which students respond negatively, like the disturbing avatar of V. that abuses Mélanie. Rereading passages that illuminate the characters refreshes students' memories, builds their confidence, and stimulates further thought. From here discussion often moves into critique of the characters' traits and actions. If Paola has so strong a father, why does she seem such a passive character? Why does *Vineland*'s Frenesi leave her family? As the class attempts to answer such questions, I prompt students to consider familial explanations, if they seem plausible and potentially fruitful. For instance, considering the enigma of Paola's passivity in the light of her war-torn upbringing can initiate exploration of the important themes of historical discontinuity and disturbances of identity.

As discussion develops, teachers should contribute knowledge that illuminates characters and incidents: define the Oedipus complex, explain the importance of violent families in Jacobean tragedy, or distinguish between Pynchon's and received versions of twentieth-century events. Such interventions show students that the confusing narratives are worth deciphering for their revelations about what it is to be human. Pynchon's proposition, for example, that to be human is to be artificial, a "stencil" of one's parents or of earlier generations, is a challenge to received wisdom that stimulates lively debate.

Family-related discussion questions often provide useful starting points for students struggling with the texts. The suggestion that V. "seduced" Stencil's father (488) invites the question of whether she could be his mother and can lead first to a discussion of V.'s many identities, then to tracking the literal and figurative ways that she functions as a mother, and then to the difficult question of the identity of the author of the narrative that makes her a mother. In a class on Pynchon's novels, consideration of V.'s complexity can be extended to examine the nature of resemblance in texts that complicate identity by multiplying versions of the same entity (V., the Tristero, the villains of the Zone). Students respond well to the idea that such figurative resemblance in Pynchon is much like family resemblance. A perceptive student of mine saw an intertextual metaphor in which both V. and the Tristero function as vehicles of desire for a lost mother. Questions about family can give students a way to approach the questions about metaphor and identity that Pynchon's texts insistently raise.

Pynchon's fictional children and families yield no end of rewarding discussion topics. Why does Mélanie become V.'s fetishized sex object (410–11), just as the girl was for her father (401)? What does this repetition of abuse say about abusive families generally? Thinking about abusive parent-child relationships in *Lot 49* raises questions about the parody of child abuse enacted through Metzger. What does he tell Oedipa about family relationships? What can we make of the correspondence between his menacing stage mother and the ineffective father of *Cashiered*, who kills Metzger's child-star character in a submarine named after the character's dead mother (31–32)? How does this parody of bad parenting relate to the similarly familial silencing of youth in *The Courier's Tragedy*? The inquiry can show students how close such recognizable family relations lie to more impenetrable aspects of the novels, like perversion and uncanny repetition, thus helping them move their interpretations from the simple to the complex. A combination of open and guided discussion takes students beyond agreeing that a character like V. is weird or repulsive to articulating what she tells them about motherhood or death.

Like discussion questions, writing topics can allow young scholars to see how family matters resonate with larger ideas. In a sophomore novel course including *Lot 49*, I had good results when I encouraged the class to use research from psychology and religion to discuss ways in which Inverarity functions as an absent father figure (e.g., leaving Oedipa with an inheritance, determining her life like God the father). A rewarding writing topic for an American novel course including *Vineland* was a study of Frenesi as mother that asked what justifies or condemns her leaving her family, in the light of what students knew of the representation of marriage in other contemporary novels such as Don DeLillo's *White Noise*. A reader-response approach to this topic resulted in several individualized, well-developed papers about marriage in relation to students' own conceptions of real and ideal marriage.

An assignment involving analysis of voice in *V.* proved challenging and edifying for a senior in a thesis class. The student remarked that the voices of the Profane and Stencil sections differ. She investigated the significance of this difference in view of her initial impression that the Profane sections seem adolescent and the Stencil sections mature. Her paper studied these shifts of register, showing how diction and style created them and examining what these "impersonations" (59) as Stencil would have it, of youth and maturity meant for the substantiality of characters in the novel. This assignment might be revised for undergraduates interested in the mystery of Pynchon the man. They can speculate why the young author chose to adopt such different and ambiguous voices instead of his "own." Can we, as Pynchon seems to in *Slow Learner*, blame his inconsistency of voice on his youth and a predilection for "literary theft" (16)? Or are there less personal, historically mediated forces at work in his early parodies of spy fiction and beat novels? Struggling with these questions, students learn how literature and society interact to produce what we think of as characters and authors.

## *Benefits*

This family-centered approach to Pynchon, which tends to focus on matters close to students' hearts, like children, instead of on the teacher's dauntingly informed readings of Pynchon, has in my experience greatly improved the quality of class discussion. In one of my classes, disgust with the abuse of Mélanie led to frank talk about the prevalence of sexual abuse in a society that fetishizes the female body. In several reaction papers that followed, students spoke of women they knew who had been abused; the novel had helped them learn something important about the connection between objectification of women and child abuse. Family-centered discussion is often wide-ranging, as students shift between observations about the "real" world of lonely youth and bad families and interpretations of textual worlds in which characters are just as confused as real people. Students realize with Oedipa how complex the world is and how difficult to understand. They learn through investigating the familiar text of life and the strange text of literature together that life must be read.

Another benefit of this strategy is that it elucidates puzzling aspects of Pynchon that frustrate many readers. For instance, discussion of neglectful parents helps explain the author's interest in entropy. An idea like entropic information loss is clarified by linking it with the idea of the information loss between uncaring parents and their children. Similarly, Pynchon's confusing "procedures that interrupt narrative progression" (Cornis-Pope 107) can be familiarized by seeing them as representative of the interrupted stories that are abusive childhoods and as resembling childhood's challenge to authoritative narrative modes. Once students see that the novels are much concerned with childhood, they are less disturbed by narrative strategies borrowed from comic books, adventure stories, and daydreaming. Digressions like Profane's alligator adventure, the Metzger episode, or the *Gravity's Rainbow* tale of Byron the Bulb seem no longer trivial but expressions of youthful energy directed against repressive parental forces.

A further advantage of the approach is that it demonstrates that character is constituted in fiction just as much through relations among figures as through "character" understood as "individuality." This concept leads directly to important theoretical questions about the constitution of the extraliterary subject. As Mendelson indicates, for Pynchon the subject is often shaped by impersonal relations, "structures of government or convention" outside of which the individual barely exists ("Encyclopedic Narrative" 1273). The family-centered approach suggests that families (like Slothrop's) can be complicit with the impersonal forces (like the rocket cartel) that determine personality.

Indeed, discussion of families generates consideration of larger ideas in the novels: attention to the physical and mental harm done to Gottfried or the children of Malta by the forces of war can initiate discussion of key ideas in *Gravity's Rainbow* and *V.*, such as repression, technology, and the persistence of trauma. Similarly, attention to the absence of living parent figures in *Lot 49* can initiate discussion of the related themes of death and denial of death that Diana York Blaine rightly suggests are central to that novel (52). Characters embody ideas in Pynchon, and parents and children embody them with instructive clarity.

Not the least important benefit of teaching Pynchon through families is the insight gained that a deep concern with family characterizes postmodern novels just as much as it does traditional novels like Dickens's and Tolstoy's. Students learn how to discover their own experience in the seemingly alien narrative lines and themes of difficult contemporary fictions. All good teaching of postmodern novels works to foster this discovery, but families provide an easier beginning than less personal, more abstract lenses. The personal approach is especially beneficial for lower-division undergraduates not majoring in English, from whom it has generated intelligent papers: a formerly hippie mother wrote on Oedipa as 1960s woman; a paper on Pynchon as slow learner and "thief" was informed by a student's dyslexia and growth as a writer; and another student related Stencil's impersonations to a personal struggle to recover from psychosis. All these papers showed clear understanding of the ways that literature reflects and does not reflect life, a starting point for investigating the greater questions that literature teachers want young scholars to be able to address.

By beginning an examination of Pynchon's work with what is already familiar to students, the instructor brings them to understand sophisticated aspects of the texts gradually and gratifyingly. Such an approach can also help undergraduates study other difficult writers who focus on families, such as Joyce. After a well-guided exploration of Pynchon's parents and children, undergraduates may feel "totally familied out," but they will not think like the incorrigibly immature Profane that they "haven't learned a goddamn thing" (454).

# Reading Race: *The Crying of Lot 49* and Early Pynchon

*Steven Weisenburger*

Readers of Pynchon's second novel interested in critical studies of its racial politics will search the MLA database and skim texts from their library stacks in vain. Beyond mentions of characters' ethnoracial identities as ascriptive signs of membership in a modern American underclass, the available scholarship offers nothing approaching a sustained analysis of race. This lack makes initial sense because the story's all about white folks . . . isn't it? Mostly it is, though I contend that in a thoroughly racialized society where "white" is the central yet unexamined identity category, attending to what Toni Morrison names the "Africanist presence" (5) in a novel like *Lot 49* unlocks rich potential both for close reading the text and for historicizing its depictions of race and social struggle in 1960s United States culture.

Approaching Oedipa's sojourn as detective quest, a common interpretive tactic, provides a good starting point because detection requires reading carefully the ensembles of textual and contextual evidence before one. Thus I guide classroom discussion toward a sense of how Pynchon's narrative has sequenced Oedipa's encounters with an array of men who each, as John Johnston has shown, supply what may be clues about the Tristero as a network for (potentially) subversive communications among America's "disinherited" (164). We also map out how these men's disclosures send the bourgeois Oedipa into a steep descent among those disfranchised San Franciscans she glimpses in Chinatown (117), in an "all-night Mexican greasy spoon" (119), in an "exhausted busful of Negroes going on to graveyard shifts" (121), and in dingy city streets teeming with alienated souls who may be living out "a calculated withdrawal . . . from the life of the Republic" (124). This mapping helps students see that Oedipa returns from that underworld with basic questions about political power: Who wields and who resists it? How, and with what results? Focusing on power and control orients our reading of the narrative's more off-the-wall plot digressions.

Even though Pynchon's humorously named array of professionals and entrepreneurs (e.g., Manny Di Presso, Genghis Cohen) possess relatively less power than Pierce Inverarity, it is significant that every one of them is white, an invisible trait so long as whiteness remains the default racial category. Moreover, the narration identifies two of those men, Hilarius (the former Nazi concentration camp psychiatrist) and Winthrop Tremaine (the Los Angeles swastika salesman), with a mid-twentieth-century fascist white supremacy in its (anti-Semitic) German and (anti-black) United States versions, thus also stipulating a historical link or inheritance joining American to European imperial and racial desires. Here discussion might detour from close reading into historicist critiques of race, but first I take up Oedipa's brief encounter with Tremaine.

The most overtly racist man Oedipa meets, Tremaine describes how his government surplus store sells simulated Nazi armbands and SS uniforms:

> "Got this little factory down outside of San Diego," he told her, "got a dozen of your niggers, say, they sure can turn them old armbands out. You'd be amazed how that little number's selling. I took some space in a couple of the girlie magazines, and I had to hire two extra niggers last week just to take care of the mail." (149)

Here Tremaine's second-person possessives ("your niggers") extend the fraternal hand of a white racist solidarity (for "[w]inners") that Oedipa belatedly realizes she cannot name but ought to have rejected, if only for its obvious sexism (note that Tremaine advertises in "girlie magazines"). The belatedness of her response practically assents to Tremaine's racism (one reason it persists socially) and casual sexism. This scene also spotlights how subordinate Oedipa feels to masculine power, from her relations to Inverarity at the novel's beginning through to its conclusion, when she prepares to face a roomful of suited businessmen. Finally, Oedipa's lapse in this scene also lets slide, with no challenge, Tremaine's commodification of genocidal Nazism into a set of empty signs to be marketed in a contemporary American fashion system. One might well critique this moment using Fredric Jameson's analysis of late capitalism's eviscerated histories, the "cultural logic" of a postmodernity and its ceaselessly marketed derealizations of the past, its amnesias in the face of historical fact and process, and its wholesale flattening of affect (*Postmodernism; or, The Cultural Logic of Late Capitalism*). Such a reading would require one to locate Oedipa in her time, at just the historical moment (1965–66) when George Lincoln Rockwell's brown-shirted, swastika-banded American Nazi party members claimed national headlines as they hounded and at times physically assaulted black civil-rights activists—including an infamous 1965 assault on Martin Luther King. While Pynchon wrote, Rockwell was espousing exterminationist solutions to "The Negro Question" (see Simonelli, esp. 75–76).

Which turns attention back on Tremaine's black sweatshop workers. Oedipa passively condones racism; Tremaine's "niggers" manufacture badges for white men who are their worst nightmare. How can they aid a fascist white supremacy? The question requires that readers analyze the complicity of Pynchon's disinherited Americans with their disinheritors; and that analysis finally obliges one to reckon with the Tristero system's alleged subversive communications system in terms of co-optation and complicity. And since the structure of either-or propositions that drives Oedipa's (and thus potentially our) interpretive (detective) effort is itself built on the supposition of an oppositional, subversive Tristero, reading Tristero's messages as working in cahoots with rather than in opposition to white domination enables readers to see Oedipa's propositions as forming an interpretive cul-de-sac for us to leave behind—like a so-called dead letter.

A powerful way to begin historicizing a reading of this novel is to turn to Pynchon's June 1966 essay, "A Journey into the Mind of Watts," published when *Lot 49* was in press. The Watts essay is overclouded with pessimism at the prospect of an oppressed people who have persisted for too long in believing "the white version of what a Negro was supposed to be" (78). Although Pynchon images a few sharp-dressed militant Black Muslims and Black Power advocates, Watts remains for him a brutally oppressed and perversely narcissistic subculture. The essay reads Watts as a space as well as a "mind" recognized within its closed circle and by its closed circuit, an anticommunity where white oppression and black complicity recognize their identities in each other.

That self-reflexivity so vital to colonialist domination may be seen as defining the novel's fictional California through place names like San Narciso and the Echo Courts motel, where Oedipa's runaway hairspray can shatters a mirror (37). But I also like to suggest in broader strokes the relation between essay and novel. Understood equally well as a Conradian "journey into," the novel eventually finds Oedipa wandering among the Bay Area's deeply impoverished minority population, including not only African Americans but also Asians quarantined in San Francisco's Chinatown and Latinos riding bus lines over roads whose names recall their once-dominant status in California. Her descent into this racialized underclass thus concentrates politically and morally the novel's thematics of history, inheritance, property, and the proprietary values inherent in stories and storytelling.

An advantage of this approach is that it tends to reorient students' ideas about what is this novel's crucial scene. Reading *Lot 49* as detective story means emphasizing the auction scene at narrative's end, because that's where the text ought to realize the detective's conventional task of fully disclosing criminality and arresting it. But because Pynchon's narrator pulls up short of that moment, the conventional response is to see the ending as giving way, in Alan Wilde's influential rubric, "to postmodern quandary, to suspensiveness" (146). Resisting that impasse, I read *Lot 49* as Oedipa's quest into an American space of colonial oppression and racial alterity, especially emphasizing her sojourn among San Francisco's outcasts and oppressed minorities in chapter 5. For there is where (if we must see it as detective story) she witnesses the crime (of disinheritance, of alienating oppression). Just there, moreover, we observe Oedipa failing that witnessing in two related ways. First, one finds no textual evidence that she recognizes these people's poverty and utter marginality as the consequence of a certain criminality, in the sense of a power relation diminishing and scarring their humanity. I see this as cognate with her failure, in chapter 6, to respond immediately to Tremaine's bigotry. So when she feels the need "to touch" a drunken flophouse denizen while almost simultaneously admitting, "I can't help" (126), Oedipa states the political consequence (here, an ethical paralysis) that results from her moral failure to discern the larger, systemic injustice metonymically right before her eyes. And I argue that this happens because, in the second place, she is persuaded that in such men's desperate poverty she has "discovered the irreversible process" (128)—something like their supposedly natural fate.

Here again close reading the text should join with a careful historicizing. As the historian Kenan Malik has shown, the 1960s marked a crucial shift in Western discourse: after the Nazi holocaust, it became less and less acceptable to designate racialized bodies according to the classic pseudologics of phenotype—that whole panoply of somatic stigmata. Not simply a rejection of racial epithets (such as Tremaine's "niggers") predicated on what Frantz Fanon theorized as the "epidermalization" of caste differences (11), 1960s liberal intellectuals sought new, transracial ways to represent and address inequality. In the United States, the master text in this effort was Michael Harrington's 1962 study *The Other America*, a now classic formulation of the theory that poor people (and especially the minority poor) are different from normative society not biologically but culturally. Using then current theories of a "permanent underclass," Harrington argued that inequality persists because the poor are distinct from the dominant society as a consequence of habits and morals handed down through generations—different, thus, as the consequence of a self-perpetuating "culture, an institution, a way of life" (23) that had to be destroyed in order for America to win its war against poverty.

Despite its best intentions, Harrington's theory of a self-replicating "permanent underclass" or "culture of poverty" seemed only to reinscribe something like biological differences or inherited "traits." Especially for conservatives, this theory sponsored claims that "no amount of intervention could transform poverty . . . [that] the poor were distinct, different, apart from society" (Malik 202). As such it had the effect of reracializing the poor and of reinscribing their degradation as, in Oedipa's word, "irreversible," a matter if not of biology then of providence or nature's God.

Widely disseminated through the United States media, the "culture of poverty" thesis represented in Harrington's book is an important context for *The Crying of Lot 49*. Advanced students will do much with a comparative analysis. They are quick to notice how Harrington presents his study as travelogue, as journeys into enclaves of American poverty and racial alienation; also, how his array of subjects—day laborers living at a subsistence level, Hispanics and African Americans doing service jobs at odd hours and in segregated conditions, the elderly poor, alcoholics and addicts, the mentally ill and physically handicapped—corresponds to Oedipa's episodic encounters in San Francisco. Beyond these surface comparisons, though, Oedipa shares with Harrington's sociological observer a reading of the other Americans as "increasingly invisible" and almost ghostly (Harrington 2), as "atomized" individuals lacking social solidarity (4), and as having their own psychology and communicating through their own languages (17). As for Harrington, so for Oedipa the minority and outcast figures she encounters are all defined by traits of invisibility and atomized alienation—think of those "isolates" composing the Inamorati Anonymous (116). The novel's Tristero system may well be seen as reprising Harrington's claims of secretive, mystified communications among the minority poor. The key difference is that Pynchon's narrator imputes to the Tristero a subversive, resisting function—a "calculated withdrawal . . . from the life of the Republic" (124). Harrington's other Americans exist "separate, silent, unsuspected" (Pynchon, *Lot 49* 125), but Harrington never sees them as having the degree of purpose, even if atomized, that Pynchon's narrative suggests here—or more exactly, that Oedipa attributes to that underworld.

We therefore need to play textual detective and ask: when, where, and from whom does Oedipa get her first hard clues about the Tristero? Interestingly, they come not from Harrington's other Americans but from representative middle-class men of the military-industrial-complex patronizing the Scope bar. In fact, initially (at the Scope) she thinks the Tristero must be "some inter-office mail run."(52) And what are these communications about? Illicit sex, in an ad seeking multiple partners (52). Or lost love, in the case of the aging alcoholic who hands Oedipa a letter for a wife he abandoned "long ago" in Fresno (125). Standing between those twin poles of insatiable and unrequited desire we have, in the only actual message that Oedipa reads, this note addressed to Mike Fallopian, a gem not of desire but of inertia: "Dear Mike, . . . how are you? Just thought I'd drop you a note. How's your book coming? Guess that's all for now. See you at The Scope." The note consists of nothing more than clichéd and listless interrogatories and pathetic (and self-referential) performatives ("Just thought I'd drop you a note"), which is why Fallopian laments, "That's how it is" (53). Thus we might think of the Tristero as a messaging system without message content, as a performative rather than a declarative and certainly not an interrogative (critical) sociocultural instrument. The emptiness of the messages not only suggests how the Yoyodyne bureaucrats and engineers' involvement in the Tristero occurs under some higher official aegis, it also proves politically useful in white management of minority resistance. Certainly their message system works concertedly with oppression, because any minority population's withdrawal from the life of the Republic would be tailor-made for a segregationist and colonialist regime of power.

Advanced students might also be directed to another important mid-1960s text, Fanon's *Black Skin, White Masks*, especially its theory of the colonized mind: "the replacement of the repressed spirit in the consciousness of the slave by the consciousness of the master, a symbol implanted in the subsoil of the collective group and charged with maintaining order in it as a garrison controls a conquered city" (145). Depending on how adept my students are with theory, I also summarize for them or have them read Robert J. C. Young's analysis, in *Colonial Desire*, of complicity and oedipalization (166–74). This subchapter supplements Fanon and moves discussion beyond the commonplace Freudian readings of *Lot 49* because, in sharp contrast with conventional psychoanalytic theory, Young defines oedipalization as pathological rather than normative; he understands it as an engine for sublimating the terms for one's own brutal degradation. Young's theoretical work thus suggests how Oedipa earns her name.

Her sojourn takes Oedipa into virgin territory (for her) that, like Pynchon's Watts, reveals United States racial oppression functioning in a recognizably regulated space of colonialist control and minority complicity. Finally, readers may find that her narcissistic nonresponsiveness to that other America makes it ethically imperative for them to set aside the narrator's either-or box of interpretive possibilities drafted for us at the novel's end.

There we are invited to understand the narrative's disclosures as evidence of a hidden, overarching history describing ordinary Americans' disinheritance; or nothing more than extravagant coincidence; or a massively articulated plot designed to fool Oedipa into believing that history; or a paranoid delusion. Alternatively, in the approach sketched here, *Lot 49*'s raced space never was the site of a previously unsuspected resistance to main forces of United States history. That site and the signs of its inhabitants' co-optation were always legible, as Mucho Maas hazily realizes from the detritus in the cars traded in by "people poorer than him . . . Negro, Mexican, cracker" (13). Given its rigorous colonialist logic, that place could never have taken shape as merely a natural happenstance or accident. Nor could it unfold as plot laid out for Oedipa to stumble into or a plot that a delusional Oedipa believes she stumbles into, because none may claim such total authority over such a plot. The plot's main roles—of master and slave—are wholly systemic, interlocked and interlocutory. Like everyone else, masters like Pierce are positioned by and in that dynamic of capitalist colonization and differ from their counterparts, the disinherited, only in having relatively greater privilege to humor—or ineffectually critique—that system. Finally, the awful irony is that, absent critically informed frontal assaults on a colonial power's fundamentally unjust parsing of civic and economic rights, seeking to escape or resist that power tends instead to further manifest or work in complicity with the Man's authority. As *Gravity's Rainbow* puts it: "The Man has a branch office in each of our brains" (712).

*The Crying of Lot 49* stops short of exploring racism's genocidal dark side, though the mention of Dr. Hilarius's work at Buchenwald ought to haunt any reading of the novel. Therefore one might well conclude classroom work on *The Crying of Lot 49* by indicating how exterminationist white supremacy is a major theme in both Pynchon novels bracketing the text, particularly in the Herero episodes so crucial to *V.* and *Gravity's Rainbow*.[1]

## NOTE

[1] A reading of McHugh suggests that scholars are no longer neglecting race, white supremacy, and colonialism as key rubrics for reading *Gravity's Rainbow*. McHugh understands especially how the complicity of disfranchised people is not only the deep desire of white oppressors but also a key logic in the self-perpetuation of racial oppression (see esp. 2–11).

# Teaching the Epochal Oedipa: *The Crying of Lot 49* as Political Dialogue

*Jerry Varsava*

*The Crying of Lot 49* examines, on the one hand, the nature of individual rights and freedoms in contemporary American society and, on the other, the claims of various collectivities for political recognition. The individual versus the group, the individual versus society, the private sphere versus the public sphere—these are structural conflicts that have been played out over the course of American history, though always with a specific local, historicized inflection. Political life in the United States in the immediate postwar period is nuanced by cold war urgencies, the dominant economic ethos of the day, a rapidly evolving hyperconsumerism, and the emergent rise of identity politics. As Oedipa Maas moves through her travels and travails, up and down California in the early 1960s, she encounters an America sundered by two competing ideologies—the libertarianism of Pierce Inverarity and his ilk and the recognition politics of various nascent micropolitical groups—neither of which is able to envision what comes to be called by the novel's end "excluded middles," a site of liberal accommodation and compromise (181).[1] As classroom discussion of the novel proceeds, students should be challenged to (re)consider their definitions of the public and private spheres and to examine those ideological rifts that order political events in their own day.

In teaching *Lot 49* as an extended political dialogue that deals with specific, temporally conditioned issues and concerns, I have found a couple of texts to be useful pedagogical adjuncts. J. Kerry Grant's *A Companion to* The Crying of Lot 49 provides a painstaking explication of the novel's many obscure, and not so obscure, references. *America: A Narrative History* (1989), by George B. Tindall and David E. Shi, is a highly readable overview of American history—political, social, cultural—that runs through to the 1988 presidential election, and it is my source for historical fact and context. Finally, to position topics and themes not only in time but space as well, I also use maps in the classroom when discussing this and other political novels.

When we first encounter Oedipa, her existential condition is likened to that of an entowered "captive maiden," though she is as much ensconced in her metaphorical confinement as she is entrapped in it, comfortable in her political quietism and general passivity (21). Her appointment as executrix of the will of her former lover, Pierce Inverarity, provides the impetus for Oedipa's odyssey through contemporary America and leads ultimately to the formation of an active critical view of her country at mid-century. Inverarity is a practitioner of economic libertarianism. Symbolically enough, he keeps a bust of Jay Gould (1836–92) on a shelf over his bed. An unscrupulous investor and promoter during the Gilded Age, Gould, like robber barons and corporate rogues of all eras, embodies the worst instincts of *homo economicus*—an unflagging pursuit of personal aggrandizement that is unenlightened by either elemental business ethics or social conscience. And the many entrepreneurs and commercial interests we encounter in *Lot 49*, notably Inverarity, Yoyodyne, Tony Jaguar, and Winthrop "Winner" Tremaine, are little better. To enliven class discussion, one can prompt students for the names of miscreant businessmen they might have encountered of late in the media. (There's usually no shortage of such characters.)

Robert Nozick has advanced the most developed and most widely cited contemporary defense of American libertarianism. In his *Anarchy, State, and Utopia* (1974), he argues for a "minimal state" whose powers are restricted to a few basic functions: "protection against force, theft, fraud, enforcement of contracts, and so on. . . ." Any attempt by a state to do more—for example, to compel redistribution of economic shares or to limit citizens' rights "for *their* own good"—amounts to an unjustifiable constraint on individual liberty (ix). Social conscience is solely the product of individual choice and not of governmental legislation or policy. Or, as he axiomatically puts it, "From each as they choose, to each as they are chosen" (160).

The appearance of *Lot 49* predates that of Nozick's major work by a number of years, so Nozick is in no way a direct influence on Pynchon's views on libertarianism. It is rather another apologist for libertarianism, Ayn Rand, who serves as Pynchon's immediate ideological antagonist. Throughout the 1940s and 1950s Rand promotes her own version of libertarianism—inelegantly termed "reason-individualism-capitalism" in *Capitalism: The Unknown Ideal* (151 [1966])—in her many essays, as well as in novels such as *The Fountainhead* (1943) and, especially, *Atlas Shrugged* (1957). Rand's defense of economic liberty and personal selfishness is strident and uncompromising. And, however simplistic her views may now appear, they have received a broad hearing, judging from the number of reprints her novels have gone through. Students might be asked what elements of Rand's philosophy still manifest themselves in American society and how they do so.

Oedipa confronts evidence of economic libertarianism at every turn as she seeks to understand the manifold mysteries in which she is enveloped. Exploring Inverarity's hometown of San Narciso, the place where he first put down the "plinth course of capital," she learns that he was involved in several legally dubious undertakings, ranging from obtaining tax concessions for Yoyodyne, of which he was a major shareholder, to the commercial exploitation of human bones for both Fangoso Lagoons, his gated-community development, and Osteolysis, a developer of cigarette filters made from bone charcoal (24–26). Yoyodyne, a major aerospace company headed by warmongering "Bloody" Chiclitz, seeks its place alongside the likes of Bendix, Grumman, and Boeing, among many others in America's burgeoning military-industrial complex. (A brief digression on the Eisenhowerian origins of the phrase "military-industrial complex" is generally rewarding for students.) When Oedipa becomes distracted from her role as executrix, the lawyer Metzger reminds her that her "first loyalty, legal and moral, is to the estate she represents," clearly establishing the priority of private interests over public ones (76). Indeed, as Oedipa surveys her immediate surroundings, there is little evidence of any operative public sphere that might countervail the powerful self-interested machinations of local entrepreneurs. Government "of the people, for the people, by the people" is nothing more than a dated eloquence.

In the words of Nancy Rosenblum, an exponent of liberalism, libertarians posit "an imperial self that is a whole world" (220). In *Lot 49*, San Narciso stands in large part as a narcissistic monument to Inverarity. The unconstrained economic self-determinism sought by these imperial selves, irrespective of whatever broader trickle-down benefits may flow to the broader population—Reaganomics *avant la lettre*—cultivates alienation and discontent among a variety of constituencies. Oedipa's political (re)education will be defined in large part by her recognition of alterity, of the other, in American society.

Oedipa's declaration that she is a "Young Republican" is more an admission of political acquiescence than a statement of ideological conviction (76). Narcotized by the consensus history of the cold war period and the easy, if unevenly distributed, consumerism of the booming 1950s and early 1960s, Oedipa has, like so many Americans, left politics up to the politicians and the policy makers. Wandering across the campus of the University of California, Berkeley, she compares her college experience some ten years earlier with that now unfolding differently for others here. A victim of the political conformism of her professors, Oedipa must now use the critico-analytic skills she acquired for ends more socially relevant than completing degree requirements. In discussing Oedipa's Young Republicanism, students should be encouraged to consider what this ideological perspective means to them.

The 1960s sees the rise of new social movements in the United States. The period's many manifestations of social dissent—marches, sit-ins, teach-ins, demonstrations, and riots, even—all bear testimony to the yearnings of one group or another for recognition and social influence. Any number of historical markers document the emergence of identity politics: Lyndon Johnson's Civil Rights Act of 1964 and Voting Rights Act of 1965, as well as the emergence of various Black Power groups; the appearance of Rachel Carson's *Silent Spring* (1962) that sounded the alarm on environmental destruction; the rise of youth-led organizations like the Students for a Democratic Society and the Free Speech Movement; the establishment of the National Organization for Women (NOW) by Betty Friedan and others; the founding of United Farm Workers (UFW) by Cesar Chavez; the establishment of the American Indian Movement (AIM); and the beginning of the Stonewall movement at the end of the decade.

Over the course of her peregrinations through contemporary America, Oedipa encounters representatives of various distinct groups with divergent degrees of political awareness. African Americans quietly accept their consignment to the economic underclass, whether they work for the racist Winthrop Tremaine or Yoyodyne or indeed trudge along to "graveyard shifts" for other employers (149, 82, 121). Jesús Arrabal, an anarchist in exile from his native Mexico, separated from one country and alienated within another, finds no possibility of social integration as he fights a doomed battle against the economic oligarchy that Pierce Inverarity and others represent (119–20). Similarly, she confronts a group of gays who sequester themselves socially in North Beach clubs to pursue their lifestyle without censure or menace (110–11). Finally, Oedipa, the quiescent Young Republican, frightened as her men are stripped away, "one by one" (153), slowly evolves into an independent young woman who, through her actions, extends the range of possibility for at least one woman and therein challenges the gender stereotyping endemic in her society.

Subordinated to the establishment—figured in the libertarian Pierce Inverarity and his fellow oligarchs—each of these constituencies has rather limited options: either to accept a condition of political nullity or to embrace a nebulous countercultural phenomenon called Tristero. Either way, they will continue to suffer a common fate; each will be denied broad-based political recognition and the prospects for enfranchisement and influence that recognition brings. In his *The End of History and the Last Man*, Francis Fukuyama takes up recognition at some length (162–65, 168–91). Building on earlier discussions by Plato in *The Republic* of *thymos* and by Hegel on humankind's fundamental yearning for recognition, Fukuyama provides a serviceable taxonomy of recognition in contemporary civil society. For him, Plato's *thymos* is akin to what we might today call "self-esteem" (Fukuyama 165). And, further, it suggests "something like an innate human sense of justice: people believe that they have a certain worth, and when other people act as if they are worth less—when they do not *recognize* their worth at its correct value—then they become angry" (165). Some people embrace "megalothymia," the "desire to be recognized as superior to other people" (182). Alternatively, there are those that endorse what Fukuyama calls "isothymia," "the desire to be recognized as the equal of other people" (182).

Throughout *Lot 49*, we find a conflict between megalothymic and isothymic sensibilities. Thus, Inverarity and his associates—as with distant Puritans and their fantasies of the elect and preterit and like self-aggrandizers of all ages—seek ever-increasing shares of material well-being and political influence to sate their presumptuous notions of self-worth and entitlement at the expense of workers, Jesús Arrabal and his "CIA" compatriots, the sick, the urban poor, African Americans, and so forth. Thus, the Republic and its cybernetic agent, the United States Postal Service, stand as guarantors of a status quo predicated on inequality of opportunity and a vacant public sphere. And the consequence? A fractionated society where polarities abound. Possessors of little enough, the disenfranchised are at least proprietors of their own retreat from society into a counterculture vaguely designated as Tristero. One might pose at this point a variety of questions. Who are the disenfranchised today in America? Is there still a need for micropolitical agency in America? What shape might or does such agency take? All these questions can yield productive classroom dialogue and advance students' understanding of the novel and current events.

Unlike Inverarity and his fellows (for whom self-definition is determined by personal actions and private commitments that operate beyond communal constraints and concerns), the disenfranchised derive their sense of identity and indeed their sense of disentitlement from that series of predicates that define their given group or given community. And the various groups are but local figurations of a much larger umbrella phenomenon—Tristero-W.A.S.T.E.—which becomes effectively, however nebulous and inchoate it may be, a sort of community of communities.

In *Habits of the Heart: Individualism and Commitment in American Life* (updated in 1996), Robert Bellah and his colleagues provide a detailed analysis of the civic dangers of unbridled individualism. Individualism holds that "the individual has a primary reality whereas society is a second-order, derived or artificial construct" (Bellah, Madsen, Sullivan, Swidler, and Tipton 334). This privileging of the private over the communal yields a society of the type described in *Lot 49*, in which there is no sense of the commonweal and certainly no equitable distribution of economic shares and social prestige. Such a society is bereft of "social capital," which Robert Putnam defines as those "features of social organization, such as networks, norms, and trust, that facilitate coordination and cooperation for mutual benefits" (qtd. in Bellah, Madsen, Sullivan, Swidler, and Tipton xvi). Similarly, other communitarians such as Michael Sandel and Alasdair MacIntyre give precedence to group identity because they see in it a source of social harmony (Sandel) and virtue (MacIntyre).

*Lot 49* is often or even typically regarded as bereft of closure, its conclusion an inconclusive preamble to more excellent if generally inscrutable adventures for Oedipa. I have found it pedagogically useful to ask my students if in fact the opposite might not be true. Arguably, by novel's end, Oedipa reaches a moment of conceptual clarity that is firm and defining, if contingent. How can her encounters with America be viewed as an endorsement of a historicized postmodern version of traditional liberalism that seeks to mediate the competing political philosophies of different social constituencies: notably, libertarianism (with its promotion of individual rights and a minimal state), and communitarianism (with its privileging of group rights and an involved state)? Cannot her meditation on "excluded middles" at the end of the novel be seen as her personal intervention into this rancorous debate, one that continues today, though with shifting points of reference and valence?

At the end of the novel, Oedipa laments that in San Narciso and America human possibility has been reduced to a simplistic polarity involving "storm-systems of group suffering and need" and "prevailing winds of affluence." And Oedipa knows that, whatever it might amount to in material terms, Inverarity's legacy is an "America" in which the negotiation of individual and collective rights has failed to achieve meaningful dialecticality and balance (178–79). The circumstances of the disenfranchised appear to her to be beyond remedy, and she wonders if she herself will one day go over to Tristero, "if it existed, in its twilight, its aloofness, its waiting" (181).

The conflicting demands of the individual and the collectivity have, predictably enough, been a focal point of much discussion among political and social theorists over the last several decades. In his celebrated 1958 essay, "Two Concepts of Liberty," Isaiah Berlin differentiates between two types of liberty or freedom. "Negative liberty" is "liberty *from*"; its preservation "consists in the 'negative' goal of warding off interference" from others (127; emphasis in orig.). For its part, "positive liberty" is "freedom *to*"; this form of freedom asserts that personal self-realization should be determined by oneself, and not by "external forces of whatever kind" (131; my emphasis). Negative freedom enshrines the libertarian value of total personal freedom and refuses to address those inequalities of opportunity that many encounter through little or no fault of their own. (See Patell for an application of Berlin's two types of liberties to selected fictions by Pynchon; and Varsava, "Dialectics," for a discussion of Patell's position.) Such inequalities may derive from any number of random local circumstances (for example, illness, accident, and climatic disaster) but also from, as John Rawls states, individuals' "social fortune or their luck in the natural lottery"—that is, their acquired socioeconomic status or their particular range of exploitable talents such as intelligence or physical strength (75). When positive liberty is socially embraced, individuals and groups operate freely, unconstrained by either past injustice or present misfortune.

In *Lot 49*, conflictuality derives from America's incapacity to achieve something like a functional synthesis of personal and communal interests and the views of liberty that underwrite each. And it is the hallmark of liberalism that it pursues the negotiation—"haggling," Berlin terms it—between the two positions, not once and for all but as an ongoing series of discussions that are responsive to the exigencies of the day (124). The political locus of this negotiation is the lamentably absent "excluded middles" that Oedipa cites, with the pluralization of "middle" suggestive of liberalism's inherently contingent, historicized nature. In her America—or is it Inverarity's?—the melding of private and communal interests has not occurred. The United States is a place of illiberality bereft of, variously, Berlin's "pluralism" (171), Ronald Dworkin's "integrated liberalism" (233), and George Kateb's "mutuality" (225–26).

By the end of the novel, Oedipa has taken to heart a suggestion of Pierce Inverarity, the inveterate trickster; she will "[k]eep it bouncing" (178). If political (and moral) entropy in America is to be overcome, it will be through the active and balanced engagement of citizens like Oedipa who are intent on overcoming the restrictive ideological dichotomies, and this is the liberal lesson that she teaches us and that we might teach to others.

Here's a final pedagogical suggestion. A schematic overview of the ideological debates undertaken in *Lot 49* will look something like the chart opposite:

Overview of Oedipa's Political Dialogues[2]

| **Ideology** | **Representative Figurations** | **Key Passages in *Lot 49*** | **Primary Sources** |
|---|---|---|---|
| Libertarianism (Private rights, negative liberty) | Pierce Inverarity, defense industry scions, Winthrop Tremaine | 24–26, 58–63, 82–89, 149–50 | Rand, *Atlas Shrugged* (1957), Nozick (1974) |
| Liberalism and "Excluded Middles" (Private and communal rights, negative and positive liberty) | Oedipa | 177–82 | Berlin (1969), Rawls (1971) |
| Communitarianism (Communal rights, positive liberty) | Various social groups, Tristero, W.A.S.T.E., the other, alterity | 94–99, 155–74, 109–32 | MacIntyre (1981), Sandel (1982), Bellah, Madsen, Sullivan, Swidler, and Tipton (1985) |

In presenting the novel as political dialogue, one might offer this figure to students in one of two ways. They might receive it at the end of the unit, where it would serve as a useful summary. Another more dynamic and, I think, more pedagogically effective use of it would be to develop the figure through discussion and debate in class. One might, for example, provide to the class the four headings at the top of the figure—Ideology, Representative Figurations, Key Passages, and Primary Sources—and then slowly fill in the spaces as they come to be identified and defined. In achieving the completed figure after much critical engagement with both the novel and contemporary political events and issues, students will, in their own ways, have emulated Oedipa in her journey of personal and ideological self-discovery. They will have, in their own ways, kept it bouncing.

NOTES

[1] The analysis of *Lot 49* that I offer here derives in part from an earlier examination of the novel found in my "Thomas Pynchon and Postmodern Liberalism" (1995), in which I discuss politics and political philosophy in both *Lot 49* and *Vineland*. Interested readers may wish to refer to this article.

[2] Will Kymlicka's *Contemporary Political Philosophy* offers an excellent overview of liberalism, libertarianism, and communitarianism, and I strongly recommend it for the clarity of its analyses and its detailed bibliography.

# *Lot 49*: Science and the Novel of Systems

*Stacey Olster*

To many of the undergraduates who enroll in my upper-level Novel of Systems course, we may as well be living in the world that C. P. Snow described in *The Two Cultures and the Scientific Revolution* (1959) as split between science and the humanities. My syllabus attempts from the start to redress this division by introducing the three novelists to be covered—Thomas Pynchon, William Gibson, and Don DeLillo—as writers whose fiction illustrates today's concern with systematizing constructs. In the literature by these writers, the discourses of science and the humanities have been fully integrated.

The opening chapter of Tom LeClair's *In the Loop: Don DeLillo and the Systems Novel* (1–31), which traces the inception of systems theory to the biologist Ludwig von Bertalanffy, provides an especially useful catalog of the metascience's key concepts (9–12). Systems theory originates in response to the future-shock conditions of the late 1960s and 1970s. It uses scientific ideas to comment on the conditions of late-twentieth-century life, reflects a sociopolitical experience scaled to multinational corporations and a global economy, and depicts human beings in reciprocal relations with their environment rather than as entities exerting force over that environment or in causal sequences. The systems novel that is characterized by these traits functions as a metasystem itself, yet one that admits to the tenuousness and artificiality of its own metaphors. Not surprisingly, students have relatively little difficulty applying these criteria to the fiction of Gibson (with its depiction of high-tech corporations and information acquisition) and DeLillo (with its focus on pervasive mass media and their effects).

Pynchon's fiction, however, proves much more challenging because it deals with subjects much less familiar. For one thing, the disciplines of physics and cybernetics—a rich source of metaphor and plot in Pynchon's works—have no immediate (or apparent) correlation to the daily lives of most of the English majors at my university. For another, the brand of free-floating paranoia and shadowy conspiracy that characterizes life within the systems delineated in those works and that once provided a hook for students who experienced, at however great a remove, the late 1960s seems almost sentimental to students today, for whom the existence of plots—as evidenced by the 1995 bombing of the federal building in Oklahoma City and by 9/11—and clearly defined enemies is decidedly real. Afforded no certainty that the Tristero system that forces Oedipa Maas on her maddeningly labyrinthine journey even exists, students who read *The Crying of Lot 49* feel only frustration.

An obvious way to deal with the science phobia that serves as the initial obstacle to students who open *Lot 49* is to assign secondary reading written by literary critics that sketches, in layperson's terms, the paradigm shift from Newtonian to quantum physics that Pynchon's works take as their given (e.g., Friedman; Nadeau 17–64; Hayles, *Cosmic Web* 31–59; Strehle 1–26). Instructors who wish to assuage their own science phobia or at least refresh their own knowledge of scientific principles might consult some of the many books written by scientists that also trace that paradigm shift, such as Peter Coveney and Roger Highfield's *The Arrow of Time*, Richard Feynman's *The Character of Physical Law*, and, for a general overview, Jim Breithaupt's *Physics*.

Rather than add to an already heavy reading list, however, my approach has been to prepare a handout (see app.) that summarizes for students the scientific information they most need (e.g., Newton's laws of motion and the law of universal gravitation, the three laws of thermodynamics, Einstein's special theory of relativity and general theory, Heisenberg's uncertainty principle) and immediately turn to Pynchon's early short story "Entropy" to examine the application of those scientific principles in literature (see Mangel).

There are several advantages of assigning this text as the first fiction the students read. First, the story explicitly introduces the scientific principle of entropy and dramatizes two contrasting efforts to counteract entropic decline. The apartments of Meatball Mulligan and Callisto—one on top of the other—act as two competing systems within the universe that is their shared building. The inhabitants of both apartments are subject to the same environment, described by Callisto's idiomatic version of the second law of thermodynamics: "you can't win, things are going to get worse before they get better, who says they're going to get better" (282). Does one attempt to defer the inevitable, as evidenced by Meatball's lease-breaking party that is moving into its fortieth hour in the story's first sentence, by remaining open to the reinvigorating chaos of party crashers and latecomers? Or does one attempt to stave off the inevitable, by creating a "tiny enclave of regularity in the city's chaos" and "ecological balance" that Callisto's "[h]ermetically sealed" flat incarnates (279)? Second, the story provides students with the opportunity to see, as Callisto does, the variety of ways in which the concept of entropy also can serve as "an adequate metaphor to apply to certain phenomena in his own world" (283), both scientific and nonscientific, and hence—to invoke a central concern of *Gravity's Rainbow*—be mapped onto different sets of coordinates.

Third, the story enables me to introduce audiovisual samples of those nonscientific phenomena directly into our discussion and thereby avoid the glazed-eyes response that uninterrupted discussion of science can produce. If entropy in communications theory is a measure of the inefficiency of a signal (N. Wiener, *Human Use* 31), the characters in Pynchon's story who ponder qualitative differences between Sal Mineo and Ricky Nelson (photographs of whom I exhibit) and view the word *love* as adding an element of leakage into statements that otherwise might be deemed closed circuits (284, 285) display the prospects of an increase in entropy—hopelessly muddling the communication—that are no less frightening than those contemplated by Callisto. Yet when the members of the Duke di Angelis quartet, in homage to the minimalist orchestrations of Stravinsky's *L'histoire du soldat* and Gerry Mulligan's "Love for Sale" (recorded sections of which I play), eliminate all instrumentation entirely and end up with just silence (289–90), they illustrate in musical terms the same phenomenon that has just been portrayed in the conversation above—no communication.

One of the most important phenomena to which Pynchon's scientific metaphors are applied in *Lot 49* is history, a *social* science, the writing of which is portrayed as a form of systematizing or order making. Indeed, *Lot 49* is filled with characters that contextualize the events of the present with respect to ongoing processes of the past. The Peter Pinguid Society traces the cold war back to an 1864 naval confrontation between Russian and American ships (49–50). Genghis Cohen and Emory Bortz see philatelic forgeries in the late-twentieth-century United States as reflecting a tradition of mail fraud that originates in the late-sixteenth-century Low Countries (158–60, 163–65).

Given this fact, I end our discussion of "Entropy" by focusing on Callisto's invocation of Henry Adams. Because the attempts of both men to chart temporal continuity (history) are portrayed as threatened by developments in the hard sciences—Callisto is aghast at thermodynamics, Adams is shocked by power (280)—their efforts show that any reconstruction of history now necessarily involves a systematizing of history, an ordering process that is itself subject to noise and entropy. To pursue that comparison further, I distribute a handout with excerpts from *The Education of Henry Adams*, the model for the autobiography that Callisto is in the process of dictating.

Because the world defined in terms of "physics stark mad in metaphysics" (381–82) that Adams's turn-of-the century "new American" (497–98) faced can just as easily encapsulate the situation in which the suburban housewife Oedipa Maas finds herself in *Lot 49*, the Adams autobiography provides a useful transition from Pynchon's 1960 short story to his 1966 novel. At the same time, because Adams's recognized need for systematizing, for man to "invent a formula of his own for his universe, if the standard formulas failed," came with the caveat that "[o]ne sought no absolute truth" (472)—Adams viewed his "Dynamic Theory of History" (474–88) as failing to uncover what he called "Unity" (484)—his book offers a qualification to which Oedipa only comes at the novel's conclusion, if then.

This is not to suggest that students must wait until they finish Pynchon's book to appreciate the relevance of Adams's approach. On the contrary, such qualified systematizing underlies the operation of the Nefastis Machine (85–87, 104–09), which links two otherwise unrelated equations for entropy by virtue of an atomic gatekeeper, Maxwell's demon, who violates the second law of thermodynamics by ordering a vessel's air molecules with respect to speed, and a "sensitive," who is defined as "one that can share in the man's hallucinations" (107). But Pynchon's portrayal of Maxwell's demon does not come until the midpoint of the novel, too late for students struggling to understand how the preeminent system in the novel, the Tristero system—whose cultural markers at first denote just evil to Oedipa (e.g., black garb seems an index of stealth and subversion)—can function as the formula she "invents" for her universe when the "standard formulas" fail, to recall Adams's phrasing.

To assist them in their early reading, I ask students to identify what might constitute the "standard formulas" underlying Pynchon's novel. By encouraging them to think of Adams's language as broadly as possible and to focus on words that recur frequently enough to suggest a unified discursive system, I help students become aware of the religious dimension that terms like "revelation," "redemption," and "Word" connote. I then ask students to question the degree to which a universe created by the Judeo-Christian God with which most are quite familiar differs from a universe imagined by Newton as operating by laws of motion and gravitation put into action by a mover. To solidify the similarity, I draw their attention to Adams's reminder that "[n]one of the [early] astronomers were irreligious men; all of them made a point of magnifying God through his works" (484).

With this congruence between the systematizing of seventeenth-century science and religion thus established, we turn our attention to the Calvinist variant of religion that Pynchon's text most incorporates, first specified when Randolph Driblette accuses Oedipa of being as "hung up with words" as "Puritans are about the Bible" (79). After briefly outlining for students the preordained movement toward redemption that forms the basis of the Puritan formulation and noting the economic success that became a measure of spiritual status, I ask them to speculate about the ways in which the early chapters of the novel portray this Puritan formula as having failed. Some note the Paranoids' blown fuse (42) and *The Courier's Tragedy*'s two blackouts (73–75) as examples of light extinguished rather than revealed. Others—unknowingly anticipating the slaughter of trees and selling of offspring that will mark the Slothrop family's entrepreneurial impulse in *Gravity's Rainbow*—cite a consumerism run rampant (product names for character names), the vulgarity of which (cigarette filters made from the bones of dead GIs [60–63]) suggests what Pierce Inverarity, Yoyodyne's "founding father" (26), has inaugurated. Many point to evidence—such as the trajectory of Oedipa's hair spray can (37–38)—that randomness rather than order is the defining characteristic of the universe. This, in turn, leads to debate over whether that trait is best interpreted as Augustinian absence (Slothrop's suspicion that Providence may have stepped out for a beer [378]) or Manichaean malice (*Lot 49*'s Scurvhamite Other [155–56]).

Discussion then shifts to the question of whether the "gemlike 'clues' " to a Tristero system that Oedipa uncovers actually "make up for her having lost the direct, epileptic Word, the cry that might abolish the night," or serve as "only some kind of compensation" (118), never equal to the original in its ability to provide psychological succor. As a means of approaching this issue, I ask students to do what Mike Fallopian challenges Oedipa to do near the end of the book: "Write down what you can't deny. Your hard intelligence. But then write down what you've only speculated, assumed. See what you've got" (168). What they "get," among other things, is the fact that the mention of a "tryst with Trystero" (75) that ends act 4 of *The Courier's Tragedy* the night that Oedipa happens to see it is the result of its director's idiosyncratic decision to follow the pornographic Vatican version of the text instead of the version in Emory Bortz's edition, as is his common practice (153–54). And that the mark traced in the dust by one of the Wells, Fargo men killed by masked marauders in 1853 can signify a cross as easily as the letter *T* (89). And that the muted post horn emblem that Oedipa repeatedly sees during her walk through San Francisco reflects so much her own expectations that "perhaps she did not see it quite as often as she later was to remember seeing it" (123–24). And that there may just have been too much kirsch in the opening Tupperware party's fondue (9).

With the previously hard evidence of Tristero's existence shown to partake of whimsy and wish-fulfillment in equal measure, the connections that bring Tristero into being increasingly emerge as the products of Oedipa's systematizing imagination. Once students come to this crucial realization, they are ready to focus on the Nefastis Machine as emblematic of the dynamic underlying the entire novel. For twentieth-century physicists, the subjectivity (the demon) that fuels that machine simply reflects the role played by the position and synthesizing grip of the observer in any attempt to garner knowledge about the universe. For mythologists who view infusions of the self as indications of narcissism, which the text's references to San Narciso and Echo Courts readily encourage, it confirms the transformation of person into the "servomechanism of his own extended or repeated image" that left the Greek youth in a "closed system" (McLuhan, *Understanding* 41). And for students more comfortable with psychology than physics, it suggests that the "true sensitive" who witnesses pistons move as a result of Maxwell's demon (107) is merely a "true paranoid for whom all is organized in spheres joyful or threatening about the central pulse of himself" (128–29). Tristero, they then can conclude, is the product of a "growing obsession, with 'bringing something of herself' . . . to the scatter of business interests that had survived Inverarity" (90), an obsession that can be traced back to Oedipa's egocentric "[s]hall I project a world?" (82).

Nudged to view Oedipa's behavior in the terms of thermodynamics' tenets, however, and in comparison with that of characters who renounce all claims to conspiracy, students start to realize that paranoia need not denote mental illness. After Mucho Maas, who "believed too much" in his used-car lot, forfeits his N.A.D.A. nightmares to work at a radio station in which "he believed not at all" (15), he becomes "less himself and more generic" (140)—closer, in other words, to that state of uniformity toward which entropic processes move. Nudged even further, to see Oedipa's sifting among clues as analogous to their own activity as readers, students find that the urge for "pulsing stelliferous Meaning" that animates her efforts is the same impulse that prompts observant critics to link Oedipa's clues "woven into The Tristero" to that other woven "tapestry which spilled out the slit windows and into a void, seeking hopelessly to fill the void," embroidered by girls in a Remedios Varo triptych (82, 81, 21). (This triptych is another image that I exhibit.) With this repetition, students begin to see the novel itself as a system of words designed to elicit their own tendencies to find systems in the universe of their reading. Confronted with this similarity, students become aware that, even more than a function of Oedipa's imagination, Tristero is "nothing but a sound, a word," that in Oedipa's search for meaning becomes "a metaphor of God knew how many parts" and hence is ultimately the function of a language system (109).

With this in mind, I ask students to reconsider what they have read from the perspective of communications theory, based on the assumption that, as John Nefastis reminds Oedipa, "[e]ntropy is a figure of speech" that "connects the world of thermodynamics to the world of information flow" (106). To assist them, I reproduce Claude E. Shannon's schematic diagram for a communication system (5), in which an information source sends a message through a transmitter, whose signal is picked up by a receiver, which then transmits the received signal as a message to a destination. Students have little difficulty citing examples of the myriad ways in which information is distorted or interrupted by noise in Pynchon's text: the telephone calls from Inverarity and Hilarious in chapter 1, the mixed-up reels of baby Metzger's televised film in chapter 2, all of Mucho's radio broadcasts. These last prove especially helpful in enabling students to pinpoint how the state of uniformity that results from thermodynamic entropy manifests itself in cybernetics; as Mucho illustrates both verbally and personally, "Everybody who says the same words is the same person" (142).

As in the short story "Entropy," Pynchon predicates the health of a nation on the ability of its citizens to communicate with one another, just as the "salvation" of the Holy Roman Empire, as the history of Thurn and Taxis illustrates, has depended on communication among competing German princes (164). This focus on communication leads logically to the accent on language in the novel's final pages. Much like John Dos Passos incarnating "U.S.A. [a]s the speech of the people" in the preface to his trilogy (vii), Oedipa recalls itinerant "Americans speaking their language carefully, scholarly," and mourns

America as a land in which "the chances [were] once so good for diversity" (180–81).

In analyzing these wonderfully elegiac last pages, I emphasize how great the stakes of such linguistic diversity are. For if the word "America" suggests to Oedipa only two meanings—either "a transcendent meaning, or only the earth," "[a]nother mode of meaning behind the obvious, or none" (181–82)—the stakes could not be higher. We then evaluate evidence that might be construed positively as pointing to a range of possible meanings rooted in the human act of metaphor.

The Puritan devotion to the Word with which Oedipa's search is repeatedly compared (79, 156) was the product of attributing divine origin or status to the language of scripture. In Pynchon's hands, this Puritan reflex becomes a strategy for restoring multiple meanings by way of metaphor. Thus, "DT's" can signify "delirium tremens" on the one hand and time differentials and spectra on the other (128–29). "Nada" can denote "nothing" in Spanish, and "N.A.D.A." can identify a trade union (144). And not least, "waste" can mean "trash," and, taken as an acronym, W.A.S.T.E. can signify the slogan of a secret society (87–88). As a result, language in *Lot 49* is shown to operate like a sacred text, a source of proliferating meaning within a monologic society threatening to be in an irreversible process of entropic decline.

In asking students, as the final part of our examination, to evaluate how successful Pynchon is in this restorative endeavor, I juxtapose two passages: John Nefastis's claim that Maxwell's demon makes the metaphor of entropy "not only verbally graceful, but also objectively true" (106), and Oedipa's qualification of the act of metaphor as "a thrust at truth and a lie, depending where you were: inside, safe, or outside, lost" (129). Immediately dismissive of the first in a universe in which no objective truth exists, students remain dubious about the second until reminded that the fictional framework of Pynchon's novel allows his book to function as a closed system "inside" of which they remain for as long as their reading continues. As long as they "share in the man's hallucinations," to recall the feedback required by Nefastis's demon, and, as "sensitives," take part in an admittedly subjective system, they reap the same benefits as Nefastis when looking at the machine he has constructed: information flows and chaos is pushed back a bit. Work may not progress—pistons may not rise and fall—but, in terms of language, history moves from linguistic equilibrium to metaphoric dynamism.

Having come to appreciate the way in which metaphor in Pynchon's fiction can bridge the divide between science and the humanities that C. P. Snow described nearly a half century ago, students can better appreciate the union of voodoo and cyberspace that informs the fiction of William Gibson, the next author we study in the Novel of Systems course. Far from being an anomalous writer, consigned to that all-purpose student category of "weird," Pynchon has become for them a prescient writer, whose influence continues to promote universes of wonder.

# APPENDIX
From Newtonian to Quantum Physics

## Seventeenth-Century Newtonian Physics: The Universe as Clockwork

### Laws of motion

Any mass tends to remain at rest or in uniform motion.
Acceleration produced is related to the mass of the matter and the net force applied ($A = F/M$ or $F = M \times A$).
For every action there is an equal and opposite reaction.

### Law of Universal Gravitation

The gravitational force that exists between any two masses depends on a universal constant factor, the amounts of the masses, and the distance between them.

## Nineteenth-Century Thermodynamics

### Three laws of thermodynamics

Law of conservation of energy: Energy cannot be created or destroyed. It can only be changed from one form to another.

> Changes occur through chemical reactions, and free energy becomes defined as that form of energy capable of doing work under conditions of constant temperature, pressure, and volume.
>
> Chemical reactions can go in two directions, forward or backward, from reactants to products or vice versa, depending on things like concentration, pressure, and temperature. Some reactions will yield free energy (e.g., transformation of glucose to carbon dioxide, water, and energy from the stored glucose bonds upon eating food). Some reactions will require energy (e.g., photosynthesis, which needs sunlight). Some energy-producing reactions also produce heat, which is energy dissipated or wasted since it cannot be used by organisms for work.
>
> Equilibrium is defined as a state of balance between opposing forces or actions. An equilibrium is dynamic when the forward and backward rates are equal in velocity. An equilibrium is static when a body is acted on by forces whose resultant is zero—the practical effect of such an equilibrium is that no work is done.
>
> The free energy of a system will always decrease to a minimum.

Second law of thermodynamics: The entropy (defined as randomness or disorder; term introduced by Rudolph Clausius in 1865) of the universe increases until equilibrium is attained, at which point the entropy is the maximum possible under the prevailing conditions of temperature and pressure. Or, the ultimate driving force of all chemical or physical processes is the *tendency* of the entropy of the universe to be maximized.

Unattainability statement: On the Kelvin scale of temperature, absolute zero can never be reached, only approached.

### Crumbling of Newtonian Determinism since the Mid–Nineteenth Century

Charles Sanders Peirce (1892): "Try to verify any law of nature, and you will find that the more precise your observations, the more certain they will be to show *irregular* departures from the law. . . . Trace their causes back far enough and you will be forced to admit they are always due to arbitrary determination, or *chance*" (331; emphasis mine).

Ludwig Boltzmann (1895): "I will mention the *possibility* that the fundamental equations for the motion of individual molecules will turn out to be only *approximate* formulas which give *average* values" (449; emphasis mine).

Franz Exner (1919): "[T]he laws of the macrocosm are not absolute laws but rather laws of *probability* . . . to predict in physics the outcome of an individual process is impossible" (qtd. in P. Wiener 588; emphasis mine).

Charles Galton Darwin (1919): It may "prove necessary to make fundamental changes in our ideas of time and space, or to abandon the conservation of matter and electricity, or even in the last resort to endow electrons with *free will*" (qtd. in P. Wiener 588; emphasis mine).

### Twentieth-Century Physics

Albert Einstein—special theory of relativity (1905), general theory of relativity (1916): Time and space are no longer the universal, absolute concepts they were but may change, dilate, and contract depending on the nature of the observations made of them. The interactions among time, mass, and gravity change.

Niels Bohr, Erwin Schrödinger, Werner Heisenberg, and Max Born—quantum physics and the introduction of indeterminacy (1920s): The universe itself becomes fuzzy, not just human beings' limited knowledge of it. The smaller the mass observed, the larger the degree of uncertainty.

> Heisenberg uncertainty principle (1927): The act of observing the motion of wave particles disturbs them to such an extent that no accurate information can be gathered about them.
>
> The predictions of quantum physics often tell us not of a single expected result but of two completely different possible behaviors for an experiment

and the odds of observing each. Branch points lead to a distinct number of possibilities.

Ramifications of quantum physics' uncertainty in relation to apprehension of "reality": Reality understood is reality changed.

Werner Heisenberg: "In view of the intimate connection between the statistical character of the quantum theory and the *imprecision* of all perception, it may be suggested that behind the statistical universe of perception there lies a hidden 'real' world ruled by causality. Such speculation seems to us—and this we stress with emphasis—useless and meaningless" (qtd. in P. Wiener 589; emphasis mine).

Hermann Weyl: "We have tried to storm Heaven and have succeeded only in piling up the Tower of Babel" (qtd. in Girvetz 433).

# Humor and Decentered Meaning in *Lot 49*

*Alison T. J. Preston*

Wordplay, puns, satire, parody, burlesque, and black humor are manifest throughout Pynchon's work. For many readers, such humor is an entertaining trademark of his style, for these comic elements contribute to a novelistic world that is at once potentially meaningful and possibly absurd. *The Crying of Lot 49* is representative: not only is humor prevalent, it also provides a key to understanding the simultaneous processes of decentering and reconstructing meaning that characterize the novel.[1] Much of the humor in *Lot 49* grows from the parody of Oedipa's attempts to create order and significance from the miscellaneous clues that (may) govern an underground world signified by "Tristero"; at the same time, such order creates the possibility of social meaning. The novel calls attention to the underlying logic of this comedy, when Oedipa thinks to herself that "there was [a] high magic to low puns" (129), for puns and other forms of humor simultaneously create sense and nonsense, meaning and meaninglessness.[2]

## *Comic Absurdity*

To help contextualize the function of humor early in the novel, the instructor might encourage students to speculate about a few of the character names, since they represent one of the first comic devices to which the reader is exposed. Oedipa's name evokes rich allusions to Greek tragedy and Freudian psychoanalytic theory, which further connect to Oedipa's quest for insight and requisite psychotherapy sessions from her hallucinogen-furnishing doctor. But even while considering these serious, meaningful, dimensions of Oedipa's name, readers can't help laughing at the name itself and the idea of using it for the main character in a novel. As a result, readers must consider the possibility that Oedipa's name is merely comic. Her name becomes a site of instability.

Other names, too, invite speculation, pointing either to meaningful allusion or to comic arbitrariness. Pierce Inverarity, whose posthumous demand on Oedipa entails either her discovery of penetrating truths or their inverse; Mucho Maas, who is periodically overwhelmed by too much input, who works for the radio station KCUF, and who has a thing for young women; Dr. Hilarius, who plies Oedipa with LSD tablets and makes distorted faces to promote cure; the Paranoids, both a parody of the Beatles and a band whose name calls attention to Oedipa's suspicion of a great, unknowable plot—all these names create reader amusement while also inviting interpretation that defies determinate significance.

As students explore other comic elements in the novel, I continue to focus on the ways Pynchon's humor is designed to keep readers poised between comic response and serious implication. The opening paragraph of *Lot 49* shows how the narrative voice establishes ambivalence in the reader, for the entire scene is a satire of a tipsy housewife who arrives home to find a rather weighty burden placed on her shoulders. Oedipa herself reflects mockingly on her predicament, and her apparently random memories of her time with Pierce are given a comic slant to convey, among other things, how unprepared she is to be propelled out of her comfortable world. This sequence of thoughts and ideas often strikes first-time readers as nonsensical, symptomatic perhaps of anyone in a kirsch-induced state; the sequence's lack of coherence makes it amusing, but the tone of the passage also conveys a mood of melancholy and underlying gravity that is vaguely threatening.

The indeterminacy and lack of connection that Oedipa experiences in this episode and periodically throughout the novel thrusts both her and the reader into a perception of the absurd. Because students can appreciate the inherent absurdity of the plot, a useful exercise is to ask them to define the concept of absurdity and indicate what they consider to be its main sources in the novel. Do they see the absurd residing in the superficial world of Tupperware and Muzak in which Oedipa is initially immersed or in the mysterious, incomprehensible world of the Tristero or in both?

As students are likely to mention both the idiomatic and philosophical definitions of the absurd, they find valuable discussion of the philosophical counterpart to the everyday meaning. Albert Camus defines the experience of absurdity as a perception of strangeness or a "divorce between the mind that desires and the world that disappoints" ("*Myth*" 37). To help students understand the concept of philosophical absurdity, they may be asked to question whether or not some of the patterns and conventions they follow are to a certain extent arbitrary, for the experience of the absurd entails recognizing the simultaneous necessity and futility of imposing meaning on events that are not inherently meaningful.

Oedipa seems to undergo precisely this experience as she attempts to define meaning through the imposition of her own arbitrary categories and connections. Unable to distinguish between reality and illusion, her confusion is projected onto the plot, which dissolves into a seemingly random array of intimations and unconnected clues. However, Oedipa's experience differs from Meursault's in Camus's *The Stranger*, for example, because Oedipa is navigating a world she has inherited from a person—Pierce Inverarity. She responds first in the spirit of a caper and then, as the conspiracy deepens, with the desperation of one who finds herself the victim of a bad joke. Unlike Camus's "gentle indifference of the world" (122), Oedipa's world seems at times too meaningful. The complexity of Pynchon's vision reveals a world that is simultaneously absurd and meaningful, as the potentially arbitrary categories of meaning and meaninglessness are conflated by humor.

## *Verbal Play*

Like absurdity, the extensive verbal play in *Lot 49* also functions on two levels, creating an infinite range of possible linguistic connections. Puns, double entendres, and other linguistically based forms of humor momentarily juxtapose associations and share meanings. Sigmund Freud observes:

> In every instance, the psychological process which the joking remark provokes in us, and on which the feeling of the comic rests, consists in the immediate transition, from this attaching of sense, from this discovering of truth, and from this granting of consequences, to the consciousness or impression of relative nothingness. (*Jokes* 12)

The reader's recognition of alternative meanings in the novel's wordplay produces a spark of pleasure, not unlike the way Oedipa's connection-making transforms her mundane existence with an element of surprise, momentary connectedness, and the multiplication of possible meanings.

A useful exercise to explore the types and function of verbal play in the novel is to ask students to identify a particular humorous device, define or categorize it, and attempt to explain how it functions in context. Initially, the exercise might focus on puns. Students may have discussed previously the punning quality of Pynchon's character names. Other puns function as acronyms: W.A.S.T.E., D.E.A.T.H., and N.A.D.A. appear to broadcast significance as literal signs—namely, signs of waste, death, and nothingness—that compete with the clues and intimations that Oedipa reads in them, yet they may point to literally nothing. A more evocative pun is the word "Tristero," which seems to point to a revelation of ultimate sadness of love and life, an ominous possibility that becomes all too immediate later in the novel. The variant "Trystero" complicates the possible meanings still further.

As students analyze the instrument and implications of the pun, the discussion may then focus on developing one or two examples to establish the similarity between the way the pun works as the reader interprets it and Oedipa's own attempt to make connections and establish meaning. San Narciso is an obvious pun that satirizes the southern California city as an urban realm in which Narcissus is the patron saint. Students can be asked to identify how Pynchon works or elaborates this pun: just as Narcissus saw his own reflection in the pool, Oedipa sees something of herself reflected in the unspecified revelations that surround her. As Oedipa enters San Narciso, she pulls into a motel aptly named Echo Courts, with an enormous nymph on its sign—like the nymph who pined after Narcissus—that resembles Oedipa (26). Later, during *The Courier's Tragedy*, she is exposed again to references to a Saint Narcissus (65, 72). The elaboration of this pun, though amusing as satire and parody, at the same time draws the reader into seeking the novel's deeper meanings. As Oedipa begins her quest for the Tristero, her anticipation of a metaphoric message conditions her to read the miscellaneous clues, signs, and intimations of meaning as if they contain a message she is entrusted to decode.

Puns, therefore, are kin to metaphors: both expand rather than constrict meaning in the "high magic" they possess. The centerpiece of the novel's use of verbal play comes in the scene in which Oedipa tries to comfort an old sailor. As Oedipa holds the man, who is suffering from delirium tremens, she perceives that behind the initials "DT" is a metaphor for "a trembling unfurrowing of the mind's plowshare" (128). She also makes her own pun, for "dt" is also the symbol for a "vanishingly small instant" (129), and imaginatively makes the connection that recognizes their similarity. She knows that "the sailor had seen worlds no other man had seen if only because there was that high magic to low puns." It occurs to her that the pun is a "thrust at truth and a lie" because its field is infinite (129); the pun is a means of short-circuiting language to yield up new connections and higher levels of meaning.

## *Satire*

In contrast to linguistically based forms of humor, satire is contextually based, just as the novel's jibes at Tupperware parties and southern Californian culture are. Most conventional versions of satire combine mockery with didacticism in the enfranchisement of certain humanist values. Joseph Heller's *Catch-22*, for instance, is an attack on the military establishment and American political values. I ask my students to identify as many targets of satire as they can and then ask what moral values this satiric humor embodies. They note the critique of suburban existence, of car salesmen and radio disk jockeys, of psychiatry, and such right-wing elements as the Pinguid Society and Winthrop Tremaine; altogether these targets may constitute a sustained critique of a corrupt society, an America without meaning.

But the novel's humor keeps the reader from taking this satiric critique too seriously. For example, when Oedipa reflects on the painting by Remedios Varo, which pictures a tapestry filling the void of the world, she identifies with the girls in the painting, since she too had been trapped in the tower of her ego, weaving her own incidental reality. The tone of this passage is complicated, for it both satirizes Oedipa and her mundane world and reveals her confusion and the situational absurdity of her predicament. Overwhelmed by the arbitrariness of her situation, she wonders if there is a meaning beyond the obvious. Yet the profundity of this passage and of Oedipa's realization is undercut by her conclusion that she too might take up embroidery. Even this joke, however, anticipates Oedipa's search, in which she takes up a kind of embroidery, weaving the Tristero system.

To help students perceive the difficulty in establishing a stable tonal perspective for the novel's satire, I ask them to study another scene in which the satire simultaneously presents a qualified promise of significance and undermines the legitimacy of any such attempt. As Oedipa continues her pursuit of the unutterable word, she winds up at a deaf-mutes' ball. The joke is obvious: the word can be neither heard nor spoken. Yet, as Oedipa is waltzed around to the silent music, she speculates that just as the many dances occur simultaneously in a random pattern, so may an indefinite number of alternative interpretations occur simultaneously, each with its own perceived coherence. Here, too, a deeply philosophical and political meditation is extracted from a patently ludicrous scene, yet Oedipa undercuts her own insights. On the brink of a miracle, she "curtsied and fled" (132). Which is to say that the agent of the novel's satiric critique, and the one who constructs an alternative world of meaning, is herself an object of satire.

## *Parody and Burlesque*

Like satire, which ridicules social convention, parody and its close relative, burlesque, mock the literary for comic effect. Each raises interesting critical questions regarding the role of the reader, the relationship of texts, and the social and literary contexts in which the target is situated. Since students are familiar with parody through popular sources such as *Monty Python* and *Saturday Night Live*, an interesting exercise is to have them inquire into what makes such parody work. They may be led to realize that parody requires the audience's position of objective distance from and familiarity with its source: one gets the joke when the juxtaposition between the original and the imitation are clear.

An effective scene to illustrate how the parody becomes complicated is Oedipa's attendance at *The Courier's Tragedy.* On one level, the drama is Pynchon's obvious parody of a Jacobean revenge play with its convoluted plot, vengeful characters, and gruesome conclusion. Students may be shown passages from John Webster's *The Duchess of Malfi* or *The White Devil* to familiarize them with the object of the parody. Students can also be asked to compare Pynchon's play-within-a-novel with *Hamlet*, which contains Shakespeare's play-within-a-play. Literary forms are here mocked for comic effect, yet this drama also plays with the reader's system making, for its title invokes the underground postal system Oedipa is in the midst of pursuing and seems to comment on the novel's theme of communication. As happens throughout, satire, parody, and burlesque simultaneously elicit laughter and sustain the profound ramifications of Oedipa's quest—even while that quest parodies the modernist quest at the heart of Eliot's *Wasteland* and while the quest itself is mocked as the activity of the Puritan and the English major.

At the end of the play, the word "Tristero" hangs in the air, either pregnant with meaning or utterly meaningless. The numerous literary allusions and descriptions of presumably historical events raise the question of whether these are actual reference points on which to base contemporary formulations or merely the continuous layering of fictions on fictions. The fictional plot of the drama is no more real than either the elusive citations Oedipa tries to track down or the literal Tristero system she tries to discover. For the reader as literary sleuth, assembling the various clues into a cohesive interpretation parallels Oedipa's attempts at plot making. Likewise, Pynchon slyly satirizes the unsuspecting readers looking for clues to make sense of Oedipa's plot, for their hopes for a coherent plot must inevitably be frustrated, if not dashed altogether.

In a related scene that establishes a similar purpose but magnifies the comic effect of burlesque, the "blooming" of the Tristero in Oedipa's life is compared to her attendance at a literal burlesque. As Oedipa gropes her way toward the lure of a revelation that the structure of the novel seems to suggest, the plot beckons her to become involved. The Tristero appears to her like a striptease dancer on the stage of history, teasing her with its secret while she attempts to undress it and see through its "historical figuration." Though her search has begun as a caper, the narrator wonders if once the dance ends the Tristero may "begin to speak words she never wanted to hear" (54).

## Black Humor

Oedipa's difficulty is that the more she comes to learn, the less she seems actually to know. As she suspects that she is approaching the truth of the Tristero during her night walk, the novel's tone becomes more sinister. Previously, the decenteredness of meaning is comically conceived; now the absurdity of her quest assumes the darker tone of black humor. A critical discussion can effectively focus on the implications of this shift: what defines black humor, what makes it funny or not, and how this episode takes on a different meaning from the satire and parody of earlier episodes. Instructors might provide students examples of black humor contemporaneous with Pynchon's *Lot 49*, such as Stanley Kubrick's *Dr. Strangelove; or, How I Learned to Stop Worrying and Love the Bomb* (1963) and Kurt Vonnegut, Jr.'s *Slaughterhouse-Five* (1968). Black humor is characterized as the juxtaposition of grotesque or horrifying elements with humorous or farcical ones, whose aim is to shock or disorient the reader, forcing one to laugh while simultaneously recognizing a disturbing and disoriented world. In *Lot 49*, three elements of black humor dominate: the caricature of the human, the nightmarish distortion of events, and the blurring of the real and surreal.

In some ways, Oedipa's night journey is the most terrifying of her experiences and the darkest vision in the novel. The people appear strange, like caricatures of human beings, and her surroundings distorted, like the landscape of nightmare. Normal certainties break down, and the nighttime world is suddenly rendered inexplicable though vaguely familiar as it would be in a dream. If students are familiar with the works of Vladimir Nabokov, Samuel Beckett, or Eugene Ionesco, they may be accustomed to the effect of black humor; otherwise, the instructor might also point them to the scene of Yossarian's night journey in *Catch-22* for comparison (Heller 420–29). The story in *V.*, Pynchon's first novel, of the sailor painting the side of a ship that is sinking into the ocean displays in a nutshell the dark vision of black humor (Schulz).

Events are so confused in Oedipa's perspective that they become inexplicable to the reader as well. As her night walk assumes the tenor of nightmare, it occurs to Oedipa that she "would have trouble sorting the night into real and dreamed" (117). The unfamiliar setting appears unreal to her; as Oedipa tries to rationalize the world that she sees in terms that she knows, her distorted perception of it makes it alien and hence absurd.

Reality and unreality become nearly indistinguishable in Oedipa's mind as the normal bases for judgment are subverted. The world of Tupperware and Muzak that Oedipa constructed in her tower is replaced by a world of post horns and isolates for which she has no explanation other than her Tristero hypothesis. Black humor often creates such an atmosphere of disorientation by crossing the familiar boundaries of the rational and irrational, combining extremes of perception that resist reconciliation. For Oedipa and the reader, the gap between the real and surreal is also the thin line between hilarity and horror.

## Creative Function of Humor

A discussion of the end of the novel should raise questions regarding how the pervasive humor either contributes to or undermines the possibilities for meaning implied at the conclusion of Oedipa's quest. The indeterminacy that Oedipa faces at the end of the narrative subverts the basis of her reality but at the same time extends a promise of significance that is also creative. Even as Oedipa tries to reconstruct the logic holding the plots together, the novel's binary poles of ultimate connection and total randomness prevent resolution. Such uncontrollable diversity and lack of resolution challenge the reader's desire for order, while also offering more possibilities for interpretation. With the courage one finds "when there is nothing more to lose" (182), Oedipa goes to the auction to hear the crying of lot 49, but even here humor intrudes on the reader's desire for stable seriousness. Few characters can make their last words a pun as they await final judgment. Oedipa whispers to her possible enemy, "Your fly is open," and the narrator plays along: Oedipa "was not sure what she'd do when the bidder revealed himself" (183). Oedipa's triumph is Pynchon's own success in the discovery of a high magic to low puns. This is his vision and his grand joke: the multiplicity that humor provides is the meaningful embrace of the absurd.

NOTES

[1] See Jasper for a further discussion of Pynchon's use of humor.

[2] See Henkle's description of Pynchon's comedy as "the metaphorical reduction of the fearful into the playful" ("Morning" 274).

# Tragic Satire: Chasing Nazi Symbols in *The Crying of Lot 49*

*Inger H. Dalsgaard*

The suspicion, raised in *Gravity's Rainbow*, that a Nazi mind-set has entered the postwar United States is fueled by the presence of its varied representatives in *The Crying of Lot 49*: SS-affiliated immigrant Dr. Hilarius, government surplus swastika armbands made to order near San Diego, and swarms of VW "Bugs" on California freeways.

When discussing *Gravity's Rainbow* and *The Crying of Lot 49* in class, students never fail, in my experience, to find the presence of Nazi symbols and totalitarian systems especially provocative, not least because these are often offered up in the context of humor, ridicule, puns, or gags. When a passage makes us smile uncomfortably, there is a trace of guilt at having been amused by a topic not usually considered a laughing matter. But as was true for the fictional musical *Springtime for Hitler*, from Mel Brooks's *The Producers* (1968), neither the camp pleasure of an amused audience nor the knee-jerk refusal to entertain such a distasteful subject in class must become an obstacle to a serious and conscientious reading of Pynchon's novel. The embarrassed giggle can be the one thing that prevents us from passing over descriptions unreflectively, as just sad or just funny or as comfortably relegated to history.

History, in Pynchon's texts, is not a regrettable but static past: Buchenwald experiments can suddenly surface in California suburbia, as they do when Dr. Hilarius's concentration camp research project appears to have metastasized among housewives in Kinneret-among-the-Pines and when swastika armbands and uniforms of the Third Reich enjoy renewed "street cred" on the West Coast of the USA, thanks to the surplus outlet run by one Winthrop Tremaine, a man whose name recalls America's Puritan heritage. In *The Crying of Lot 49* the past is neither distant in time or place nor ever really laid to rest.

In the course of her duties as executrix, Mrs. Oedipa Maas discovers what seems to be the existence of a fashion industry based on SS uniforms. Long before Oedipa lists insanity, hallucinations, an elaborate hoax, or a deep conspiracy as possible explanations for her many other findings (170), a careful reading of the passage in which Oedipa (wary of government monopolies) thinks she has caught Winthrop Tremaine selling government surplus swastikas presents the reader with alternative interpretations (149). In one the reader sympathizes with Oedipa's apparent suspicion that the nation's core is falling prey to Nazi glamour. In another the reader maintains distance from Oedipa's ballooning paranoia and takes statements by "the spirited entrepreneur," Winthrop "Winner" Tremaine, at face value, which indicate merely that his marketing strategies are reaching only a limited audience, although he does intend to supply "one of the big ready-to-wear outfits in L.A." with teenage and ladies' models of SS uniforms (149).

When the validity of Tremaine's claims about manufacturing and selling Nazi emblems and fashions is weighed against Oedipa's reading of the sorry state of an America where back-to-school outfits are modeled on the uniforms of the Third Reich, students may become aware not only of their dependence, as readers, on the protagonist, whose experiences and discoveries they share as they go through the novel, but also of the interpretive instability humor adds to a text. Tremaine's claims seem absurd, outrageous, and laughable, like those of several other characters, but even if they are dismissed as one of Pynchon's zany asides, they soon manifest themselves again when Mike Fallopian confirms he is "already in touch" with what Oedipa dubs "Tremaine's Swastika Shoppe" (168), a hint that he might have been the kind of "[f]ella" who bought Nazi armbands and rifles (149). Tremaine's activities may seem fantastic, but intratextual connections, as much as extratextual arguments about resurgent National Socialism, lend them reality and presence.

We learn from the passage where Tremaine explains his business to Oedipa that history is not just a used thing, lodged comfortably in the static past of dusty chronicles, but an idea, which can be resurrected in a government surplus outlet or in a classroom where a topic such as Nazism's living legacy seems combustible. History is like the unreliable Gewehr 43 Dr. Hilarius has carried over from his Nazi past, which he brings out to confront the return of the repressed in the Hilarius Psychiatric Clinic twenty years later (133). Not solely nostalgic relics, such used rifles (or ideas) also signify a future. Though they represent excess armament production of the past, Tremaine's surplus goods find new markets (through contacts to militias or Klan members, we suspect) and revive and nurture the symbols, attitudes, and practices of old repressive systems in the shape of swastika armbands and the African Americans (whom Tremaine terms "niggers") "hire[d]" to make them (149).

When required to investigate closely the deeper significance of Tremaine's choice of words, students may identify the presence of an old supremacist mind-set (of a Nazi or Confederate past) that invites us to read "to hire" here in the sense of "to rent," not "to employ." Yet these words also suggest the historicity of the novel in the emergence of right-wing militias, neo-Nazism, and John Birch Clubs in the United States during the 1950s and 1960s. Furthermore, Tremaine's use of "the *n* word" may be used to encourage students to situate *Lot 49* in the civil rights struggles then ongoing. Any number of historical anecdotes might be adduced. I often recount the experience of Werner Holzer, former editor-in-chief of the *Frankfurter Rundschau*, who interviewed a leader of a white supremacist group in Florida when covering the South in the 1960s. Holzer recalls that the appropriately named Reverend Lynch "looked at me and said, 'You know what you do when boll weevils get into your cotton? You exterminate them.' I told him, 'You know I am German. I have heard that before' " (qtd. in Willis 19). In Pynchon's novels Nazism can be seen as a metaphor for a sick American society—if not the disease itself, which was what Holzer suspected. In *The Crying of Lot 49*, Pynchon uses the swastika as a symptom of social malaise; in *Gravity's Rainbow*, he imports the whole Third Reich to reenact the lack of morals and principles afflicting the United States and suggests that a deadly virus has passed from the old world to the new by fathers infecting their sons (722–23).

Accentuating Tremaine's Nazism is the all-encompassing, global, cartelized war-economy, which thrives regardless of which political systems it supports. This unprincipled global capitalism seems in Pynchon's novels to be founded on a pragmatic, money-motivated Puritan mind-set passed from the original Winthrops and Slothrops to twentieth-century descendants for whom everything is for sale—be it sons, New England forests, or surplus swastikas—to anyone who pays the right price. The financial mechanisms that allow Tremaine to operate successfully and controversies such as the ethics involved in sabotaging logging (instead of saving trees by hugging) touch immediately on my students' personal experiences and opinions and can provide better starting points for discussions than do Nazism, white-supremacy movements, and totalitarianism. While the factory making swastika armbands suggests that the production of German historical artifacts reproduces (or rekindles) totalitarian and racist systems in an American setting, it also suggests that history has become a product—a possession rather than a series of events—and reminds us of the free choice of consumers to buy and identify.

My students are of a generation that has lost faith in the power of political action and democracy to deal with the injustices of the world. Their few and disparate options seem to be to choose between lapsing into apathy, buying fair-trade chocolate, or joining Battle of Seattle–style protests at various World Bank, World Trade Organization, and G7 or G8 summit meetings. The only power left to those with a social conscience seems to be their purchasing power or the use of violence. Oedipa considers clubbing Tremaine with his own merchandise to vent her indignation or to stop his activities. In a disguised second-person address to the reader, Oedipa reminds herself of her personal responsibility: "This is America, you live in it, you let it happen. Let it unfurl." Students usually express sympathetic amusement at Oedipa's frustrated reaction when she "drove savagely along the freeway, hunting for Volkswagens" (150). They often volunteer that, though her feelings are justified, her limited means of action are rendered both futile and comic: a position of powerlessness with which they can identify.

I always ask them to articulate why, exactly, a Volkswagen is chosen as the target of Oedipa's attack. Two explanations tend to emerge: usually, students say the VW is chosen because the historical memory of Nazism leads to a primitive rage at things German; and sometimes, they say it is because the car is a symptom of conscience-free consumerism (in the past and the present) and she is seeking material(ist) revenge. If these are the only two explanations, I follow up with the question, why not target some other German car? As a possible answer, one may point out that the VW is a nexus of the tragedy and comedy that characterize Pynchon's historically conscious writing strategies—and that are thematized in the novel's aphorism that there is a "high magic to low puns" (129).

The VW Bug (or Beetle) is a comical-looking car with a sinister prehistory. Recently made over, the Bug is still popular in the United States and is another example of buying the past off the shelf without moral conscience or historical consciousness. Few of my students know that in the 1930s (while the public works on the German Autobahn system proceeded and Hitler's political power consolidated) a "Volkswagen," literally a "people's car," was promised to every German family. As Henry Ford and Herbert Hoover had proved in the United States not long before, the car was a symbol of a future prosperity generated by the car itself: people who worked in automotive plants should be able to afford cars themselves, and the auto industry was considered a key multiplier, since it bought the products of the oil, rubber, and steel industries and required public-works projects like the construction of freeways. The incestuous production and purchase of cars was in this sense considered an economic engine capable of pulling (or keeping) national economies out of recession—whether in the United States or Germany. The automotive industry is model proof of Pynchon's critique of morally corrupt global corporations. The moral corruption was so thoroughly international during World War II that the Ford Motor Company still finds itself subject to litigation over the use of slave labor in its Cologne plant. Today the stylishness and design of the Bug override the history of slave labor in VW factories or the intimate links with Hitler's populist politics, which attach to his "people's car." This superseding of VW history may be an analogue of Tremaine's racist use of African Americans to produce stylish swastikas for a reactionary fashion market in the 1960s. In an era when VW minibuses are the hippest of hippie vehicles and her husband enjoys the musical stylings of Sick Dick and the Volkswagens, a British Beatles copy, Oedipa's chasing Volkswagens on the freeway shows a historical conscience as oddly rare then perhaps as it is now.

My students readily agree that cars are commercial (if not political) symbols of prosperity as well as conveyors of personal style or character, which allows me to bring in Mucho's perspective on the relation between humanity and automobiles. Oedipa's husband is a used-car salesman sensitive to the banal human histories contained in poor people's cars: "motorized, metal extensions of themselves" (13). Nazism, whether symbolized by the VW or the V-2 rocket in *Gravity's Rainbow* (known in British slang as a "doodlebug"), is a "bug" that has infected Oedipa's America. To the masses, political systems are as easily interchangeable as cars.

The residue of human history horrifies us, as it did Mucho, and through the image Pynchon's tragicomic narrative implies that the present, too, is just such a residue. If we become habituated to Tremaine's story because—outrageous as his merchandise is—the framework of selling and advertising seems relatively mundane, if students become absorbed in arguments about the intricacies of the text to the exclusion of debates about militias and neo-Nazism, I point out and ask them about this exclusion: did my perceived authority as a literature teacher suppress their impulse to discuss current politics, or were they preoccupied by the nature of the signal rather than the message? We sometimes start referring to such "Mucho readings" and "Oedipa readings" of the text. Mucho's way of reading has absorbed the "banality of evil," which Hannah Arendt described in *Eichmann in Jerusalem* (231 [1962]): anyone can become evil when evil is an integral, routine element of an all-encompassing bureaucracy like the Third Reich. Oedipa's approach to reading clings to the idea of forces of good and evil at work in the system and holds isolated "Hitler Hilarius" figures individually responsible (138).

How do readers respond to the return of the repressed when confronting it in the novel? I find the most difficult passage to handle (emotionally) that of Hilarius's paranoid breakdown when he realizes he cannot atone for his past by practicing Freudian psychotherapy, a therapy that promised that the light of truth would convert Buchenwald to "a soccer field, [while] fat children would learn flower-arranging and solfeggio in the strangling rooms. At Auschwitz the ovens would be converted over to petit fours and wedding cakes, and the V–2 missiles to public housing for the elves" (138). This grotesque image of cloying cuteness clashes with the mental category in which we usually keep the concentration camps or the terror weapons of World War II. At best such a disturbing combination forces us to renew our view of what these Nazi symbols stand for. Unlike the *Springtime for Hitler* audience, for whom confronting the specter of the repressed renders it innocently amusing, Hilarious realizes that Freudian catharsis cannot keep the world safe from the specter of Auschwitz or Buchenwald. Time cannot turn tragedy into comedy nor keep the potential legacy of history from reasserting itself in the future.

Instead, I ask students to recognize the indignant, suburban housewife in themselves. Oedipa is a woman brought up with 1950s values responding to a 1960s universe, where anything goes; pursuing the roots of this newly permissive and superficial society but exposed to resurgent Nazism, she reacts with disgust and a desire to put things right. Comparably, my students have grown up in a postmodern period where—in theory, at least—anything goes and where a text playfully using the hilarity of madcap Nazis and incongruous peddlers of sacrilege might easily be passed over. But Tremaine and Hilarius can be used as catalysts, allowing students to rediscover (just as Oedipa does) moral outrage, personal responsibility, and the value of responding emotionally rather than treating everything as superficial texts.

If we consider emotional response to be a part of the interpretive process and provide space in the classroom for the concerns of students, we may learn history's lesson from literature. Literature did not fall silent or become useless or meaningless after Auschwitz, nor did it after 9/11. Discussing the function of Nazism in Pynchon's novels, new generations of students may find ways to adapt their reading strategies for the world they inhabit.

# EMPIRE, HISTORY, AND POSTMODERN SPACE

## Teaching Pynchon's *V.*

*David Cowart*

I normally ask my students to read a novel in its entirety before we begin discussing it in class. But a text such as *V.* might profitably be assigned in two stages, perhaps to coincide with the institution's mid-semester break. For the last meeting before the break, students would read the first three chapters of the novel and the short story "Under the Rose" (another, more straightforward version of chapter 3). The rest of the book would then be due when classes resume. This strategy allows one to deal, in a timely fashion, with the confusion generated by the problematic chapter in which the author, shifting historical gears for the first time, introduces Victoria Wren and her calling through the polyhedral lenses of eight points of view. Students have fewer difficulties if they can be swiftly oriented (whether by pedagogical intervention or by reading the short story) to what Pynchon does with historical circumstance: the confrontation of French and British detachments at Fashoda, on the Nile, in 1898. Pynchon imagines that two German agents, Lepsius and the deceptively named Bongo-Shaftsbury, plot to assassinate the English consul in Cairo, Lord Cromer. The agents hope that such a timely assassination, mistaken for French incendiarism, will precipitate a war between France and England that will weaken both sides, leaving Germany a clear field to realize its own dreams of imperial expansion. Unfortunately, Cromer does not take the threat seriously enough. To make him more cautious, two British agents, Porpentine and Goodfellow, stage a mock-assassination attempt. Although the English agents succeed in foiling the German plot, Porpentine perishes, and in Sarajevo, sixteen years later, Goodfellow will stand alone.

Victoria—or V., as she will come to be known—plays a minor role here (she has a liaison with Goodfellow), and this very inconsequence will prove meaningful. But first-time readers will appreciate being told to pay careful attention to the appearances of Victoria and her avatars. To this end I would suggest that students be asked to hand in a written record of appearances by V. under her various noms de guerre. Such an assignment might be especially helpful if the novel is to be read in increments of a certain number of pages or chapters per meeting. A class exercise in which V.'s appearances are listed on the board allows for the catching of any omissions in students' logs. Or one can, with an overhead projector, put up for discussion and possible correction a chart such as the one on page 90. Various possibilities for discussion of this chart present themselves: one can, for example, consider whether shifts in point of view from chapter to chapter and within chapters raise questions about the reliability of these sightings. Are some of them more grounded than others? Similarly, one can consider whether the scrambling or fragmentation of the historical sequence is to be understood as a modernist invitation to reassemble the pieces and so recover a vision of cultural wholeness and meaning. Students should note that all the chapters set before 1914 seem to depict V. in proximity to international fuses (to modify a Pynchon image) awaiting the spark that will bring the Great War. The epilogue and chapter 9 orient V. to the currents that will bring World War II, "whose etiology was also her own" (387). This conflict occupies the foreground only in chapter 11, closest in time to the novel's present (1955–56).

Whenever I teach V., I point out Pynchon's propensity, in the fictions of his early career, for quest plots and thematic material related to paranoid obsession. I invite students' perceptions of just how such subject matter functions thematically. Who, I ask, quests here? What is the object of his quest? And what is paranoia? A quotation from *Gravity's Rainbow*, transcribed on the blackboard, can help: "If there is something comforting—religious, if you want—about paranoia, there is also anti-paranoia, where nothing is connected to anything, a condition not many of us can bear for long" (434). This observation often leads to an immediate insight or at least a pregnant question or two: does not all sanity and all civilization require a vision that, like paranoia, connects dots that may, after all, be random? And who connects the dots? Some classes will want to compare and contrast the dot-connecting of science and religion with that of the historian or artist. All such connecting of dots yields meaning—but which enterprises do so most reliably? Eigenvalue the psychodontist calls into question the connections made by one especially important viewpoint character:

> Cavities in the teeth occur for good reason, Eigenvalue reflected. But even if there are several per tooth, there's no conscious organization there against the life of the pulp, no conspiracy. Yet we have men like Stencil, who must go about grouping the world's random caries into cabals. (153)

## Timeline-Chronology: Avatars and Congeners of V.

*"Victoria was being gradually replaced by* V.*;*
*something entirely different, for which*
*the young century had as yet no name"* (410).

| | |
|---|---|
| 1880 | Born in Lardwick-in-the-Fen, Yorkshire (ch. 3). |
| 1890 | Sexual encounter with Ralph MacBurgess (later known as Maxwell Rowley-Bugge; ch. 3). |
| 1898 | Appears in Alexandria and Cairo during Fashoda crisis; affair with Goodfellow the spy (ch. 3; cf. "Under the Rose"). |
| 1899 | Appears in Florence during riot of Venezuelan expatriates; meets Evan and Hugh Godolphin (ch. 7); seduces Sidney Stencil (488). |
| 1901 | Apparently in England, gives birth to Herbert Stencil (489, but cf. 54). Is Sidney the father? (Epilogue). |
| 1913 | V. in Paris. At Mélanie's death, goes off with Sgherraccio, an Irredentist (ch. 14). |
| 1914(c.) | As Veronica Manganese, arrives on Malta with Sgherraccio, now a Mizzist, to wait out the war (Epilogue). |
| 1919 | On Malta still, involved in pro-Italian (and proto-Fascist) espionage. Evan Godolphin, mutilated, is her companion. Involved with Father Fairing, who later cracks in New York; resumes affair with Sidney Stencil, to his confusion. She has the sapphire and the eye, perhaps a false arm, desires a false foot (Epilogue). |
| 1922 | In Fiume with decadent D'Annunzio, much admired by Mussolini and the fasci di combattimento (ch. 9). |
| 1922 | In South-West Africa as Vera Meroving; encounters and engenders the corruption—the decadence—of old Godolphin. Weissmann will turn up as an astonishingly perverted Nazi in *Gravity's Rainbow* (ch. 9). |
| | (Word of V.'s spending a year on Mallorca and appearing in Spain, on Crete, on Corfu, in Asia Minor, in Rotterdam, and in the Roman Campagna [388]). |
| 1943 | *Qua* "Bad Priest," on Malta again "to wait out" hostilities (387); evidently dies during air raid, disassembled by callous children (cf. Benny Profane's dream, 39–40). How reliable is Maijstral at this moment? (ch. 11). |
| 1956 | Stencil touches base on Malta, refuses to believe that his quest ends there, yoyos off to Sweden after another lead. Crises in Hungary, Poland, Suez (ch. 16). |
| 1963 | Pynchon's novel published, as if to warn readers that presently (in 1965) they will be twenty years beyond World War II—time for another great conflict, the most destructive and final of all. Hints of apocalypse (461, 472, 479–80). |

One should not, however, take Eigenvalue's patronizing observation as definitive. Paranoia in Pynchon frequently symbolizes the process by which human beings organize knowledge, and "men like Stencil" include every philosopher or theologian or scientist who undertakes imaginatively to stitch together the buzzing, blooming confusion of the phenomenal world. Stencil's little quest for V. parodies the more serious system making that, in any age, models reality.

Students should eventually see what complicates any search for meaning—whether in history or in what Linda Hutcheon calls a "historiographic metafiction" such as this one (*Poetics* ix).[1] They may also see how, as readers, they undertake a quest congruent with or parallel to that of Herbert Stencil. The twinned quests of reader and character involve the pursuit of pattern and meaning, one in a novel, the other in the text of history. Some students may be able to flag the passages in which Stencil—through the narrator—speculates about what he may be on to: "The Big One, the century's master cabal" (226).

Stencil's name identifies him as a pattern maker, and, indeed, he attempts to impose a pattern on the mystery of V., the woman he has read about in the journals of his father, Sidney Stencil. Central to the book, Herbert Stencil links the aimless, mid-century present and its immediate historical antecedents, whether World War II or the more generalized currents of violence that rocked the century before and after that conflict. "Born in 1901, the year Victoria died, Stencil was in time to be the century's child" (52). But born to whom, this representative of twentieth-century humanity, this witness to two world wars and the routine carnage of political struggles in forgotten corners of the earth? In the epilogue, in which point of view does not appear to be "Stencilized" (228), the author seems to identify V. as Stencil's mother. Even if one takes the epilogue as free indirect discourse grounded, still, in the projections of the younger Stencil, the suggestion regarding a baleful maternal parent seems nonetheless valid. The conceit of being mothered by some terrible idea of violence will recur in *Gravity's Rainbow*, where Roger Mexico declares, "My mother is the war" (39). Indeed, in the twentieth century, she is the mother of us all.

As the book unfolds, then, Stencil's quest for V. becomes the quest of humanity to understand the violence of our times. In V. Stencil discovers (or thinks he discovers) the Zeitgeist, emblem of the age's love affair with carnage. Those who come into contact with her are presently ruined (Ralph MacBurgess), corrupted (the Goldolphins, father and son), or destroyed (the English agent Porpentine, the ballerina Mélanie, Father Fairing, "Ugo Medichevole, a minor magician" [388], and perhaps the Sidney Stencil who runs disastrously afoul of V-shaped bad weather—a waterspout—in the Mediterranean). Through Stencil *fils*, Pynchon shows modern humanity trying to give history a shape, a structure, a myth, a meaning. But neither meaning nor myth is more than mirage.

To provide some cross-disciplinary contextualization, teachers may want to include in their course packets a selection on postmodern historiography—perhaps the introduction to Hayden White's monumental *Metahistory* (1973). Influenced by Northrop Frye's *Anatomy of Criticism*, White demonstrates how written history, like literature, tends to take on certain formal qualities—to be, in the work of Leopold von Ranke, Jules Michelet, Alexis de Tocqueville, and Jacob Burckhardt, now comic, now tragic, now romantic, now ironic. The implications are obvious. Historians shape their material: the writing of history, like the writing of fiction, involves selection, subjectivity, emplotment. Even the simplest, most uninterpreted compilation of facts tends to be compromised by the disappearance from the record of other facts. As historian, then, Stencil creates a picture of V. that is too shapely, too fictive. The mythic V. that he produces betrays the shapeless, uncentered actuality of the past.

But what kind of mythographer is Pynchon? How does his "mythical method" (Eliot 178) differ from that of James Joyce or T. S. Eliot? Students need to see how, under its fragmented surface, Pynchon's narrative at once coheres with machined precision and subverts or betrays that wholeness. They should recognize in this seeming conundrum something of how postmodernism differs from modernism. Ideally, they will know a modernist text or two (*To the Lighthouse*? *The Waste Land*?) against which they can gauge the new aesthetic. If Pynchon does not share the syllabus with a modernist exemplar such as Joyce, Virginia Woolf, or Eliot, a teacher can derive the same benefit through assignment of an excerpt from one of the most significant works to which Pynchon alludes. In fact, a prior or concurrent assignment from *The Education of Henry Adams* (e.g., the much anthologized chapter 25, "The Dynamo and the Virgin") will go far toward clarifying both the immediate meanings and the larger cultural significance of Pynchon's novel. Adams simultaneously participates in the modernist exploitation of myth (as universal, instinctive truth) and anticipates its postmodern debunking. He salutes the divine female principle in Western history: the Venus of the ancients, the Virgin of medieval Christianity. But the West, he says, has declined from cultural unity to chaos. Thus both Venus and Virgin, quondam embodiments of sexual energy and fertility, find themselves sidelined in the modern age, vitiated, emptied of power. In 1900, Adams can no longer affirm spiritually grounded meanings for terms such as "force" or "energy." Nor can he affirm any direction or telos to history.

Where Adams ruefully concedes the displacement of the numen by the forces that positivist science describes, another mythographer insists that, however neglected, the goddess abides. This second major referent for Stencil's mythmaking is Robert Graves, explicitly mentioned (along with Adams) at the beginning of chapter 3. Given its resistance to excerpting, a handout or lecture excursus describing the premise of Graves's *The White Goddess* would be helpful to students. More seriously than E. O. James, Erich Neumann, Jane Harrison, or Johann Jakob Bachofen (author in 1861 of *Myth, Religion and Mother Right*), Graves argues for the supremacy of a female deity disastrously eclipsed, early in the preclassical West, by the rise of the male-dominated Greek pantheon.

Further eclipsed with the rise of patriarchal Christianity, the White Goddess remains potent, and like repression itself she exacts a terrible price for humanity's whoring after—no, pimping for—strange gods. In Graves's view, this apostasy, this deference to divine usurpers, has warped the course of more than two thousand years of history.

Like Adams and Graves, Pynchon takes a keen interest in the history of his times, but he views historiographic mythopoesis with great skepticism. His V. is a *parody* of history's divine female principle, the variously named goddess that Adams and Graves see as icon of cultural continuity. The twentieth century's character can be seen in its mythic avatar, then, but where both Adams and Graves could look back to a prior standard of cultural wholeness against which to measure (and by which to rebuke) their present—where they could, at least by implication, envision some recovery of a cultural arche-order, whether preclassical, classical, or medieval-Christian—Pynchon's V. embodies by contrast only the darker, entropic, self-destructive energies of a civilization on its last legs. Thus Pynchon foregrounds a factitious historical myth only to subvert it—and with it all such mythopoesis.

As V. parodies various female archetypes, so is she recursively parodied by the secondary female figures in the story, and the class might want to look at this feature in some detail. Again, students can be asked to generate a little chart, with Victoria Wren and her pseudonyms on the left, other women on the right (the side-by-side configuration may promote attention to the ways in which the female characters and V.'s avatars complement one another, all subsisting in the same fictional universe):

**Women in V.**

| | |
|---|---|
| Victoria Wren (Cairo, Florence; see 209, riot) | Fortune, La Donna Libertà<br>Mélanie l'Heuremaudit<br>Mara the sorceress-spirit, "Maltese for woman" (461) |
| V. at 1913 theater riot ("Nobody knew her name in Paris" [406]) | Veronica (1930s New York sewer rat, wants to become nun [121], as had Victoria; cf. Elena Xemxi)<br>Hedwig Vogelsang<br>"Sarah" (South-West Africa, 1904) |
| Veronica Manganese (on Malta) | Mrs. Buffo<br>Paola (notice her as the anti-V. at the riot [16]—cf. V. in Florence or Paris—and, at end, reconciling with Pappy after yet another riot, on the Valletta docks) |
| Vera Meroving (South-West Africa, 1922) | Rachel Owlglass |
| The Bad Priest (besieged Malta) | Esther Harvitz<br>Lucille at street fair |
| | Fina (see 144–45, 151)<br>Hanky and Panky<br>Flip and Flop<br>Brenda Wigglesworth |

Itself in decline, itself subject to entropic drift, the female mythic archetype defined by V. recurs throughout the novel in steady diminuendo. Like V., the secondary female figures gravitate toward either the inanimate or violence. Rachel Owlglass and Esther Harvitz answer the call of the inanimate, the one fetishizing her MG, the other undergoing rhinoplasty and abortion. Josefina Mendoza ("Fina") seems to thrive at the periphery of violence (that of New York's gangs)—but presently she becomes the sexual victim of her whilom acolytes. Mass rape will also be the fate of Sarah, the unwilling concubine of the channeled trooper in von Trotha's army. Mélanie l'Heuremaudit will become the fetishized object of V.'s passion, serve as another riot's focal point, and perish in a horrifically literal consummation with the inanimate (she turns up alive, however, in Pynchon's 2006 novel *Against the Day*). Mrs. Buffo, whose "dragon-embroidered kimono" (13) recalls the dragon-embroidered tights of both Mélanie and V. (397, 388), presides over Suck Hour as barroom version of the White Goddess. Paola Maijstral Hod hovers, V.-like, near riots at both the beginning and end of the book. She spends a season as the prostitute Ruby before reconnecting with her estranged husband in one of the book's rare sanguine moments.

In considering the women in the novel, one can also pause to solve the puzzle of sometime viewpoint character Benny Profane. Though he evinces a healthy dread of the inanimate, he represents the passivity of clueless, late-twentieth-century humanity—small wonder the Whole Sick Crew swiftly clasps him to its decadent bosom. But what, one asks students, makes this "great amoebalike boy, soft and fat" (36), so appealing to the story's most attractive women—Paola Maijstral, Fina Mendoza, Mafia Winsome, Rachel Owlglass? Students should recognize in women's attitudes to Profane some kind of counterparody of the V. phenomenon. He is almost a complete cipher, yet one woman after another "constructs" him according to her own desire for mythic masculinity.

Herbert Stencil, by the same token, constructs V. according to his desire for some key to history's chaos and his own identity. Through Stencil's eyes, the reader sees that Victoria Wren and the personages she becomes (especially the generic V.) have a valence for violence. Riot is her element, "the state of siege" her "natural habitat" (62). Hence the teasing intimations that V. somehow explains the century's drift toward greater and greater violence and disorder (386, 387, 410, 460–61). The V. antitypes all batten on violence, first crudely, then with gathering horror. In Lardwick-in-the-Fen the ten-year-old Victoria destroys only one man, then goes on in Cairo (1898), Florence (1899), and Paris (1913) to hover near and perhaps foster, as tutelary spirit, the Great War itself. Subsequently, she finds herself within the orbit of forces that will "improve" on the carnage of that first war (for the horrors of World War II—on and off the battlefield—will put the prior bloodshed into perspective). But does V. really die in 1943, as Fausto Maijstral's testimony seems to affirm—or is her baleful influence everywhere seeking the true apocalypse of World War III? The book will end with Armageddon seemingly at hand in the form of the Suez crisis of 1956 (Egypt again, where V. began her adult career). Though the first readers of this novel knew, in 1963, that the Suez crisis would be defused, they may have been less comfortable when they reflected that World War II began twenty years after the end of World War I. A similar twenty years of fitful, interbellum peace would end within a year or two of V.'s publication. Would 1965 see the beginning of World War III?

Early in the century, Sidney Stencil (Herbert's father) thinks in terms borrowed from Christian eschatology (Descent of the Paraclete, Armageddon, apocalypse), but the author encourages the reader to question the premises behind such terms: notions about history as something that has form and moves toward a promised end. Thus Sidney Stencil's theory of "Paracletian politics" (472, 480) is exposed as merely the thinking of patternmaker-senior. Both Stencils have theories of history, then, and both are mistaken. *Accident* reigns—the kind of accident that, cataloged in a bravura passage in chapter 10 (290–91), claims the life of Sidney in the Mediterranean on the novel's last page. Whether as ultimate war or simple fulfillment of entropic drift (culminating in a triumph of the inanimate, of nothingness), only secular apocalypse looms, an apocalypse of collapse or self-immolation, not biblical fulfillment. The horror that V. legitimately embodies is that humanity repeatedly conspires to promote, rather than resist, this end.

V. organizes and makes sense of the age only in our fevered desire that there be such sense, such a rationale. At some point in their scrutiny of this text, students should see (or be nudged into seeing) that V. is *not* present for the important violence of the century. Unlike Brigadier Pudding's Domina Nocturna (in *Gravity's Rainbow*), she puts in no appearance at Passchendaele or the killing fields of the Spanish Civil War—nor does she gravitate to Gallipoli, the Somme, the Battle of Britain, the Bulge, Dresden, or Hiroshima. Even in Cairo, Florence, Paris, German South-West Africa, and the siege of Malta, she figures only at the periphery of such violence as occurs. Once this dawns on readers, they see the novel as a grand demonstration of humanity's enormous need to rationalize the past, the need that forces the historian—Herbert Stencil, for example—into dubious acts of emplotment. Perhaps, too, they see humanity's conceptual crucifixion between history as concatenation of aimless accident and history as coherent narrative (one option impossible to live with, the other false). As a representative figure, Stencil is not to be despised if, last seen en route to Sweden to check out another lead on V., he cannot give up the quest. The human mind cannot live with the wholly random character of history and the phenomenal world.

Little more than a vast Brownian motion, history enacts the steady conversion of the animate into the inanimate. How, one asks students, does Pynchon's heteroclite heroine exemplify this entropic tendency? They should see that she comes to instantiate a principle of incremental—and deadly—objectification. The pattern here concerns the conversion of living flesh into something mechanical or moribund. The conceit receives its greatest elaboration in V., who seems to delight in inanimate replacements (the wig, the clockwork eye, the navel sapphire, the silver foot) for her own living tissue and so embodies—literally—the love affair with the inanimate. "Even in Florence," the narrator reminds us, Sidney Stencil "had noted an obsession with bodily incorporating little bits of inert matter" (488). She naturally comes also to embody the fascism that promotes the progressive objectification of human beings in this century, notably in the slave-labor camps of German South-West Africa, which prefigure the more dreadful camps in World War II.

By this reasoning, fascism would seem to exemplify the decadence that keeps cropping up here. When Profane, reproached for giving his name as Benny Sfacim ("jism"), corrects it to Sfacimento, meaning "destruction or decay" (140), both words seem to pun on *fascismo*. Even as Pynchon squarely faces up to what might be called existential decadence, the human fate articulated by Mehemet the xebec captain ("The only change is toward death. . . . Early and late we are in decay" [460]), he deplores our age's tendency toward the ideological promotion of what in *The Crying of Lot 49* he calls "the irreversible process" (128). Fausto Maijstral defines decadence as "[o]nly a clear movement toward death or, preferably, non-humanity" (321). Similarly in the reflections of Itague, in 1913 Paris, the reader sees that the decadence theme complements or subsumes the inanimateness theme: "decadence . . . is a falling-away from what is human, and the further we fall the less human we become. Because we are less human, we foist off the humanity we have lost on inanimate objects and abstract theories" (405). Thus fetishism pervades the Paris chapter, as Mélanie, addressed as *fétiche* and known professionally as La Jarretière (the garter), pantomimes intercourse with a lay figure, dreams of herself as wind-up doll, and dances with automatons. In turn, she will become the "object" of V.'s twisted love. Itague's reference to "abstract theories" may reflect proleptically on those of Herbert Stencil (or Mafia Winsome), but it also gestures toward the aestheticism, the artistic decadence, that influences such characters as Evan Godolphin and Rafael Mantissa.

One of the more subtle historical elements of the novel is its attention to purely artistic decadence in a variety of forms. The term *decadence* can refer specifically to the international movement that embraced late-nineteenth-century French and British aestheticism and the Generation of 1898 in Spain—or it can refer more generally to any artistic movement's period of exhaustion and decline. Thus the author of *The Crying of Lot 49* characterizes Jacobean drama as decadent, and many would so characterize the Stravinsky-like Porcépic's compositions. Not necessarily inferior, such art features highly unconventional subject matter and a style that can seem by turns chaotic and precious. The term can characterize any period—including, I should think, both modernism and postmodernism—of extreme artificiality and excess. The late-twentieth-century "crisis of representation," which fosters a self-referential art disinclined to mimesis and disengaged from reality, can be understood as a postmodernist version of the aesthetic or decadent assertion of art's superiority to nature. One can see why artistic decadence properly figures as subtheme in Pynchon's novel, which constantly resists ideologies that assert the superiority of the inanimate (even art) to living flesh. If one must recognize this rhapsodist of rhinoplasty, this allegorist of cloacal alligator-hunting, as himself a decadent, one must also recognize his profound humanism, decidedly at odds with occasional critical perceptions of alleged postmodernist nihilism.

Decadence, then, has aesthetic meanings both specific and generic, and in the course of his story Pynchon modulates suggestively from the one to the other. Chapters set before World War I include a number of specific allusions to the aesthetes, decadents, and their fellow travelers. With the exception of a brief reference to D'Annunzio in chapter 9 and to Rimbaud in chapter 13, the chapters set after World War II tend to invoke only the generic decadence represented in Roony Winsome ("king of the decky-dance" 220), the novels of his wife Mafia, and the Cheese Danishes of Slab's Catatonic Expressionism. In between, during World War II, Fausto Maijstral weaves together observations about decadence both moral and aesthetic. Fausto, as it happens, is Herbert Stencil's spiritual brother, for Fausto's mother Carla would have destroyed herself and her unborn son were it not for the intervention of Stencil's father, Sidney. Seeming to echo Eigenvalue, Fausto observes in his journal what he calls "life's single lesson: that there is more accident to it than a man can ever admit to in a lifetime and stay sane" (320–21). But Fausto goes on to affirm the artist's responsibility vis-à-vis the accident-filled cosmos:

> Living as he does much of the time in a world of metaphor, the poet is always acutely conscious that metaphor has no value apart from its function; that it is a device, an artifice. So that while others may look on the laws of physics as legislation and God as a human form with beard measured in light-years and nebulae for sandals, Fausto's kind are alone with the task of living in a universe of things which simply are, and cloaking that innate mindlessness with comfortable and pious metaphor so that the "practical" half of humanity may continue in the Great Lie, confident that their machines, dwellings, streets and weather share the same human motives, personal traits and fits of contrariness as they.
>
> Poets have been at this for centuries. It is the only useful purpose they do serve in society: and if every poet were to vanish tomorrow, society would live no longer than the quick memories and dead books of their poetry.
>
> It is the "role" of the poet, this 20th Century. To lie. (325–26)

More than a pose of weary iconoclasm, Fausto's assertion regarding the mendacity of the artist represents an enlightened aesthetic. Pynchon, who shares it, also "lies," but he contrives to tell the truth about life's shaky foundation in accident. In addition to symbolic brothers, Fausto Maijstral and Herbert Stencil are Pynchon surrogates, types of the artist who spins narrative gold from the straw of life's disconnected circumstances. Only art manages to be comfortable shuttling between formless actuality and the emplotment that makes it graspable. Only the artist, as Keats famously remarked, "is capable of being in uncertainties, Mysteries, doubts, without any irritable reaching after fact & reason" (193). F. Scott Fitzgerald said much the same thing in *The Crack-Up*:

> [L]et me make a general observation—the test of a first-rate intelligence is the ability to hold two opposed ideas in the mind at the same time and still retain the ability to function. One should, for example, be able to see that things are hopeless and yet be determined to make them otherwise. (69)

Artists, then, are uniquely empowered—especially in certain fictions that display their own artifice—to lie, to recast the world as narrative even as they show that whoever makes history into story must inevitably traduce and misrepresent it. Pynchon calls into question the sense-making discourses, the organizations of data that cohere to explain history. He demolishes historiography and eschatology alike. Further, he deconstructs myth and with it the modernist pretense of postreligious metanarrative.

Pynchon's novel invites its readers to see history and other forms of system-making as necessary fictions, products of the collective human need for pattern. This recognition animates not only the deceptive pattern of V. sightings but also the author's predilection for the quest plot and the theme of paranoia. Insofar as Pynchon interrogates the fictive emplotment of history, he exposes its foundation in cultural assumptions analogous to (and generally as unexamined) as the hegemony of Antonio Gramsci, the ideology of Louis Althusser, or the *doxa* of Pierre Bourdieu. For a long time history was blind to its own totalizing ideologies. *V.* is one of the works that have obliged recognition of radically different perspectives. In Egypt, Malta, and South-West Africa, the reader of *V.* encounters early postcolonial discourse: counternarratives to the chronicles of victorious colonizers. If Edward Said's *Orientalism* (1978) began postcolonial studies and Hayden White's *Metahistory* inaugurated postmodern historiography, Pynchon's *V.* was one of their most important harbingers. But intellectual history was ever so: before Freud, Sophocles and Shakespeare; before Said and White, Pynchon.

## NOTE

[1] Introduced and defined in *A Poetics of Postmodernism: History, Theory, Fiction*, historiographic metafiction blurs the boundaries between "story" and "history," revealing that history is always fictive—and not necessarily less fictive than historical fiction. Major practitioners: Pynchon, Barth, Coover, Doctorow, Fowles, Eco.

# To Historicize Is to Colonize: Colonialism in V. and *Gravity's Rainbow*

*Michael Harris*

Thomas Pynchon's work might be understood as a continual effort to chart the history and the effects of European rule of the so-called Third World. The move from Pynchon to postcolonial studies forms a logical step: reading V. and *Gravity's Rainbow* might lead one to Frantz Fanon, Chinua Achebe, Ngũgĩ wa Thiong'o, Edward Said, Salman Rushdie, Homi Bhabha, and Kwame Anthony Appiah. Although Pynchon may not be a solely postcolonial writer, his work, with the possible exception of *The Crying of Lot 49*, composes a sustained interrogation of European colonialism from the eighteenth through the twentieth centuries. In his review of *Mason & Dixon*, Louis Menand put the case well: "nearly everything Pynchon has written is, essentially, a lament over colonialism—political, economic, cultural, sexual" (25).

## *The Course*

In the course I teach on V. and *Gravity's Rainbow*, I supplement the novels with selected readings in postcolonial theory as well as in Pynchon criticism—especially essays focused on colonialism, such as Douglas Ivison's "Outhouses of the European Soul: Imperialism in Thomas Pynchon" and David Seed's "The Preterite: Hereros, Kazakh and Others" and "Appendix: Pynchon's Reading for *Gravity's Rainbow*" (*Fictional Labyrinths* 179–86, 240–43)—and Pynchon's introduction to George Orwell's *1984* and "Is it O.K. to be a Luddite?"

Once we get to *Gravity's Rainbow*, I offer my students the option of keeping an extended reader's journal in lieu of doing a formal research paper. I require them to hand in five installments of this journal, one installment for each section of the novel, beginning with "Beyond the Zero" (*Gravity's Rainbow* 1–177). The final installment is a coda, reflecting back on their experience reading the novel. Our model for this journal is Clifford Geertz's "Deep Play: Notes on the Balinese Cockfight," and I encourage students, throughout their journals, to strive à la Geertz to open up Pynchon's text rather than close it down with verifiable conclusions. The journal as a whole need not be unified: their lines of pursuit can be exploratory, provisional, and tentative—like Geertz's responses to the cockfight recorded in the seven separate sections of his essay. Usually, every student takes up my offer, and the strategy works by and large for two reasons. First, the students read the novel more attentively, and, second, the nature of the assignment creates a spirit of unity in our classroom.

## *Approach, Part 1: Colonialism*

Teaching *V.* and *Gravity's Rainbow* back-to-back works well. Many of Pynchon's preoccupations in *V.*—especially those dealing with colonialism—carry over to *Gravity's Rainbow*. Although the chief setting of *Gravity's Rainbow* is World War II, the narrative also contains references to the horrors of World War I, a war in part caused by competing European colonial ambitions. Weissmann and Mondaugen, featured in chapter 9 of *V.*, both reappear in *Gravity's Rainbow*. The V-1 rocket, briefly referred to in *V.*, has now been upgraded to the V-2 and given center stage in *Gravity's Rainbow*. And there are again references to the Herero people of South-West Africa and the great Herero rising put down by General Lothar von Trotha in 1904–07. In the World War II setting of *Gravity's Rainbow*, however, we follow a later generation of "Zone-Hereros" who have settled in Germany, signaling a shift to a postcolonial future: "Now the Herero lives in his stepfather's house . . ." (74–75). The connections between the two novels make it beneficial to use *V.* in the classroom to set up and anticipate some of the issues and tropes—especially those relating to colonialism—in *Gravity's Rainbow*.

Much of the colonialist content of *V.* comes from the fact that Stencil's father, Sidney, worked in the British foreign office, with a notable stint in Malta, where he died in 1919. Many of the leads Stencil pursues about the elusive V. either come from his father or take him back to the colonial era when his father worked in the foreign office. Through Stencil's search, Pynchon provides the reader with detailed background into several different colonial settings. As the narrative skips from one international locale to another, the chapters set in the past—representing Stencil's ongoing pursuit of V.—repeatedly return to those years leading up to World War I, hinting at the significance of the historic period roughly "between 1859 and 1919" when "the world contracted a [fatal] disease" (461). Chapter 9, "Mondaugen's Story," examines a strand of that colonial history, vacillating back and forth between two events: the 1904–07 Herero rising and the 1922 Bondel Rebellion against the German colonial force in South-West Africa. In this chapter the narration becomes relatively somber, tragic, and prophetic, and Pynchon positions the reader to see von Trotha's historic campaign "to exterminate systematically every Herero man, woman, and child" (245) as a little-known forerunner of Hitler's campaign to exterminate the Jews of Europe during World War II.

Pynchon emphasizes the psychosexuality underlying colonial rule, allowing us to witness the dehumanization of the German colonizers, whose genocidal viewpoint is described through a disconcerting second-person narration:

> The voluptuous feeling of safety, the delicious lassitude you went into the extermination with was sooner or later replaced by a very curious—not emotion because part of it was obviously a lack of what we commonly call "feeling"—"functional agreement" would come closer to it; operational sympathy.
> (261)

This dehumanization of the colonizer, made apparent in the officer's analytic and complacent attitude toward genocide, is reenacted during Foppl's siege party, which displays a self-destructive nostalgia for "the days of von Trotha" to be "back again" (233).

It is easier to bring up the issue of colonialism in the context of *Gravity's Rainbow* than it is with *V.* Many parts of *V.* suggest a connection with the European colonial era, but only in a mysterious, indirect way (such as the reference to the Fashoda crisis). In *Gravity's Rainbow*, by contrast, Pynchon launches a direct, broad-based critique of the colonialist enterprise. For example, Lieutenant Weissmann, who appears only briefly in *V.*, is transformed into a major allegorical figure in *Gravity's Rainbow*. As *Dominus Blicero*, Weissmann ("White Man") represents the human impulse to colonize, control, and dominate the environment. In the novel's underlying life-death struggle, Weissmann is the chief representative of death: his alias Blicero comes from the word " 'Blicker,' the nickname the early Germans gave to Death" (322). As such, he is linked with a decadent sexuality, evident in his relations with Oberst Enzian, the Herero he brought back from South-West Africa, and with Katje and Gottfried, whom he "adopted" during Germany's occupation of Holland. Bhabha's conceptualization in "The Other Question" of colonial rule as operating on two ambivalent levels—a manifest, conscious, administrative level and a latent, unconscious, erotic level—can be helpful in explaining Weissmann to students. In a 1969 letter to Thomas Hirsch, Pynchon describes German colonial relations with the Herero as "the imposition of a culture valuing analysis and differentiation on a culture that valued unity and integration" ("Pynchon's Reading" 241). Throughout *Gravity's Rainbow*, Pynchon presents European colonialism as a movement toward death, based on a repression of Europe's own life-giving instincts. This lesson is one of the first that Enzian "learn[s]" from Weissmann (324).

If the repressed is that which always returns, then European repression, brought on by European culture's high valuation of analysis and differentiation, found release with a vengeance in the colonies. "Out and down in the colonies, life can be indulged, life and sensuality in all its forms, with no harm done to the Metropolis, nothing to soil those cathedrals, white marble statues, noble thoughts" (317). Pynchon shows in an assortment of ways the consequences of this European repression: German genocidal practices against the Herero, the senseless extinction of the dodo by the Dutch in Mauritius, the calculated use by the British of opium addiction against the Chinese, and the removal of cocaine from Coca-Cola, creating "an alcoholic and death-oriented generation of Yanks ideally equipped to fight WW II" (452). Late in the novel, Weissmann himself sums up the fruit of the European colonial enterprise: "In Africa, Asia, Amerindia, Oceania, Europe came and established its order of Analysis and Death" (722).

## *Approach, Part 2: History*

In *V.* and *Gravity's Rainbow*, Pynchon's treatment of colonialism is linked to a suspect historiography. This link between colonialism and historiography becomes even more pronounced in *Mason & Dixon*, where Wicks Cherrycoke conducts a running critique of history as "hir'd, or coerc'd, only in Interests that must ever prove base" (350). In effect, history is an interview with the winners, and part of Pynchon's project is to re-vision and problematize our understanding of the past, to call attention to history as a construct. Rather than completely do away with history, however, Pynchon presents history as a narrative with multiple strands. As Michael Bérubé has said, Pynchon's "revisionary, postwar paranoid politics fashions preterites within preterites, and in so doing constructs histories within History" (225).

A large part of Pynchon's critique of the colonial enterprise is directed at the way the colonizer planted memory in the colony, the renaming of towns and geographic locations to commemorate the colonizer's past and to erase the already existent oral history of the subject people. It is surely not coincidental that many postcolonial writers, including Chinua Achebe and Ngũgĩ wa Thiong'o, changed their names, excising the European parts to reflect more accurately their African heritage. Indeed, Pynchon's revisionary historical work in *V.* and *Gravity's Rainbow* aligns him with many postcolonial writers who set about repairing and recasting their nations' histories following independence. This historiographic aspect of colonial rule, however, will not be immediately apparent to many students. Reading some of the following texts will provide students with a context for understanding postcolonial history: Achebe's "Named for Victoria, Queen of England"; Norman O. Brown's *Life against Death: The Psychoanalytic Meaning of History* (chs. 1, 2, 7, and 15); Said's "Overlapping Territories, Intertwined Histories" and "Resistance and Opposition" (*Culture*, ch. 1 and ch. 3); Molly Hite's "The Arc and the Covenant: *Gravity's Rainbow* as Secular History" (*Ideas* 95–157); Kathryn Hume's "Pynchon's Mythological Histories"; and Thomas Schaub's "History and Fiction: From Providence to Paranoia" (*Pynchon* 76–102). Students might also be asked to report on aspects of colonial history, such as Germany's intervention in South-West Africa, the Fashoda crisis, and the decolonization movement.

If, as Robert Holton has argued, it is in "themes of race and colonial history that the continuity of *V.* lies" (333), then chapter 3 becomes an excellent place to focus students' attention on the underlying coherences of the novel. We might see this chapter as a study in orientalism, although Pynchon's novel preceded Said's study by some fifteen years. The narrator in each Stencil impersonation is a marginal figure—in some cases, Arabic—in turn-of-the-century Egypt, looking on a group of British imperial representatives. The narrators, in their scattered ways, overhear whispered references to "Fashoda," but they have little or no understanding of what that means. Each narrator also has his or her own story and set of material circumstances, and thus Pynchon demonstrates in dramatic fashion the many strands of history that counter and disrupt the master narrative of European colonial history. Reversing the colonial gaze, he has P. Aïeul, a café waiter in Alexandria, consider his lone European customer: "Another fat Englishman, fair-haired, florid—didn't all Northerners look alike?" (64). Here the colonial representatives are seen essentially as tourists: all live in a "Baedeker's world," where the joke on all such visitors is that "the permanent residents are actually humans in disguise" (78). The backdrop of these shifting fictional narrators is the actual Fashoda incident of 1898, in which British and French colonial forces came close to conflict after the French seized the town of Fashoda for its strategic position on the Nile. Competing "claims" to this territory notwithstanding, this satiric chapter leads the reader to wonder what, if any, material effect this European crisis would have on the indigenous people's lives.

In *Gravity's Rainbow*, Pynchon demonstrates how history serves the ends of empire by highlighting the plight of the Zone-Hereros. The Herero people of South-West Africa, first described in *V.*, now find themselves displaced in Europe at the end of World War II. These transplanted hybrids living in an imposed history must work through an array of stereotypes, openly displayed and undercut by the narrator: "Hyperthyroidal African eyes, their irises besieged as early cornflowers by the crowding fields of white . . . Ooga-*booga!* Gwine jump on dis *drum* hyah! Tell de res' ob de trahb back in de village, yowzah!" (*Gravity's Rainbow* 656). The Zone-Hereros strive to hold onto their own cultural history based on unity and integration, as evidenced by the mandala symbol and their ability to "carry on business every day with their ancestors" (153). Their group, however, has splintered into two factions, one of which views the Rocket as their destiny and the other which aims to complete von Trotha's attempted genocide through mass suicide. Enzian, leader of the former faction, has developed "some peculiar ideas about survival" as a result of his long stay in the Raketen-Stadt (452). Pynchon reverses the old colonial phrase when Enzian tells Slothrop that he "may have gone a bit native out here. . . . Stay in the Zone long enough and you'll start getting ideas about Destiny yourself" (362). Enzian thus acknowledges his own colonial mentality.

Pynchon's metropolis-colony metaphor, linking history to empire, also suggests Slothrop as a colonial subject: "His erection hums from a certain distance, . . . wired by Them into his body as a colonial outpost here in our raw and clamorous world, another office representing Their white Metropolis far away" (285). Perhaps to a lesser extent, we might see Roger Mexico as a figurative colonial subject as well. All three—Enzian, Slothrop, and Mexico—struggle to free themselves of "sterile history—a known past, a projectable future," born out of "superstition and fright," giving them "someone else's paper words to say" (126, 626, 627).

Students might be reminded that by most historical accounts World War II marked the beginning of the end for the European colonial era. *Gravity's*

*Rainbow* shows, however, that colonialism still remains alive and well in the form of a multinational corporate empire, the Raketen-Stadt, that knows no boundaries and touches every sphere of life. Pynchon insists that we understand colonialism not only as a political-historical-economic phenomenon but also as a way of seeing the world and experiencing life. As if to counterbalance his three colonial resistors (Enzian, Mexico, and Slothrop), Pynchon depicts Weissmann as representative of the colonial mentality in the political sphere, Pointsman in the social sphere, and Laszlo Jamf in the scientific. Weissmann's desire to carry out a personal and national destiny and Pointsman's emphasis on cause and effect underscore empire's compulsion to connect events into a self-serving linear sequence. As Ivison puts it, the empire needs to historicize, in part to justify its existence: "the absence of a narrative threatens the imperial order" (139).

To concretize their understanding of colonial history in this novel, students might focus on Enzian, who serves as a representative colonial subject and thus a casualty of history. Enzian's obsessive drive to assemble Rocket 00001 ironically mirrors his stepfather Weissmann's desire to assemble 00000. Like so many others, Enzian is seduced by the charisma of the Rocket; by firing it he could equal Weissmann's feat and also exact vengeance on his stepfather. Thus Enzian, like the "Moon, like Ndjambi Karunga" in Herero mythology, "is both the bringer of evil and its avenger" (322). Even though Enzian believes that the Rocket represents a means to escape history that will enable the Hereros to find the "Center without time" (319), his pursuit of 00001 is largely determined by those before him, like Weissmann.

Observing the Herero attempt to escape history through the Rocket or cultural extinction, students should consider the significance of this obscure African culture's extinction. Besides the loss of a culture valuing integration and unity, it would also represent one less strand in the world's multiple histories and thus a dangerous step toward monocultural history. Having students read Ngũgĩ's "Moving the Centre: Towards a Pluralism of Cultures" helps them see what is at stake in such a loss. Even more important, given the novel's many references to magic, the Other Side, revenants, and specters, extinguishing the Hereros would represent a loss of belief in the mystery and sacredness of life. Signs of life in this novel exist in those who react to this imminent loss by challenging history's "stone determinacy of everything" (86). Roger Mexico, who "wrecks the elegant rooms of history [and] threatens the idea of cause and effect itself," is one such example (56).

Slothrop, too, turns away from history and the detriment of war to pursue a more localized, personal historiography. From Enzian's "Herero beliefs about ancestors," Slothrop begins to "feel his own, stronger now as borders fall away and the Zone envelops him, his own WASPs in buckled black, who heard God clamoring to them in every turn of a leaf or cow loose among apple orchards in autumn" (281). Toward the end of the novel, Slothrop answers the question Pynchon posed in *Slow Learner*: Is history personal or statistical? Ruminating on his family leads him to adopt William Slothrop's ancestral spirit and to question the sanity of his family's obsession with paper. Slothrop's personal history is thus subversive, a threat to the imperial narrative. By contrast, Enzian, a victim of colonial corruption—first by the Rhenish missionaries and then by Weissmann—embraces the European order of analysis and death. Ironically, given the Herero belief in ancestral worship, Enzian is seduced by his European stepfather's legacy, perhaps ignorant of that of his father, Old Tchitcherine, who went AWOL from his Russian flagship off the African coast during the Russo-Japanese War. There Old Tchitcherine met "the solemn Herero girl" who would become Enzian's mother. "It was power he walked away from, the feeling of too much meaningless power, flowing wrong . . . he could smell Death in it" (351). Together they discovered a language of love "which they were perhaps the only two speakers of in the world" (352). *Gravity's Rainbow* shows us what history did to the product of that love.

# Antwerp and the Representation of the Holocaust in *Gravity's Rainbow*

*Luc Herman*

If *Gravity's Rainbow* is the "climactic war novel" of the twentieth century (Muste 9) or, at the very least, a "new kind of war novel" (Tölölyan 31), any classroom treatment of the book should start by activating the images of war cherished by the students. Teaching *Gravity's Rainbow* in Antwerp adds to the relevance of this opening, since most of my students hail from the Antwerp region and are therefore more or less familiar with the V-2 raids on the city in 1944 and 1945. Furthermore, the specific way in which Pynchon controls historical detail with respect to Antwerp allows for a more general take on his method of historical representation. His single longer passage on Antwerp amounts to a showcase for his insistent development of motif networks. Remarkably, the passage in question does not seem to mention the fate of Antwerp's relatively large Jewish population. Students can test this startling fact against the rest of the novel to assess Pynchon's potential omission of the Nazi treatment of the Jewish people. Local knowledge thus becomes essential for the discussion of a larger ethical question: does *Gravity's Rainbow* as a historical novel do justice to the fate of the Jewish people?

As Khachig Tölölyan was the first to report in a Pynchon context, "Antwerp, the Belgian city that was a major supply port for the Allies, was hit by 1,265" V-2s, over a hundred more than London (45). One particular bombing raid continues to stir the Antwerp imagination after all this time. On 16 December 1944, around twelve hundred people were watching a matinee performance of the brand-new American movie *Buffalo Bill* (starring Joel McCrea and Maureen O'Hara and directed by William Wellman)[1] in the Rex movie theater in Antwerp, when a V-2 came down and killed 567 of them. This relatively famous historical event may have inspired Pynchon to write the final episode of *Gravity's Rainbow*. Having established the potential importance for the novel of what to many students is their hometown, I usually direct the class attention to the Antwerp page (546) to check whether Pynchon's representation of the city offers any important clues for an overall interpretation of the novel.

The Antwerp page occurs in episode 24 of part 3, in which Katje Borgesius and Pirate Prentice take "an allegorical tour of a rather pleasant hell" (Weisenburger, *Companion* 233). The moment Katje and Pirate touch for the first time, she has to think of her little brother, Louis, who left home at eighteen and "got as far as Antwerp." In Antwerp, Louis fell in with a group of Catholic youngsters constantly jockeying for position in their exaggerated attempt to please and serve a priest. Antwerp has historical significance as a Catholic city—when the Spanish captured it in 1585, all the Protestants fled north across the big rivers that still more or less constitute the border between Protestantism and

Catholicism in the Low Countries—but Pynchon accomplishes far more than historical accuracy with this topical evocation of Catholicism and its wartime appeal to the young. He uses the family ties between Katje and Louis to remind the reader of the sister-brother constellation in which Katje along with Gottfried sexually attended to Weissmann-Blicero when the latter was stationed at the V-2 battery near The Hague. This hard-to-miss reminder implies a more general connection between Nazism, Catholicism, and the (youthful) craving for a leader who is able to provide (sexual) guidance.

Interestingly, Pynchon continues his Antwerp passage by reinserting this specific connection into the local context and thus "proving" it on the grounds of seeming historical plausibility: "Louis began to attend Rexist meetings." But just how accurate is this plot development? In 1930 the Walloon Léon Degrelle had become the leader of the Rexists (after Christus Rex), an ultranationalist political party of Christian renewal with close links to Fascism and National Socialism. Under the Nazi occupation it turned into a collaborationist force with a pan-European vision of the New Order, which envisaged Belgium, or even a re-created Burgundy, as an eventual partner of the Third Reich. Degrelle took his own script to heart: he became a major protagonist of the Walloon SS Brigade and went to fight against the Communists.

In *Gravity's Rainbow*'s Antwerp passage, Katje relates that Louis "went out to a soccer field and heard Degrelle tell the crowd that they must let themselves be swept away by the flood." As Degrelle's nationalism was oriented toward his own native language, French, readers are entitled to wonder whether he could have excited a largely Flemish-speaking audience in Antwerp, and even whether he would have come to Antwerp at all for a rally during the war, since there was a wide range of nationalist collaborationist movements that were offering the Antverpians Nazi redemption in their own language. Rex had a Flemish chapter, and a Degrelle speech in Antwerp is therefore not so counterfactual as it may seem,[2] but the choice of Rex as the party Louis eventually joins remains remarkable, particularly because most if not all of its Flemish alternatives were deeply Catholic as well. Maybe Louis was haunting the rich French-speaking circles in the city, a possibility supported by the fact that he starts living with a man who bears the French first name Philippe, but perhaps Pynchon was also interested in the anticipatory possibilities of the signifier "Rex," as it also refers to the destroyed movie theater.

In the Antwerp passage, Rex is described as the "realm of total souls" (546), a phrase correctly identified by Steven Weisenburger as "actual rhetoric from Rexist propaganda" (*Companion* 235). In the fictional universe of the novel, this expression connects Rex with the Other Side, the place where the dead can still be contacted by the living. This link highlights the heroic death wish of the SS Degrelle joined, and it also assumes a prophetic dimension given the other meaning the word *Rex* came to have for Antwerp during the war. Katje concludes her monologue about Louis, "When the heavy rocket attacks began against Antwerp I knew it could not be an accident . . ." (546). Louis's behavior in Antwerp makes the V-2 bombardments seem to Katje a logical consequence of his adherence to a leader (Catholic or Rexist) who inspires (mortal) sacrifice. Since Antwerp in *Gravity's Rainbow* amounts to nothing more than a locale for this dangerous loyalty, the city simply had it coming. Antwerp, in Katje's reductive view, was bombed because its men were prone to surrender their lives to reach the orgasm they could not possibly achieve with the revered leader. Unlike Slothrop, who might have received some special heterosexually oriented conditioning to magnetize the V-2s falling on London, Louis and the other Antwerp male citizens attracted the bombs because of a homosexual desire intimately connected with the allure of totalitarian systems. As a result of this connection, the whole plot development in the Antwerp passage might be summarized as one from impact (of the totalitarian system) to impact (of the bombs), or—to use Pynchon's preferred term—from Rex (Degrelle's party) to the Rex (the destroyed movie theater). Antwerp therefore also constitutes a fascinating example of signifiers taking on more and more meaning as a result of the (creatively) paranoid reader's search for connections in the hypertextual environment that goes by the name of *Gravity's Rainbow*.[3]

Once the hermeneutic potential of the Antwerp passage is in place, I face the daunting task of moving from this local key to an understanding of the treatment of history in the novel as a whole. Pynchon's use of the word *genocide*, just before the text turns to Antwerp, serves as a bridge to a discussion of *Gravity's Rainbow*'s World War II. In his letter of 8 January 1969 to Thomas Hirsch about the use of South-West Africa in *V.*, Pynchon describes the German effort to eradicate the Bondelzwart Hereros in 1904 as "a sort of dress rehearsal for what later happened to the Jews in the '30's and '40's" ("Pynchon's Reading" 240). Antwerp features a large Jewish community, part of which has remained orthodox and is therefore still quite visible in the cityscape. The tragic losses suffered by this community constitute an essential aspect of how World War II affected Antwerp, but the deportations of Jewish Antverpians do not show up in Pynchon's representation of the city focalized through Katje. The omission is somewhat strange, since the connection between these historical events and totalitarianism would be a perfect fit for the conglomerate of motifs evoked in the Antwerp passage. Does Pynchon amply compensate for his perhaps ethically questionable decision to neglect the Jewish community here? At this point in the course, I assign my students parts of the book and tell them to come up with a list of references to the Holocaust. This exercise does not exhaust Pynchon's treatment of the Jewish people in *Gravity's Rainbow*, but it enables the big leap from a local to a general reading.

The relative scarcity of Holocaust references in the novel[4] does not mean that the genocide of the Jews cannot be central to Pynchon's representation of the war. As Wolfgang Iser has suggested, a gap or *Leerstelle* in twentieth-century fiction can have a variety of effects on the reader, such as the decision to enrich the act of interpretation with those elements that must look blatantly absent or at least underrepresented to the specific community to which the reader belongs (or would like to belong). Far from entailing disrespect for the text, this interpretive procedure appeals to an Antverpian group of students who might have felt a degree of indignation because of Pynchon's "failure" to include the city's Jewish community.[5]

So instead of seeking a definitive answer to the question of how Pynchon deals with the Holocaust in *Gravity's Rainbow*, I offer his evocation of this historical event as an illustration of how his historiographical method often allows for several readings, perhaps even some with radically opposed ideological imports. This use of the Holocaust in the classroom is obviously more than an illustration of Pynchon's historiographical method: my choice implies a primary importance, one motivated locally (by presence of the Jewish community in Antwerp) and more generally (by the current grasp of the Holocaust as a pivotal event). However, the privileging of the Holocaust runs the risk of making the extermination of the Jewish people totalize the interpretation of a novel in which psychological totalization (in the form of paranoia) and the totalitarian system of Nazism (which was responsible for the genocide) amount to the proverbial two sides of the same coin. Students must at all times remain aware of this ideological risk.

Once a focus is in place, the tendency to see evidence everywhere may hamper a balanced assessment of the novel as a whole. In what follows, the choice of textual material in trying to gauge Pynchon's treatment of the Holocaust has been motivated not only by a didactic wish to explore the limits of relevance but also by the need to hold students' attention. The word *holocaust* appears at least eight times in *Gravity's Rainbow* (69, 112, 118, 134, 205, 415, 688, and 716). Elsewhere I have shown that its first occurrence, in the western parody at the end of Slothrop's famous trip down the toilet, leads to the creation of a triad of victimized peoples in that it connects Jewish people with Native Americans, whom the episode has already linked (and will continue to link) to African Americans ("Parody"). The narrator relinquishes his report of the "coming holocaust" in favor of a description of a dog, whose slaying (combined with the reader's association with the events of World War II) may unsubtly suggest the genocide of the peoples in question. If the dog is thought to stand for Jews, Native Americans, and African Americans, then the narrator's move may also suggest the level of existence on which "the white man" situates them (*Gravity's Rainbow* 69). The remainder of this episode includes a move from death to regeneration, but this shift does not do away with the evocation of genocide. Pynchon has apparently felt it necessary to infuse a parody of a western with a word basic to his understanding of the period covered by the novel.

The other instances of the term *holocaust* in *Gravity's Rainbow* all seem to underscore what, using a concept borrowed from psychoanalysis, could be called its latency in the novel. Whether in the sunset panorama of London observed by Pirate Pentice and Osbie Feel (111–12); Slothrop's focalization of the disgusting candy drill (118) and of the Himmler Spielsaal on the French Riviera (205); the description, occasioned by Roger Mexico and Jessica Swanlake, of

London anticipating Christmas in 1944 (134); a statement by Leni Pökler about Pluto, "the planet of National Socialism" (415); a brief reference, probably by the narrator, to St. Veronica's hospital being consumed by fire (688); or in a description of terraces near the end of the hilarious culinary pranksterism scene (716), *holocaust* proves a highly noticeable component of the novel's more or less dormant vocabulary. The Leni statement is similar to the paragraphs from the parody of the western in that it contains a (veiled) reference to the scapegoating of the Jewish people under Hitler (Weisenburger, *Companion* 199).

The concept of latency solves the question concerning the Holocaust's absence or presence in favor of presence. In a constructive effort similar to Richard Crownshaw's,[6] it endows Pynchon's Holocaust with an importance that meets the expectations raised by its historical weight. This radical reading may not readily convince, and it does not amount to a complete explanation either. At this point, I ask students to revisit the parts of the novel each has been assigned and to provide the group with all passages related to the Jewish people. As I see it, the first appears on page 105, where Pynchon connects their fate with what might be an insight into the essence of war: Katje's definitive crossover from Blicero to the Allied Forces in episode 14 of part 1 entails memories of the spy work she has done for the Allies "in the months out at Scheveningen" with Blicero. Three Dutch Jewish families have been lost to the Germans during the search for a specific rocket site, and Katje's argument that she has compensated for this makes her comprehend the underlying economic logic of the ongoing conflict: "Don't forget the real business of the War is buying and selling." The fate of Jewish people is subject to capitalist reason; they are "negotiable," just "as cigarettes, cunt, or Hershey bars" (105). Does Pynchon perhaps subsume the Holocaust under an economic explanation of the war, as he has Katje do in the ruminations about her job in The Hague? Or does he somehow compensate for this relegation so as to do (what a Jewish-oriented or just plain responsible understanding of history might like to call) "more justice" to the horrors of genocide? Students at this point invariably bring up Dora. The presence in *Gravity's Rainbow* of the Dora labor camp (originally a subcamp of Buchenwald) provides a test of the potential disproportion between the novel's representation of economic imperatives and that of the Holocaust. When it first appears in the text on Slothrop's arrival in Nordhausen, Dora is mentioned for its "slave laborers" (289). Next it is simply identified as "the prison camp next to the Mittelwerke" to which Micro, who will guide Slothrop through the V-2 production facility, knows "the secret doors" (296). Jewish prisoners are not isolated from the rest of the internees. Although Slothrop and the other visitors are warned about a potential encounter with dead prisoners, the description of the underground factory quickly shies away from this topic to concentrate on the Mittelwerke's special architecture and assorted characteristics. Slothrop's take on Dora clearly fits the Katje mold. The mention of a prison camp allows for an automatic association with the Holocaust, but Pynchon lets Slothrop become acquainted with this metonymic location as a supplier of cheap labor.

Engineer Franz Pökler's experience of the Dora camp is different. When working in the Mittelwerke, he acquires firsthand knowledge of what's going on: "he could *see*—the starved bodies, the eyes of the foreign prisoners being marched to work at four in the morning in the freezing cold and darkness, the shuffling thousands in their striped uniforms" (428). Again the Jewish prisoners are not singled out. On his last day at the factory, Pökler decides to cross over into Dora to complete his understanding: "Had the data, yes, but did not know, with senses or heart . . ." (432; ellips. in orig.). While Pökler briefly considers the camp in connection with his existence as an engineer and could thus be seen to share the hierarchy inherent to the understanding of concentration-camp politics developed by Katje and Slothrop, his perception of Dora at the end of the war has the potential of shocking the reader into the sudden hypothesis that Katje and Slothrop's grasp is a defense mechanism against oppressive feelings of guilt. Pökler, in contrast, vomits and is overcome by a feeling of impotence.

In view of the absence of the Jewish community in the Antwerp passage, it is tempting to see Pökler's vision of Dora as proof of a special importance devoted by Pynchon to the systematic seclusion and killing (either by execution or forced labor) organized by the Nazis. Perhaps taking into account the latency of the term *holocaust*, Antwerp students (and those readers seeking to redeem Pynchon from the charge of underrepresenting the genocide of the Jewish people) could use this Dora description to overrule the relative dismissals of the topic by Katje and Slothrop as "wrong" subjective angles on what "clearly" assumes high visibility in what everybody will agree is an impressive passage. The problem with this argument is that Pynchon does not seem to privilege Pökler's experience, which is after all just as subjective as that of the two other characters in question. In addition, the Pökler passage does not take into account the specificity of Dora as a labor camp founded with the express purpose of accelerating the V-2 production—for that aspect, one must go back to Katje, Slothrop, and also Enzian.[7] This lack in the Pökler passage does not mean that Dora cannot function as a metonym for the Nazi policy of terror, but even then Slothrop's tour and the Pökler description do not exhaust the subject.

Dora and the Holocaust are most fully anticipated in the famous Hansel and Gretel game directed by Weissmann-Blicero. Following the Grimms' plot, the children, played by Katje and Gottfried, are supposed to end up in the oven. When Katje arrives at her insight about the "negotiability" of Jewish people immediately after the sex game flashback (105), this oven may become a metaphor for the terrible fate suffered by (mostly Jewish) prisoners at extermination camps like Auschwitz. The episode frustrates any easy equation: in Weissmann-Blicero's perspective, "his Destiny is the Oven," while the children "will survive and prosper long beyond his gases and cinders, his chimney departure" (98–99), but at the same time the metaphor seems legitimized by Weissmann-Blicero's capacity for organized destruction as he remembers it from his days in German South-West Africa. The oven as a metaphor of the Holocaust is potentially objectionable on moral grounds because of its grossness, but then the sadomasochism episode complicates the emotional reaction, and the metaphor might therefore be felt to be as subtle and complex as the other Holocaust-related aspects of the text.

Such a tour of (potentially) Holocaust-related passages is nowhere near exhaustive,[8] but it puts the Jewish community's absence from the Antwerp passage in a larger context, allowing students to reconsider the question or even the reproach arising from their local take on *Gravity's Rainbow*. They recognize that Pynchon uses a variety of representational techniques in his depiction of the Holocaust, and they perhaps see that this variety indicates a wish to steer clear from the realism associated with the accepted understanding of historical events. Given the novel's subject, the word's latency in the text may subtly alert the reader to its importance: since *holocaust* appears only eight times, one could say that Pynchon displays great measure in evoking this latency. The word, however, is so loaded that many more occurrences would probably take away its effect of shock. The characters' various perspectives on the Holocaust produce versions of history that may prevent the development of monolithic "History," which Katje defines as "sequences of violence" (105). She resolutely incorporates mass killings into this chronology, but Pynchon can be thought to depict the Holocaust with such finesse that he avoids the historiographical sweep that might destroy the event's uniqueness. The choice of the Dora labor camp as a metonym for the Nazi concentration-camp system possibly indicates that Pynchon subordinates the fate of the Jewish people to what might be considered his fetish, the Rocket, and yet this camp leads to the most stirring passage of all, Pökler's experience of Dora (432–33). If we accept a connection between Pynchon's carefully dosed disturbance of the reader and the significance of the Holocaust for his understanding of World War II, then this passage efficiently compensates for historiographical omissions such as that in the Antwerp episode.

Since Pynchon engages in a variety of procedures to represent the Holocaust, it is impossible to make definitive statements about the ideological underpinnings of his depiction. Even the special bias of a local reading like the one from Antwerp does not affect this observation. If the relative absence of a topic is hermeneutically valorized in the more general interpretation of the Holocaust evocation, then this will perhaps cause Antverpian readers to revisit the Antwerp page. The word *genocide* maybe appears too far ahead of the Antwerp passage for one to consider it proof that Pynchon was broaching the fate of the Jewish community in his representation of Antwerp. "Rex" might constitute a better candidate: because of the connection between Gottfried and Louis, the victimization of Gottfried at the hands of a Nazi officer could lead the reader to surmise a parallel between Louis's subjection to totalitarian Rexism and the consequences of Nazism for the Jewish community in Antwerp. But Louis belongs to the side of the aggressor—could the sentence "Soon my brother was out in the street with his broom, along with the other guilty sarcastic young men" therefore be taken to imply a cleanup (also) resulting in the deportation of Jewish citizens (546)? Perhaps, but it is far from unequivocal and could be said to miss the uniqueness of the Jewish fate. Whatever there is of it, the Antverpian reading, as a local version of the novel's representation of the Holocaust, calls forth the suggestive power of Pynchon's historiographical method and thus constitutes a useful inroad into his most impressive novel.

## NOTES

[1] In a brief preliminary to the collected papers of the 1998 conference on *Gravity's Rainbow* at the University of Antwerp (Herman, Introduction), I erroneously identified William Wellman as the leading actor.

[2] For the complex history of this chapter, see Conway, esp. 73 and 83–84.

[3] For *Gravity's Rainbow* and its reading as a hypertext, see McDaid and Moulthrop; Mangen; and Herman, "L'ipertesto."

[4] Laurent Milesi, who brings in relevant quotations from Pynchon's other novels, goes as far as calling this relative absence " 'the deportation' of the Jewish question" in *Gravity's Rainbow*—a "grimly functional metaphor," (220), as he responsibly deems it.

[5] Louis Mackey has described *Gravity's Rainbow* as "a sustained piece of preterition" in that it systematically passes over certain elements relevant to its fictional universe. "What is conspicuously omitted is perspicuously obscured" (20), Mackey writes, but he does not apply this insight to the Holocaust depiction in *Gravity's Rainbow*.

[6] In one of the more probing essays to date on the subject, Crownshaw has sought to valorize Walter Benjamin's concept of allegory to read Franz Pökler's visit to camp Dora as an icon of how Pynchon's novel occasionally registers "trauma and its temporality" and thus prevents the Jewish genocide from being recuperated in a collective memory that would likely answer to narrative demands of historical realism such as chronology and completeness (209). While Crownshaw's proposal is enticing because of the subversive value it places on this aspect of *Gravity's Rainbow*, his interpretation seems marred by a limited amount of evidence.

[7] For an attempt to read Enzian's meditation on war and technology against the grain, see Herman, "Enzian's Meditation."

[8] An obvious addition would be the metaphorical import of the passage about the extermination of the dodo (108–11), which appears in the same episode as the oven game and Katje's thoughts about the Jewish fate. Another relevant passage, from the perspective of Horst Achtfaden, concerns the development of "extermination camps" into "tourist attractions" (453).

# Mediating the Past: Narrative, History, and Teaching *Vineland*

*Robert L. McLaughlin*

Students, understandably I think, are frequently confused and challenged when encountering postmodern fiction, particularly Thomas Pynchon's fiction. The confusion and challenges arise from two basic causes. First, Pynchon's fiction is firmly in the postmodern aesthetic and as such not only refuses to operate by the stylistic and formal conventions of narrative fiction with which most students are familiar and comfortable but also demonstrates its own self-conscious awareness of these conventions. Second, Pynchon's fiction draws on an incredibly eclectic body of knowledge from a variety of disciplines—history, science, sociology, religion, myth, art, popular culture, and many others—knowledge that can seem overwhelming. Moreover, the presentation of this knowledge is not simply informational; it also acknowledges, examines, and critiques the structures, rules, and discourses by which knowledge is constructed in the various disciplines. The difficulty of the fiction, then, arises from its form and content but also its self-consciousness, the manner in which its narrative form comments on itself as narrative form and in which its knowledge presents itself as the product of epistemology. In teaching Pynchon's novels, I try to provide my students with the means to overcome their confusion and meet the texts' special, postmodern challenges.

The first challenge to address is the students' aesthetic and formal difficulties with the novel's refusing to play by the rules of realist narrative fiction. For example, after the first sixty-seven pages of *Vineland*, students are usually confident that Zoyd is the novel's main character; then, to their surprise, he disappears for quite some time, rather like Roger Mexico in *Gravity's Rainbow*. Similarly, students, after coming to think of the novel's main narrative as Prairie's search for her mother, are inevitably disappointed that the meeting of mother and daughter offers neither the emotional nor thematic catharsis they'd expected; it's even presented anticlimactically ("Frenesi, whom Prairie had managed at last to meet" [366–67]), rhetorically more like an instant replay of the moment than the moment itself. I encourage students to think about these and other examples of Pynchon's anticipation and playful thwarting of readers' expectations in terms of postmodern fiction's tendency toward self-referentiality, to which they were introduced in John Barth's "Literature of Exhaustion" and Charles Russell's "The Context of the Concept." Such examples provide good opportunities to talk about the rules of narrative fiction and what happens when an author chooses to break them. One thing that can happen is that these rules are exposed as rules; that is, instead of being the way narrative "naturally" works, they are constructed or arbitrary or both. This idea becomes especially important when we think later about how the novel treats history, and indeed all knowledge, as narrative based.

On a more specific level, students' difficulties with *Vineland* arise from its protean narrator. Within a section, a paragraph, or sometimes a sentence, the narrator shifts focalization and the temporal setting in complex and potentially confusing ways. For example, the sixth chapter begins with Frenesi in the narrative present (1984) alone in the Sun Belt city apartment of her latest posting, thinking about Prairie, the daughter she gave up when she threw her lot in with Brock Vond to be a snitch for the government. It then segues into a subjunctive conversation with her husband Flash—that is, the exchange is rhetorically marked as a conversation that might have taken place but did not ("She couldn't talk about much of this to Flash")—which leads to a brief flashback to 1969 and Brock Vond's reaction to what we later find out is DL's rescue of Frenesi from the reeducation camp. This flashback is followed by a conversation between Frenesi and Flash that apparently occurred sometime recently ("They were sitting in their new kitchen . . ." [69]) but before the moment of the narrative present. And so the chapter continues, shifting from Frenesi's focalization to Flash's to the narrator's and frequently to a hybrid—the narrator's discourse merging with Frenesi's or Flash's—and hopping around in time, from the narrative present to expository summaries of their lives in the post-1960s to more of those strange subjunctive conversations ("imagining often a turn of the conversation that would allow her to say" [70]). Later, the chapter gives us Frenesi's family background, starting in the 1950s Hollywood of her childhood, where, one can infer, her mother, Sasha, is telling her these stories. Again, the narrator jumps forward and backward in time and shifts viewpoint, from Frenesi to Sasha to Sasha's mother Eula, but, in a technique Pynchon will use throughout the novel, he repeatedly returns us, at least momentarily, to Sasha talking to Frenesi to remind us that this family and personal history is being filtered to us through storytelling and that the story is being distorted by its auditor, Frenesi, who insists on reimagining it as a movie ("Platters spinning, mellow reed sections" [78]). Close readings of sections like these in class, asking the students to keep track of whose eyes we are seeing the action through and at what points the view changes and to keep track of what time a scene or paragraph takes place in relation to the narrative present, can help them not only get a handle on Pynchon's technique but also understand how important it is to know from whose point of view (the narrator's, a character's, some hybrid combination's) a given utterance is made.

As the foregoing suggests, I find it useful to bring in Mikhail Bakhtin (through either a minilecture by me or a student presentation on "Epic and Novel" or "From the Prehistory of Novelistic Discourse" or both) to provide a way of thinking about Pynchon's technique. Bakhtin helps us understand the ways in which focalization is connected to discourse and how discourse analysis elucidates both the complex manner in which the narrator shifts among and layers various lenses and the manner in which discourse implies ideological belief systems that the text then propels into dialogue. We identify and discuss the various means by which Pynchon's narrator introduces a variety of discourses and thus dialogism into the novel, including parody (e.g., Takeshi's Japanese-monster-movie manner of speaking); hybrid utterances; songs; embedded narratives (e.g., Sister Rochelle's stories and Yurok legends); and character zones (my favorite example is the narrator's using the discourse of mathematics to describe the mathematician Weed Atman: "Weed saw that he was the tallest person in his vicinity, if 'vicinity' be defined as a domain bounded by a set of points partway to the next person of a height equal to or greater than his own . . ." [206]).

The easiest entrée for students into these concepts is the novel's obsession with television. Not only does watching and talking about TV dominate most of the characters' daily lives, but TV discourse has also become integral to their ways of seeing and talking about the world. This obsession includes using TV as the ultimate simile and signified, as when Zoyd tries to explain, "It's like Mr. Sulu laying in coordinates, only different" (40), and unconsciously accepting the structure of TV shows as the structure for human experience, as when Isaiah Two Four tries to reassure Prairie of an imminent happy ending with, "Only a couple more commercials, just hold on, Prair" (105). Not surprisingly, students easily relate to the ways an outside discourse, the discourse of television, can work its way into one's own discourse and, beyond that, into one's worldview.

One way to move into discussions of how Pynchon's narrative technique treats the novel's themes—particularly its historical exploration of the 1960s—is to do a close reading of the description of Zoyd and Frenesi's wedding (38–39). Take, for example, the first paragraph ("Frenesi Margaret, Zoyd Herbert . . ." [38]). Rhetorically marked as Zoyd's memory, the passage is narrated through a complex, merged point of view. Zoyd is associated with the romanticizing of the past, remembering it as peaceful (despite a reminder of the social and political tumult of the time) and harmonious. Zoyd in the next paragraph remembers a homogenous gathering: surfers, beer-riders, "bikers and biker chicks, playing at villainy," "back-to-nature acidheads," and finally the local sheriff, all interacting with no conflict (38). That Zoyd's romanticized 1960s is naive is established through the tension between his focalization and a version of the narrator's voice that parodies what Zoyd is praising. This voice is found in the quotation from the wedding ceremony with which the passage begins and in the description of Frenesi's cousin as "a tall florid girl in a minidress that bore the image, from neck to hemline, of Frank Zappa's face, thus linking her in Zoyd's mind somehow with Mount Rushmore" (39). More soberly, there is also a narrative voice of elegy, which recurs throughout the novel: a contemporary voice that seems to mourn the loss of what the 1960s could have been. This voice recognizes how in a few years Zoyd's ideal 1960s moment will have been turned into a greeting card, a product to be sold, one of many examples in the novel of political-military-industrial America co-opting its dissenters' means of opposition. This voice also laments the cutting into pieces of reality, a process seen not only in rational analysis but also in film (twenty-four frames per second) and TV (all those pixels) and a process associated here and in all Pynchon's novels with an oppressive ideology of control. Ironically, at the end of the passage, Zoyd seeks to freeze and save this moment, unaware apparently that this attempt distorts reality and serves the purposes of control. The tension among these different views of the past—romantic, parodic, elegiac—informs much of the novel's treatment of history.

Close readings in class of these passages and discussion of the ideas they generate prepare students for the presentation of history in the long central section of the novel, in which Prairie, on the run from Brock Vond with DL, hears about DL's past, the failed attempt on Vond's life, DL's partnership with Takeshi, and, most important, Frenesi's betrayal of 24fps and Weed Atman and the fall of $PR^3$. Significant for the novel's exploration of history and the way we know the past, the murder of Weed—the central moment of the betrayal and fall (symbolically, the failure of the 1960s)—is lost to us. Frenesi and the members of 24fps, who filmed the encounter between Rex and Weed, "missed the actual moment" because Howie was changing rolls. When the film begins again, "the moment" has already been mediated through the culture's ubiquitous pop culture: "Rex was staring into the camera, posing, pretending to blow smoke away from the muzzle of the .38" (246).

Moving outward from the lost moment, the novel shows us that our knowledge of the past grows out of layers of mediation. Courtesy of DL and Ditzah Pisk, Prairie learns much of the story of her mother and $PR^3$ through surviving 24fps footage. However, despite the film collective members' beliefs, film is not an objective, neutral purveyor of information: it selects, includes, excludes, frames, zooms, tracks, lingers or cuts away, all according to the consciousness behind the camera and all personalizing, making subjective, its subject. Prairie, as a child of the 1980s, is media-savvy enough to know this. On top of the film record is layered characters' memories. By emphasizing that these stories about the past are stories, being told by one character to another—like Sasha's stories to young Frenesi back in 1950s Hollywood—the novel discourages us from suspending our skepticism and accepting the stories as the objective truth of what happened. One of the first things DL says to Prairie is that the problem with talking about the 1960s is "everybody remembering a different story" (101).

Beyond memories expressed through storytelling, the novel frequently gives us more than one storyteller. For example, while Prairie watches the 24fps footage, both DL and Ditzah joke about, interpret, and comment on what she's watching. Similarly, much of DL's storytelling is dialogized with Takeshi's comments: "he was not shy about putting in with color commentary on DL's version" (149). In fact, the narrator implies that this joint storytelling becomes over time something of an act and something of a ritual. Introducing the story of their sex-act-cum-assassination-attempt, the narrator tells us, "By the ancient system, it was the hour of the cock, 'In more ways than one,' as Takeshi in later years liked to interpolate in comical accents, predictably to DL's annoyance" (151).

While gaining confidence in how to engage Pynchon's narrative and stylistic techniques, students need also to become familiar with some of the historical background for the novel's content. I use several student presentations to provide some history, especially focusing on the disparateness of the 1960s experience. The topics I assign include Charles Wright Mills's *The Power Elite* (influential for the New Left and, I think, for Pynchon); the Students for a Democratic Society, particularly the Port Huron Statement (I recommend James Miller's *Democracy Is in the Streets* and Kirkpatrick Sale's *SDS* [Sale was a college friend of Pynchon's, and Pynchon blurbed the book generously]); Berkeley's Free Speech Movement; the Student Nonviolent Coordinating Committee; Abbie Hoffman and the Yippies; and Ken Kesey and the Merry Pranksters. While far from exhaustive, these presentations fill in many of the gaps in the students' knowledge about the 1960s. (They can also be entertaining: one semester, a student played a tape of Hoffman doing a radio interview.) More important, they complicate the students' notions of the 1960s as they see that the political analysts of the SDS had little in common with the Summer-of-Love hippies and that even within a single organization or movement, there were disagreements, dissension, and the seeds of self-destruction.

With this knowledge, students can better see how Pynchon uses the College of the Surf rebellion and the personalities of the 24fps members as representative of the potential and the failure of the 1960s.

These presentations on conventionally written histories of the 1960s contrast interestingly with Pynchon's self-consciously narrative approach and the novel's structure. To facilitate discussion of the novel's treatment of history, the students read Linda Hutcheon's "Beginning to Theorize Postmodernism" for her argument that postmodern aesthetics critically reexamines the past, and I assign a student presentation on the first chapter of Hayden White's *The Content of the Form* for his ideas about how narratizing the past shapes the way that past is understood. White helps us define the tension in the novel between history as narrative and all that implies—narrative focalization, selection of events, the linking of incidents into chains of cause and effect, the shaping of the past into an interpretable story—and history as archeology, in the Foucauldian sense, as is suggested by Prairie's digging through the layers of the past, back to the key moment of the death of Weed Atman. That the novel rejects neither of these models for knowing the past seems clear. Cause and effect is at the heart of Frenesi and DL's moral struggles: acts have consequences, and one needs to take responsibility for the consequences of one's acts. The disruption of linearity that is implied by the archeological method informs the narrator's elegiac attitude toward the 1960s: though from the narrative present the 1960s are only fifteen years into the past, it seems a time completely cut off from the contemporary age, a time of great promise that was tragically lost.

Many important topics for discussion can develop out of this look at the intersection of postmodern narrative aesthetics and history in the novel. For example, it raises the question of an officially sanctioned version of history versus ad hoc, personal, or oppositional versions. Students may want to discuss Sister Rochelle's alternative narratives of Eden and hell or the Yurok legends about the *woge* and the country of death in terms of how they rewrite basic narratives of Western culture (166, 382–83, 186–87, 379–80). (They may remember their earlier reading from Jean-François Lyotard's *The Postmodern Condition*.) This exploration can lead to discussion of how power is manifested through narratives and discourse (most clearly seen in the TV and film themes) and of the potential for narrative and discourse to offer a means of opposing power.

Another, connected topic is power's ability to co-opt to its own uses the discourses of opposition. This process, which we see as early as Zoyd's memory of his wedding-day scene becoming " 'sensitivity' greeting cards" (38), is summarized in Mucho Maas's office as "revolution . . . blending into commerce" and rock and roll becoming "just another way to claim our attention" (308, 314). Students may want to talk about the political effects of distracting discourses and what "paying attention" means as a political practice. They may also want to discuss the possibilities for defining a position of opposition in the face of these kinds of operations of power.

A final complication can be offered students by pointing out how Pynchon's narrative is problematized when we note how many of its sequences—for example, the *Godfather*-esque Wayvone wedding, the *Empire Strikes Back*–inspired encounter between Prairie and Brock Vond—are filtered through the discourses and narratives of TV and film; it seems *Vineland* itself is implicated in the discursive practices it has been criticizing. What does this implication say about the possibilities for opposing the operations of power? Students may want to think about this question in terms of Hutcheon's argument that postmodern practice recognizes its position within the systems it seeks to critique (253–54).

To get students to these big-picture formal, stylistic, and thematic questions, I usually try to begin with more specific, less intimidating, discussion-fostering questions. For example:

What is the significance of the 1984 setting, especially in connection with the obvious Orwell allusion?

What do Hector and other characters mean by the repeated question about the 1960s, "Who was saved?" (with thanks to N. Katherine Hayles's essay of that name)?

In what ways do television and movies influence the way the characters see themselves and their world?

How does the concept of death implied in the Thanatoids contrast with the concept of death implied in Hector's reminder to Zoyd, "[Y]*ou are goín to have to die*" (32)?

What different kinds of storytelling can be identified in the novel, and how do they function differently?

For a given passage, trace the narrative focalization; that is, identify whose voice is narrating and at what points the narration switches to another voice.

*Vineland* is a complex and challenging novel. I think it is by encouraging our students to engage its complexities, aesthetic and thematic, that we can best help them meet its challenges and discover its rewards. The foregoing is one strategy for doing this, though hardly the only one. A text like *Vineland* can tell us many things, depending on what we choose to ask it. My goal as a teacher is to help my students find ways to frame their own really interesting questions and to discover their own answers.

# Historiographic Metafiction / Metafictional Historiography: The *Mason & Dixon* Project

*Hanjo Berressem and Norbert Finzsch*

## *Approach and Task*

The *Mason & Dixon* Project was the title of a transdisciplinary seminar on *Mason & Dixon* taught jointly by the two authors of this essay, one of whom comes from the field of American literature and the other from that of American history. After we had separately taught Pynchon from within a literary and a theoretical context (Berressem) and eighteenth-century American history from within a cultural and historiographic context (Finzsch), we wanted jointly to map the two major discursive regimes of historiography and fiction. The project would attempt to create a microversion of what we understood as interdisciplinary cultural studies. For this effort, we would use a text that was extremely concerned with mapping these two regimes and with the concept of mapping in general. Since the overall aim of the project was to stake complexity against simplicity, a text that played out complexity against simplicity seemed a good experimental site.

We chose Pynchon's *Mason & Dixon* because it bases its structure on the complex lives of "real people," thereby using in many ways contingent historical givens as a foundation for the creation of its narrative. Although this observation seems fairly obvious, it marks a decisive change in Pynchon's poetics. Real people have always populated Pynchon's novels, but always as minor characters. In contrast, as a retelling of factual lives, *Mason & Dixon* takes what closure it has from the life stories of the protagonists. In retelling the "life-lines" of two real people, the story does not allow itself to follow a preconceived, structural logic. Thus, the narrative closure shares the contingency and the complexity of any historical closure provided by death. The story follows the actions of its two primary characters, in flashbacks and flash-forwards but always along an overall chronological line, and it comes to an end when this line comes to an end. The lives of Mason and Dixon and the text of *Mason & Dixon* have this ultimate "Destination in common" (349).

In our approach to *Mason & Dixon*, we present the mapping of life and text as the great accomplishment of the novel, the central activity by which Pynchon performs the conflict between historiography and fiction, and we help our students explore with us the stakes of that conflict.

At the core of history lies the sheer complexity of the lived event: "the Event not yet 'reduc'd to certainty' " (177). This complex, incomputable event might be seen as the unrepresentable and unreachable perspective point or core of every historiography. In fact, it might be read as historiographies' traumatic kernel, which historiography tries to make sense of by inserting it into specific historical series but which it will never be able to represent in all its complexity. The program of a metanarrative historiography is to include this impossibility into its poetics and to allow this incomputable complexity—nonlinear history—to traverse its texts, while classical historiography tends to reduce complexity to a common (and simpler) vision.

The stakes of complexity are partly thematized in the novel by various simplifying forces. For example, like the conceptual surveying that informs the writing of its history, the geographic surveying of the continent causes "Conditions hitherto shapeless [to be] swiftly reduc'd to Certainty" (636). Complexity is staked against the order of the straight line. As Walt Whitman notes in "Democratic Vistas": "of all dangers to a nation . . . there can be no greater one than having certain portions of the people set off from the rest by a line drawn" (414).

In the text, maybe even more than in Mason's and Dixon's respective journeys, the utopian counterweight to a linear history and the control it confers is the idea of a multiplex, timeless moment in its sheer complexity and potentiality, the historical moment before its setting down into static writing, the moment forever traversed by "the tangle of purposes" (79), the complexity of the historical event as a result of an emergent, autopoietic system that follows a complex set of rules and machinic operations.

*Mason & Dixon*'s fundamental polyvocality results from and simultaneously exemplifies such a nonlinear historiographic method. Because it is so steeped in the eventuality of history, it remains an open, contingent, and complex story. Following this formulation of the project, class discussion focused on the ways the autopoiesis of *Mason & Dixon* keeps conventional resolution at bay, achieving a fictional representation of history's complexity.

## *Writing: Life-Lines*

We began class discussion by analyzing a passage from the middle of *Mason & Dixon*, one often identified by Pynchon scholars as a sketch of the novel's overall poetics. Here the frame tale of *Mason & Dixon*, in which the "untrustworthy Remembrancer" (8), the Reverend Cherrycoke, tells the story of Mason and Dixon to his relatives, once more emerges from the story being told, and conversation among the listeners drifts to the eighteenth-century debate about the writing of history and the writing of fiction. The chapter takes its motto and theme from a fictional text by the reverend, entitled *Christ and History*:

> History is not a Chronology, for that is left to lawyers,— nor is it Remembrance, for Remembrance belongs to the People. History can as little pretend to the Veracity of the one, as claim the Power of the other,— her Practitioners, to survive, must soon learn the arts of the quidnunc, spy, and Taproom Wit,— that there may ever continue more than one life-line back into a Past we risk, each day, losing our forebears in forever,— not a Chain

> of single Links, for one broken Link could lose us All,— rather, a great disorderly Tangle of Lines, long and short, weak and strong, vanishing into the Mnemonick Deep, with only their Destination in common. (349)

Thus, while Cherrycoke's text shares the by now common idea that historiography, like language, has no proper origin and forms a complex system, it swerves away from the prevailing deconstructive logic by relating historiography, as does the novel, directly to the individual life-lines of two specific human beings and thus directly to the body: its historical position, the various cultural inscriptions that produce it, as well as its materiality and temporal finiteness. It is this—highly innovative—move that creates the novel's link between fiction and history. Cherrycoke's historiography is a hybrid: on the one side, it is not completely contained in the field of facticity and chronology; on the other, it is not contained in the field of a living memory. Rather, it occupies the highly problematic middle ground, which is the complex ground of writing (*graphein*)—the novel itself.

From a contemporary perspective, the notions of facticity and living memory seem idealistic. If the first is based on the ideal of objectivity and thus of a transparent, unequivocal language and on a clear separation of object and subject, the second is based on the equally logocentric ideal of a subjective, living memory—an internal, psychic notation in which writing proper has no (mediating) part. If Cherrycoke positions historiography in a field that questions these two incompatible ideals, he situates it squarely in the problematic field of writing that we have come to call the universe of discourse.

Student understanding of this passage and what is at stake in it may be developed by discussing the two extreme takes on historiography as either written facticity or living memory that are addressed in the conversation among Cherrycoke, Uncle Ives Le Spark, Ethelmer, Tenebrae, and Euphrenia that follows the passage we have been discussing. In this conversation, Ives, the lawyer, takes up the position of the idealistic factualist, who proposes that one simply has to "look at the evidence. The testimony. The whole Truth," while his son Ethelmer argues a romanticism of history that is not tied to facts and thus to concepts such as truth (349). As he emphatically notes, "Who claims Truth, Truth abandons." According to Ethelmer's similarly idealistic conception, historiography can and should be separated completely from the field of power. Instead, historiography should be a moral and libidinous undertaking; an imaginative staging of history, in terms both of rhetorics and of setting.

Students should be invited to see how this conversation thus figures lawyers, other agents of power, and generally the government as standing for overcoding machines that reduce (not only historical) discourse from complexity to simplicity. As Ethelmer remarks in the face of his personal oedipal agency, "Sir, no offense meant. I was but pointing out that a single Version, in proceeding from a single Authority—" but Ives simply interrupts, "No one has time, for more than one Version of the Truth." When Euphrenia notes that in the case that history is not factual one might as well read novels, Ives takes up the common position that novels are a danger for the "moral safety of the company," and he warns everybody that he "cannot . . . energetically enough insist upon the danger of reading these storybooks,— in particular those known as 'Novel' " (350–51). If the young romancer Ethelmer argues for the truth in fables, the old realist Ives opts for the truth in facts. Cherrycoke's text—as well as Pynchon's—however, presents these options as extremes, and it argues that historiography occupies a complex field in between the two.

Subsequently, the conversation drifts off to the various positions historians have taken toward fiction and fictionality. The passage presents a panorama of the multifaceted relation between the discourses of fiction and history at the time of the narration, for the temporal backdrop to this discussion is the complex interactions among history, historiography, and fiction in the eighteenth century, compactly summarized in the statement that historiography "begins in novel and ends in essay" (see Thompson 280 [these pages are placed on reserve for students to read]). At the beginning of the debate about the nature of historiography, such an assertion could be read as a statement about the poetic principles underlying historiography; later, it can be read teleologically as referring to the progression from one genre (the novel) to another, more historical one (the essay). By the time period in which the fictional conversation takes place, historiography has freed itself from the poetics of the novel and inscribed itself in the poetics of the essay, a movement that had much to do with the growing influence of the Enlightenment.

When this debate is presented, tongue-in-cheek, in a fictional text that purports to write history and that is based on the lives and the journal of two minor historical figures, this metafictional moment reopens the debate within the context of late-twentieth-century givens. Today, after Hayden White and Foucauldian discourse analysis, history no longer claims easy access to the formerly innocent terms *truth* and *objectivity*. Teachers may assign White's useful introduction to historiography's recent linguistic turn, for the essay describes clearly how history writing has once more come to share the fundamental fictionalization of reality ("Burden"). At the least, historians recognize that every account of historical happenings is a narrative that follows certain conventions of genre, style, and structure and that therefore inevitably follows a logic of distortion, exclusion, erasure, and artifice. In our post-Foucauldian universe, Clio—muse of history—finds herself once more in the company of Thalia (comedy) and Melpomene (tragedy). Sitting in a pub—most of the discussions in *Mason & Dixon* are, programmatically, set in public houses—she tries to make sense of and set down a cacophony of voices demanding to speak (of) their own, often suppressed, histories.

Pynchon's strategy of embedding his writing into discourses and representations generally considered fact(ual) is not used to provide verisimilitude to the text, although this is one of its effects, but rather to question the concept of factuality. The fundamental textualization of history creates a complex moiré of discourses that range, in cultural acceptance, from true to false and from certified knowledge to myth. In the funhouse (as well as the prisonhouse) of the text, all these reflect each other and refract into each other.

## Zones and Zonings

From the mapping of history and fiction, the *Mason & Dixon* Project then asked students to consider the mapping of the discursive and the material—that is, how the complicated discursive fabric that makes up *Mason & Dixon* is always coupled to the complexity of the material realm, to the intelligent materialism that makes up a specific ecosystem or a specific continent. If *Gravity's Rainbow* is set in a Germany that has been disassembled by violence into a zone in which, for one timeless moment, everything seems possible and in which the future seems open, *Mason & Dixon* is set in a country on its way to being slowly assembled into the cultural and political aggregate that would come to be called the United States. The line that Mason and Dixon draw delineates the logic of zoning, which is a main American occupation. *Mason & Dixon* follows how surveying, mapmaking, and inscription replace the shifting borders of the American ecosystem called (from within a cultural, political position) a wilderness with the simplicity and exactitude of straight lines.

Discursively, it marks the replacement of "if" by "is"; the replacement of the subjunctive by the indicative. As an unmarked narrative voice (easily read as authorial) notes, the American ecosystem was

> safe till the next Territory to the West be seen and recorded, measur'd and tied in . . . changing all from subjunctive to declarative, reducing Possibilities to Simplicities that serve the ends of Governments,— winning away from the realm of the Sacred, its Borderlands one by one, and assuming them unto the bare mortal World that is our *home*, and our *Despair*. (345; emphasis added)

In this context, the frontier figures as "the Membrane that divides [the native Indian's] Subjunctive World from our number'd and dreamless Indicative" (677).

The mapping of material ecosystem and cultural system is performed by the text itself when the fictional America, which had served as "a very Rubbish-Tip for subjunctive Hopes, for all that *may yet be true*" is described, like the Foucauldian body, as a writing surface on which one genre is replaced by another (345). The fictional subjunctive is replaced by the historical declarative: "as long as its [the country's] Distance from the Post Mark'd West remains unmeasur'd, nor is yet recorded as Fact, may it remain, a-shimmer, among the few final Pages of its Life as Fiction" (650).

The novel follows the different regimes of discursivation, wondering what is happening to the capacity of wonder in the reduction of "if" to "is." In the novel's complex narrative architecture, such moments of the subjunctive (which are comparable to such subjunctive times and places as the "Eleven Days," the "notorious Wedge," and the "Hollow Earth" [191, 469, 603]) occur when, for instance, an episode is revealed retrospectively to have been doubly fictional, as when Mason has a conversation with his father that is revealed—only after one has read it as fact—as fictive and subjunctive: "All subjunctive, of course,— *had* young Mason gone to his father, this *might have been* the conversation likely to result" (208). The most comprehensive of these subjunctive stories is the one about what would have happened if Mason and Dixon had proceeded further into the continent, with sentences such as "They [Chainmen] would be rediscover'd in episodes to come, were the episodes ever to be enacted, did Mason and Dixon choose *not* to turn . . . but rather to continue West, away from the law, into the savage Vacancy ever before them . . ." (709; second ellips. in orig.). Whole passages of the text are historically fictitious even within the fiction (393). Viewed in this way, students may understand the subjunctive as one of the novel's strategies for maintaining the complexity of the possible in the face of historical resolutions, material and discursive, of the body and the nation.

In *Mason & Dixon*, the rational writing machine that transforms "if" to "is" is closely related to the Enlightenment; especially Theodor Adorno's Enlightenment, which entailed the cruel and merciless reduction of complexity to simplicity and with it, the reduction of stories to a master narrative: the reduction, ultimately, of "histories" to "history" and the congealing of dynamics into static factuality. From this standpoint, one might argue, freedom lies in the possibility of fictionalization, of turning a monological history back into a polyphonic choir of stories.

The rhetorical thrust of Pynchon's narrative plays out two logics simultaneously, those of a natural and a discursive field, a continent with its geography and its various life forms, its ecologies, its economies, its assemblages, its force fields, and its complex machineries. Through these tangled complexities, which have their own histories and their own patterns of emergence, Mason and Dixon draw a line that not only designates a local border but at the same time figures a desire and need that seems curiously, and tragically, to be part of human nature—the need to draw straight lines.

The text acknowledges this need, but students recognize how the novel leads to a discussion about that need's epistemological and systemic function and position. The implications of drawing straight lines can be put as a direct question to the class, eliciting responses that are at once aesthetic, pragmatic, and political. Different cultures, after all, negotiate the straight line in different ways. In some cultures it is something to be avoided; other cultures are built on its matrix. Straightness is not a bad thing in and of itself. There are many "straight stories." But when a straight logic has replaced all other logics, it may be that something has gone wrong.

## *Bad History: Geometry and Slaughter*

With straight lines we map the world. It should be acknowledged that for certain historical and cultural projects, the straight line has been an immensely efficient instrument. For these projects, the chain, as a figure of straightness, has been a tool of immense epistemological value. Symptomatically, on the other hand, the measuring chain that Mason and Dixon carry with them to literally enchain the land echoes with the rattling of the chains of slavery. Here the stakes of writing bear directly on the body.

If with his narrative Pynchon returns to the era of mapping, measuring, and surveying, he does so because he is interested not only in the colonizing force of these operations but also in the topology of mapping discourses, of mapping situations, and of mapping cultures. In the first context, mapping is the main occupation of Mason and Dixon, whose job is to measure the wilderness and to settle a property dispute that reaches back into the history of seventeenth-century England. Their relentlessly accurate mapping draws a line so precise that it can cut a house into two juridical halves. Although this cutting may ultimately have positive effects, the mapping and drawing of straight lines represent in themselves transgressions and the intrusion of violence into the hitherto undivided. Captain Zhang observes, "Bad History. Nothing will produce Bad History more directly nor brutally, than drawing a Line" (615).

As Michel Foucault notes, transgressions carry the limit—understood as a border—to the "limit" of its existence. Border and transgression are so inextricably related that they cannot be thought separately ("Préface" 237). Bordering is a movement of pure violence that embodies what it seeks to exclude and vice versa (245). In these dynamics, violence is no antithesis to rationality. In fact, as Foucault asserts in a gloss of Adorno, "The most dangerous thing about violence is its rationality. . . . Between violence and rationality there is no incompatibility" ("Foucault" 803).

Once acquainted with this critique of the Enlightenment, students can see the Enlightenment at work in the ruthless, violent project of colonizing both geographic and discursive spaces and of subsuming them under the violent law of a mapping performed by the powers that be. Two things that go well together and that will bring about a new war machine are, as Squire Haligast proclaims, "Geometry and slaughter!" which are "[t]he future of war, yet ancient as the mindless Exactitudes of Alexander's Phalanx" (551). Ironically, Adorno notes that this form of the Enlightenment is following the logic of a myth and as such becomes—as with its relation to violence—what it so carefully aims to exclude (Horkheimer and Adorno).

Zsuzsa replies to Haligast that the reason for exactitude is the subsuming of the single individual to the "preëmptive needs of the Manœuvre," which equalizes desire and free will: "Who is unique? Who is not own'd by someone? What do any of their desires matter, if they can be of no use to the Manœuvre" (551). Mason especially often feels similarly owned, and both Mason and Dixon are rational beings, at least in most of their professional activities. Rationality, motivates their excursion into the American wilderness, because the project of mapping and fixing borders is closely tied to the overall maneuver of the Enlightenment. Even as parts of this machine, they are constantly fascinated with myths, local stories, and the complexity of the land they are in the process of measuring. It is this superimposition that makes for their fundamental ambiguity and for their unreadability.

## *Loops and Twists*

This complicity in the prevailing cultural machines—a fundamental complicity that defines most of Pynchon's poetics—makes *Mason & Dixon* realistic. *Complicity* is a useful term to describe the workings of complex systems: each open system is complicit with other systems, from which it cannot be separated. Similarly, the novel argues (like many historians of its setting's time) that fact and fiction are in complicity.

In the final move in our discussion of the ways Pynchon's autopoiesis refuses the conventional distinctions between the regimes of history and fiction—and what is at stake in this refusal—we take up another infamous passage. Here Mason and Dixon's complicities are figured in a textual complicity: the strange loop created when the captive's tale about Eliza's abduction (Pynchon's rewriting of the captivity narrative as well as his rewriting of the story of DL and Takeshi in *Vineland*), an installment in the Ghastly Fop series that Ethelmer and Tenebrae read (527), loops effortlessly into the narrative about Mason and Dixon. During their flight from the Wolf of Jesus, Eliza and her party "arrive at the West Line, and decide to follow the Visto east, and ere long they have come up with the Party" (534). This passage, which is so smoothly inserted into the text's overall architecture as to make the shift in levels of fictionality almost impossible to detect except in retrospect, completely changes the topology of the text.

This smooth insertion is part of the implicit argument of the passage, because it shows the shifting passage from the world of fiction to the world of fact—a world that is once more a fiction. Here, one might argue, fable and romance slyly make their way into historiography. At the same time, the narratological differences between romance and historiography are erased. The planes of fiction and fact become one, a shift that implies a fundamental change in the overall topology of the text. It is no longer possible to differentiate between inside and outside, fact and fiction, historiography and romance. Here, in this topological twist, Pynchon comes closest to undeciding the general topology that has for a long time ruled over interpretations of fiction and of history.

At the threshold between historical account and fiction, *Mason & Dixon* creates a twisted topology in which questions of historiography are opened up to the complex, unrepresentable possibilities of history. Staging debates on the writing of history and fiction, *Mason & Dixon* can function in the classroom to show and explore the myriad implications of the interdisciplinary relations of the historian and the literary critic.

# Postmodern Territories: Teaching *Mason & Dixon* and the Ideologies of Space

*Amy J. Elias*

How can one teach a novel like Thomas Pynchon's *Mason & Dixon*? The novel is long, difficult, and brimming with history unfamiliar to many United States students; it is fat with Pynchonesque fabulation and thematic ideas common to Pynchon's fictional worlds. Talking dogs? Frontiersmen who shape-shift into giant beavers? The challenges of teaching the book are practical (how to fit such a monster into a one-term course schedule) and pedagogical (how to teach the book so that students are not alienated by its complexity and strangeness but also in a way that brings to the fore some of its major ideas, thematic questions, and politics). Instead of focusing on how to teach specific narrative components of the text, I would like to discuss a pedagogical context for Pynchon's novel: a course I call Postmodern Territories that is about space as an ideological territory as well as a physical fact of the material world.

Postmodern Territories is a class about how neutral places, particularly "postmodern" places, become ideological territories and how literature resists or collaborates with these ideological spatial constructions. I have run this course as a graduate seminar and as an upper-level undergraduate honors seminar; the difference between levels is the amount of reading and the writing projects. In both classes, we discussed how postmodern global culture signifies social meaning in order to explore how postmodern America reinvents space or (through theory) unveils its construction through cultural mechanisms. The goal of the course is to explore the implications of the invention and revelation of space for human beings existing in lived ethical and political communities.

In the first half of the course, students read theories about postmodern space (and, depending on the configuration of the course that term, some fiction or memoirs about specific spatial problems). In the second half of the course we read *Mason & Dixon*, a novel obsessed with cartographic, astronomical, and political space. Situating *Mason & Dixon* in relation to important ideas about postmodern space gives students an opportunity to explore current critical conversations about their material world while illustrating to them how theory from the social sciences and the humanities can be a crucial tool for the analysis of literature. One goal of the course is to help students to read the novel productively. A related goal is to teach students some important concepts in postmodern theory. A third goal is to get students to realize that space is not natural and to show them how it may be ideologically determined.

Student responses to the course in a number of its versions have been startlingly and overwhelmingly positive. Comments on course evaluations note how "[m]y head was buzzing with new ideas after every class" or how "this course made me think about my world. Driving around town now, I see the city around me in entirely new ways." The Home Spaces project described below was particularly appealing to undergraduates. Students also comment that reading theory about space at first seems like a weird idea (a typical comment is, "When I registered, I had no idea what to expect from this course") but that as the term goes on, the idea of theoretical discussion of space becomes less bizarre and increasingly more interesting to them.

Students always note that when they finally read *Mason & Dixon* in the second half of the term, they found that they had in place a set of ideas prompted by theory that made the novel less daunting than they feared. Students found it comforting to have some basic theoretical concepts to orient them when thrust into the fabulatory world of Pynchon's novel.

## Defining the Course

Postmodern Territories covers a number of spatial territories, which may include any of the following:

> defining space from feudal times to the present; perspectivism; place versus space, landscape
> astronomy and the politics of outer space
> cartography and ideology
> hyperspace, simulated spaces, consumer spaces, malls, museums, suburbs, and highways
> tourism, travel writing, and (post)colonial space
> border spaces, territories, frontiers, liminal space
> sexualized space, gendered places, queer space
> heterotopia, zones, magical realism, and fantastic spaces
> panoptic space, paranoia, and conspiratorial space
> rhizomatic space versus linear space
> moral geography and sacred space
> cyberspace, virtual space, automatons
> classed and economic space

In a fourteen-week semester, I have worked with various combinations of these topics, though the second half of the course remains constant with a reading of *Mason & Dixon*.

Texts for Postmodern Territories include *Mason & Dixon* and shorter materials such as critical articles, book chapters, novellas, memoirs, Web sites, and film clips.[1] I must say, with the requisite caveats concerning its unrefereed scholarship and openness to inaccuracy, that *Wikipedia* is a great resource as well. The course includes a strong Blackboard/WebCT (Internet course management software) component: reading assignments are posted online, and many Web sites are linked through the course site to specific days' readings.

(For example, in the unit about travel writing and tourist space, we may discuss Mary Louise Pratt's "Travel Narrative and Imperialist Vision," articles from Chris Rojek and John Urry's *Touring Cultures*, a chapter from Erve Chambers's *Native Tours*, and Jamaica Kincaid's *A Small Place*, but we also look at tourist sites online ranging from Native American reservations to Vietnam memorials to Disneyland and its controversies.) I have taught short works such as James Cowan's *Mapmaker's Dream*, Jorge Luis Borges's *Labyrinths*, Steven Millhauser's *Martin Dressler*, Cormac McCarthy's *The Road*, Art Spiegelman's *In the Shadow of No Towers*, J. M. Coetzee's *Waiting for the Barbarians*, William Least Heat Moon's *Blue Highways*, Bruce Chatwin's *The Songlines*, and Italo Calvino's *Invisible Cities* in this course on postmodern space, but there are many fictional narratives that work well with the theory presented. In some versions of the course, I have introduced *Second Life* (an online virtual reality at www.secondlife.com), MOOs (online social spaces in which many users participate simultaneously), and MMORPGs (massive multiplayer online role-playing games) in a unit on virtuality and simulation, while in other versions I have emphasized landscape theory by putting literary nonfiction about place or travel on the reading list. This sampling of readings for the course, however, is far from exhaustive and leaves room for pedagogical experimentation.

## *Teaching the Theory*

Postmodern Territories is built on two theoretical concepts key to reading *Mason & Dixon*: the ideological construction of space and the cultural dislocations of modernity. The course begins by introducing space as a historically constructed idea. We discuss "The Experience of Space and Time" from David Harvey's *The Condition of Postmodernity* (201–308) and do a unit on perspectivism (versus other spatial representations). To complicate the idea further, we also discuss Henri Lefebvre's distinctions between perceived, conceived, and lived space, Yi-Fu Tuan's distinctions between "space" and "place," and elaborations of those distinctions, such as that by Setha Low in *The Anthropology of Space and Place*. After setting up the idea that space changes through time and according to cultural needs, we examine some specific definitions of modern and postmodern space, such as gendered, queer, or classed space—defined, for example, in work by Alison Blunt and Gillian Rose, David Harvey (*Spaces of Capital*), Linda McDowell, and Radhika Mohanram. I address the question, "What are modernity and postmodernity?" by offering some basic definitions of the term in a PowerPoint presentation. We then read Fredric Jameson's essay "Postmodernism and Consumer Society" to introduce postmodern hyperspace—sometimes in conjunction with snippets from Walter Benjamin's *The Arcades Project* or selections by Jane Jacobs, James Howard Kunstler, Lewis Mumford, Andrew Ross, Neil Smith, or Michael Sorkin—and contrast Jameson's claims with more positive claims in postmodern architecture and the utopian claims of New Urbanism. (At the time of this writing, the Congress for the New Urbanism provides an online introduction defining the aesthetic and social movement at www.cnu.org/intro_powerpoint, and there are books such as Michael Leccese and Kathleen McCormick's *Charter of the New Urbanism* that illustrate its key ideas.) I also try to introduce globalization and cosmopolitanism as spatial logics; readings might include chapter 1 from Stephen Castles and Alastair Davidson's *Citizenship and Migration* or selections from texts such as Mike Savage, Gaynor Bagnall, and Brian Longhurst's *Globalization and Belonging*. The remainder of the first six weeks is divided into weekly units focusing on specific kinds of (post)modern space.

The first half of the course thus might look like this:

Week 1 Defining Postmodern Space. "The Experience of Space and Time" from Harvey's *The Condition of Postmodernity*; perspectivism; selections from Lefebvre's *The Production of Space* and Tuan's *Space and Place* or collections such as Mike Crang and N. J. Thrift's *Thinking Space*

Week 2 Postmodernism and Space. Definitions of postmodernism; discussion of globalization using selections from *Citizenship and Migration* (Castles and Davidson) or *Globalization and Belonging* (Savage, Bagnall, and Longhurst); Jameson's "Postmodernism and Consumer Society"; New Urbanism

Week 3 Heterotopias and Simulation. Michel Foucault, "Of Other Spaces: Heterotopias"; Jean Baudrillard, "The Precession of Simulacra"; Umberto Eco, selections from *Travels in Hyperreality*; MOOs and MMORPGs such as *LambdaMoo*(www.lambdamoo.info/) or *Second Life*; film clips from *The Truman Show*, *The Matrix*, *Wag the Dog*, or *eXistenZ* (New Urbanism can also be part of this unit)

Week 4 Mapping Space. J. B. Harley, "Maps, Knowledge, and Power"; selections about mapping, for instance from Derek Gregory, *Geographical Imaginations*, Anna Oliver, "The Use of Maps in Contemporary Art," Martin Brückner, *The Geographic Revolution in Early America*, or Daniel Dorling and David Fairbairn's *Mapping: Ways of Representing the World*; articles about psychogeography movements; handouts from magazines such as *National Geographic*; online map sites including *South-up Maps* and redistricting maps; Borges's *Labyrinths* or a longer text such as James Cowan's *Mapmaker's Dream*

Week 5 Travel Writing and Tourist Space. Selections from Caren Kaplan's *Questions of Travel* or Dean MacCannell and Lucy Lippard's *The Tourist* (or selections from analysis by Cara Aitchison, Nicola Macleod, and Stephen Shaw; James Clifford; James Duncan and Gregory; Roderick Nash; Henry Nash Smith; Frederick Jackson Turner; or Raymond Williams); Pratt's "Travel Narratives" or selections from *Imperial Eyes*; Kincaid's *A Small Place* and Calvino's *Invisible Cities*; various online travel magazines and tourist Web sites such as Disneyland's, Colonial Williamsburg's, and those of national parks

Week 6 Surveillance Space and Paranoia. Online materials explaining Jeremy Bentham's panopticon; Foucault's "Panopticism" (*Discipline and Punish* 195–230); contemporary surveillance technologies; Richard Hofstadter's definition of paranoia; Timothy Melley's definition of "agency panic" in *Empire of Conspiracy*; Spiegelman's *In the Shadow of No Towers*

Visualization is crucial to students' understanding that this theory is about the real world, no matter how arcane or jargon-filled it may seem in article form. It helps to have a technology-equipped classroom for this course, particularly one with Web access and projection equipment. If we read articles about simulation and hyperreality, I access Disney sites as well as those voicing political opposition; likewise, by accessing online sites, we can see immediately the opposition between the utopian philosophy of New Urbanism and protests of gated communities by groups such as Heavy Trash (http://heavytrash.blogspot.com/). When we discuss tourism in relation to globalization and simulation, I access the Web pages from travel magazines and import companies or sites from planned communities in and outside the United States (such as Celebration, Florida) as foils to Kincaid's text. When we read Jameson on the Bonaventure Hotel ("Postmodernism and Consumer Society"), the class sees pictures of the building as well as other examples of postmodern architecture; when we discuss paranoia and panopticism, students not only see a picture of Bentham's panopticon and its architectural legacies but also (if we have class time) see clips from *The Matrix*, *The Truman Show*, *Wag the Dog*, or *eXistenZ*.

Visualization is especially important when the class discusses the politics of mapping, a topic of central importance to *Mason & Dixon*. Students can report the cliché that "all maps are political," but they are weak at supporting an argument about how and why this is so or about the final significance of that observation. To clarify concepts and generate thoughtful discussion about the politics of cartography, one needs to work with theory and with real maps in class. When, for example, I show students south-up maps (world maps centered not on Europe or North America but on Australia, Africa, or elsewhere) or a contemporary map that indicates where all of the United States' Indian reservations are now located, we have a concrete visualization of how mapping the present can erase the colonial politics of the past (the reservation maps imply that these tribes have always had the same size and location they have now) and define cultures in the terms of the dominant culture.

For the undergraduate version of this course, the culmination of the theory unit is the Home Spaces project, an exercise in cultural semiotics. Students are asked to apply the theory we've read—or space theory they've researched on their own—to real spaces in their home communities. They must produce a short paper applying the theory to a specific, lived space and also give a ten-minute summary presentation (with pictures of their site) to the class. Students love this exercise. I have received papers on the gender politics of gym space, the lived values of suburban cul-de-sacs, Starbucks as a social space, discussions of the Great Smoky Mountains National Park tourist areas as nature simulations, and university housing as heterotopias combining student slums with suburban flight. The second paper (due at the end of the term) is a literary analysis of *Mason & Dixon* that attempts to apply some of the theory we've read.

In my graduate version of this course, rather than two projects on different subjects, students do a single, three-part project throughout the term that introduces writing in professional contexts. The three assignments are writing a proposal responding to a call for papers, writing an article from this proposal, and presenting a conference paper from this article research. I give them a simulated call for papers at the beginning of the term; they then write a paper proposal responding to that, which we workshop in class. They receive a grade for the rewritten proposal as well as the article it describes. Graduate students may write a cultural semiotics analysis applying space theory or a literary critique of *Mason & Dixon*. They have written wonderfully on topics as diverse as the space of the Southern flea market, downtown city revitalization, and GPS treasure hunts as well as on chaos theory and on queer space in *Mason & Dixon*. The third part of the project is a ten-minute conference presentation culled from that paper. At term's end, students present their work, sometimes at a three-hour Postmodern Territories symposium that I help them run in the English department. The symposium is open to the public—faculty members, students, and friends. Graduate students are always intimidated by this overall project and always complain about how much work it is, even though all three assignments are on the same topic. However, they also always tell me at the end of the course that the project taught them more about real writing situations in English studies than most of the other projects they've done in graduate school. Inevitably, they consider the Postmodern Territories symposium a dry run for more important public presentations of their graduate work.

## *Teaching* Mason & Dixon

After reading theory about postmodern space for six weeks, the class then turns to *Mason & Dixon*. I have found it essential to begin with historical background. My students usually don't know where Saint Helena was, don't know the colonial history of Cape Town, don't have a clue about the Transit of Venus or the Royal Society. I spend the first week on the novel going over background—historical background, authorial and textual background, genre background—using everything from maps of the world and of the Maryland-Pennsylvania-Delaware borders to scholarly articles on the use of historical detail in the novel. Most of this background is online and can be put up at a Blackboard site as links to assigned online reading.

In the first *Mason & Dixon* week, I also introduce students to Web resources that help them read the novel: the *Thomas Pynchon Wiki* by Tim Ware, the *Pynchon-L* "Mass Discussion of *Mason & Dixon*," and the novel guides available through Ware's *ThomasPynchon.com*. (See also the list of resources in endnote 2 in this essay.) A benefit of integrating the *Pynchon-L*

"Mass Discussion" into the course is that it teaches students how a list runs when discussants are genuinely excited about what they are reading and want seriously to hash through a text with fellow aficionados.

In the undergraduate class, I have tried to organize online blog discussions of *Mason & Dixon* while students read the text and work through the *Pynchon Wiki* materials or the *Pynchon-L* MDMD chapter summaries. Overall, I don't find this assignment effective because students tend to see it as busy work and do not have time to engage fully in such an online discussion. Assigning study questions has been more productive; these count as homework assignments and ask students to answer specific questions about the textual elements (plot, character, scene, etc.) and how space theory we've read might relate to the chapter under discussion. Again, however, one of the unique problems of teaching *Mason & Dixon* in a fourteen-week term is that students will be working hard simply to comprehend the text (by reading it, the chapter summaries, and all background information); to load too many written assignments on top of that is, in my experience, to court frustration and anger from these exhausted students. One answer is to assign two study questions to each student in the class for the seven-week *Mason & Dixon* period; when students come to class, they can report on their findings in relation to that day's question, but no student has to do all of the questions. I have also found it useful to have students post these reports online at the Blackboard site, for the class can then refer to these notes when studying for the final exam. Students get extra-credit points for responding online to the other students' reports. In the graduate version of the course, I assign articles on *Mason & Dixon* that are appropriate to that week's reading. Students may report on those articles as well as read the primary text.

Here is how the second half of Postmodern Territories might run, with variations for graduate and undergraduate versions of the course and for teacher energy levels:

Week 7 Presentation of Home Spaces projects in undergraduate course; workshop paper proposals in graduate course

Week 8 Beginning *Mason & Dixon*. Online background materials: *Mason & Dixon* resource discussions online; maps; background on the Old World–New World divide; Royal Society, Dutch and British East India Companies, British India, the Cape of Good Hope, Saint Helena, Black Hole of Calcutta, Transit of Venus, eighteenth-century calendar reform, Battle of Plassey, Nevil Maskelyne, Robert Clive, James Bradley, William Emerson. Introduction to main characters, class, professionalization, eighteenth-century Enlightenment setting. Articles: Charles Clerc's "Fact" and "Fact and Fiction" (*Mason & Dixon & Pynchon* 39–52, 57–86), David Foreman's "Historical Documents Relating to *Mason & Dixon*," and J. Donald Fernie's "Transits, Travels, and Tribulations, II." Literary terms to keep in mind: *historiographic metafiction*, *metahistorical romance*, *fabulation*; concepts central to Pynchon's novelistic vision such as simulation, paranoia, entropy, the power of multinational cartels

Week 9 *Mason & Dixon*, part 1 to p. 253 (with focus on space of the Cape, Saint Helena, sexualized space, moral geography and gothic, conspiracy, tourism, and colonialism). Articles such as Theo D'haen's "Postmodern Gothic" and Justin Coe's "Haunting and Hunting"

Week 10 Spring break

Week 11 *Mason & Dixon*, part 2 to p. 439. Online background: Ohio Company, British colonial grants in Americas, William Penn, Society of Friends, Maryland colony, Lord Baltimore, Lord Calvert, Great Awakening, George Whitfield, Jesuits and the Society of Jesus, Catholic Counter-Reformation, Freemasons, Jacobites, Culloden, General Wolfe, Paxton Boys, automatons, Vaucanson's Duck.

Week 12 *Mason & Dixon*, part 2 to p. 575. Articles such as Stephen Slemon's "Magic Realism as Postcolonial Discourse"

Week 13 *Mason & Dixon*, part 2 to p. 713. Online background: Mason-Dixon line and Visto, Warrior Path.

Week 14 *Mason & Dixon*, part 3, p. 717 to end.

After Week 14 Final exam for undergraduates; Postmodern Territories symposium for graduate students.

I end the unit on *Mason & Dixon* with a class discussion of moral geography (rather than theme), which includes a discussion of the frame-tale structure as well as the theme of "the subjunctive" that surfaces throughout the text.

The theory reviewed in the first half of the course provides initial contexts for discussion of Pynchon's novel. For example, after reading part 1 of the novel, students seem comfortable addressing questions such as these: By the end of part 1, what conspiracies do Mason and Dixon fear, and what panoptic surveillance do they suspect? What questions does their paranoia about the Royal Society raise concerning the relation between scholarly research and state control? What is the difference between historical pastiche and fabulation, and in what relation do both stand to the historical? What relations between capital and state power are enabled through the East India Company enterprises, and to what extent do those relations redefine space in colonial territories? How does money determine space in this text?

When we finished reading part 2, we are able to address other questions: What are the politics of cartography in this text? What cartographic politics are put in tension by the aerial view that Emerson's students learn when he teaches them to fly? What is the "subjunctive" in this novel, and how does it function as a kind of postmodern moral geography? Are the "Mate[s]" Mason and Dixon living queer space on "their Line" (768, 247)? How does the novel figure America as hyperreal and simulated space? Are Mason and Dixon tourists? When Mason and Dixon, like Huck Finn, light out for the territory and continue their Line westward, how does their postmodern "subjunctive" journey west contrast to other such journeys in American literature? In what ways is Pynchon redefining American pastoral space? Is *Mason & Dixon* an example of magical realism, and does it figure America as a postcolonial territory? What will the Line spawn? What is the (dialectical) relation between entropy and increased panoptic order in this new American space? All these ideas can be introduced through the theory in the first half of the course.

Postmodern Territories is a course about postmodern space and about Pynchon's *Mason & Dixon*. With so many aspects of space to consider and with the growing critical discourse about space and *Mason & Dixon*, teachers can experiment with numerous topics and kinds of materials. The course has the potential to put academic theory, fiction, film, the plastic arts, consumer culture, and Pynchon's novel in serious dialogue, and it also has the potential to get students (and the teacher) jazzed about looking at their world(s) in new ways. The class encourages good-natured wrangling and serious, sometimes heated, discussion, about the world in which we live now. It encourages students to consider how Pynchon's *Mason & Dixon* comments about America, past and present. And it provides opportunities for students to practice the kinds of writing they will do as they advance in language and literature studies.

## NOTES

I would like to thank the graduate students who took English 693 at the University of Alabama, Birmingham, during summer term 2002 (particularly Russ Parker, Eugene Cuevas, Mary Beth Rowland, and Mary Carol Moran) and the undergraduates and graduate students in English 499 and English 670 at the University of Tennessee for giving me feedback on this course.

[1] In this article I have omitted works of criticism pertaining to Pynchon's oeuvre, with the understanding that instructors will include these in the course. Tim Ware's *Thomas Pynchon Wiki* (http://pynchonwiki.com) is a wonderful resource for students, as is his Web guide at www.hyperarts.com/pynchon/mason-dixon/index.html. The *Pynchon-L* "Mass Discussion of *Mason & Dixon*" (www.waste.org/pynchon-l) was the first to present commentary on *Mason & Dixon* and is still useful. The *Spermatikos Logos* page is another good resource (www.themodernword.com/pynchon/pynchon_links.html). *Wikipedia* offers biographies of the major historical figures in the novel; for these, see also the information collected by Otto Sell at www.ottosell.de/pynchon/md/mdindex.html. Also important are Peter Schmidt's concordances and chapter summaries (www.swarthmore.edu/Humanities/pschmid1/engl52b/m-d1.html). Henry Holt offers a reading guide to *Mason & Dixon* (www.henryholt.com/readingguides/pynchon.htm).

## APPENDIX
### Readings for Postmodern Territories Course


Baudrillard, Jean. "The Precession of Simulacra."

Benjamin, Walter. *The Arcades Project*.

Borges, Jorge Luis. *Labyrinths*. (See also a great online version of "The Library of Babel" at http://jubal.westnet.com/hyperdiscordia/library_of_babel.html.)

Chambers, Erve. *Native Tours: The Anthropology of Travel and Tourism*.

Clerc, Charles. *Mason & Dixon & Pynchon*.

Clifford, James. *Routes: Travel and Translation in the Twentieth Century*.

Coe, Justin Scott. "Haunting and Hunting: Bodily Resurrection and the Occupation of History in *Mason & Dixon*."

Coetzee, J. M. *Waiting for the Barbarians*.

Cowan, James. *Mapmaker's Dream: Meditations of Fra Mauro*.

D'haen, Theo. "Postmodern Gothic."

Duncan, Nancy, ed. *Bodyspace: Destabilizing Geographies of Gender and Sexuality*.

Eco, Umberto. *Travels in Hyperreality*.

Elias, Amy J. "The Question of Postmodernism" (*Sublime Desire* xx–xxviii).

Fernie, J. Donald. "Transits, Travels, and Tribulations, II."

Foucault, Michel. *Discipline and Punish: The Birth of the Prison* and "Of Other Spaces Heterotopias."

Gregory, Derek. *Geographical Imaginations*.

Harley, J. B. "Maps, Knowledge, and Power."

Harvey, David. *The Condition of Postmodernity: An Enquiry into the Origins of Cultural Change*. (Early chapters defining space are very good.)

Hofstadter, Richard. *The Paranoid Style in American Politics*.

Horvath, Brooke, and Irving Malin, eds. *Pynchon and* Mason & Dixon (143–66).

Jameson, Fredric. "Postmodernism and Consumer Society."

Kaplan, Caren. *Questions of Travel: Postmodern Poetics of Displacement*.

Kincaid, Jamaica. *A Small Place*. New York: Plume, 1988.

Lefebvre, Henri. *The Production of Space*.

MacCannell, Dean, and Lucy R. Lippard. *The Tourist: A New Theory of the Leisure Class*.

McCarthy, Cormac. *The Road*.

Millhauser, Steven. *Martin Dressler: The Tale of an American Dreamer*.

Oliver, Anna. "The Use of Maps in Contemporary Art."

Pratt, Mary Louise. "Travel Narrative and Imperialist Vision."

Rojek, Chris, and John Urry. *Touring Cultures: Transformations of Travel and Theory*.

*SimCities and @Culture.*
Slemon, Stephen. "Magic Realism as Post-colonial Discourse."
Spiegelman, Art. *In the Shadow of No Towers.*
Stephenson, Neal. *Snow Crash.*
Tuan, Yi-Fu. *Space and Place: The Perspective of Experience.*

# READING PRACTICES

## Pynchon's Polyvocality

*Gary Thompson*

Reading Pynchon for the first time, students encounter a cacophony of voices that inspires simultaneous frustration and interest. His novels' verbal representations range across many discourses: the novel as a form is already hybrid, including description, exposition, narration, dialogue, letters, and so on. *Gravity's Rainbow*, the most compendious, incorporates nonliterary discourses drawn from nuclear physics, music theory, anthropology, comparative religion, calculus, and film. Down the social scale, there are popular genres: cartoons, limericks, music-hall songs, doggerel, physical humor, graffiti, and puns. Apart from students' unfamiliarity with topics such as entropy, early-twentieth-century European politics, and Pavlovian psychology, the narrative's unpredictable shifts among these discourses can be disorienting, leading readers to sympathize with the narrator's comment in the Mittelwerke that "what you thought was a balanced mind is little help" (*Gravity's Rainbow* 297). The other novels provide less imposing but still formidable versions of *Gravity's Rainbow*'s hybridity.

Any discussion of teaching Pynchon's fiction should offer some means of responding to students' confusion. Labels can be helpful to minimize confusion by directing attention to concepts. Calling a text composed of many voices *polyvocal* is a first step toward analysis and comprehension. Polyvocality, along with several other terms drawn from the writings of Mikhail Bakhtin, can help characterize some of what is estranging about Pynchon's work, furthering students' abilities to come to at least a partial understanding not only of the complexity of novelistic discourse but more generally of how literary texts serve as source material for interpretation.

Furthermore, attention to the novels' polyvocality can counterbalance the New Critical tendency to see texts as self-contained and static by connecting threads in the text to their social, cultural, and ideological sources. Attention to Pynchon's polyvocality can thus serve as a basis not only for interpreting a given text but also for building theoretically sound practices of interpretation that have resonance with fields well beyond those of English and that stress the social nature of reading and interpretation. Reading Pynchon's novels through Bakhtinian theory makes the social dimension of those texts visible. Bakhtin's emphasis on dialogism reminds us that novels re-create in textual form the social and contextual nature of writing.[1]

## *Polyvocality*

> [W]e can locate meaning in the dialogic process of interaction between speaking subjects, between texts and readers, between texts themselves.
>
> (Lodge 86)

Rather than assign difficulty, genius, and other textual qualities to an absent author, we might do better to question the supposed unity of text and canon by pointing out that even a singular text is composed of different voices (*voice* being shorthand for verbal text or utterance). Any novel necessarily brings together a variety of disciplinary contexts and social registers in an extended dialogue. The amalgamation of voices we may label as polyvocal, and as we note the shifts between voices we are observing dialogism. Bakhtin's use of dialogism spans from double-voiced phrases (called heteroglossia) to what will here be termed polyvocality, or multiple voices within a novel, or intertextuality, reading across several texts. *Dialogism* therefore may be considered any sustained attention to multiple social and cultural contexts within discourse; the term gives a useful label to a primary quality of Pynchon's fiction.

One place to start a Bakhtinian reading of Pynchon is to examine the narrative voice, illustrating at once the novels' intertextuality, polyvocality, range of social levels and contexts, and double voicing. Particularly in *Lot 49* and *Gravity's Rainbow*, the narrative voice moves with astounding fluidity between the extremes of Olympian distance above the fictional plane and an intimacy with the characters' consciousness.

In the first paragraph of *Lot 49*, for example, there are numerous double-voiced phrases in the third-person point of view, in which both a narrative voice and Oedipa's interior thoughts can be identified. A phrase such as "spoke the name of God" helps establish Oedipa's individuation early in the novel (here suggesting that Oedipa is not particularly religious [9]), but the phrase also associates the name of God with Pierce Inverarity and thus suggests the religious dimension of the search on which she is about to embark. The subsequent series of images described in this first paragraph is something like a film montage of memories associated with Pierce. "Was that how he'd died, she wondered, among dreams, crushed by the only ikon in the house?" This utterance is truly double-voiced, as Oedipa's speculation is highly literary—*ikon?*—allowing the character to share the narrator's modernist sense of irony or schadenfreude at the prospect of the robber baron's image as the effective means of eliminating his contemporary counterpart. Who is responsible for the description of Oedipa's laugh as "helpless"? Who assesses her spiritual state as "so sick" (10)? These and other phrases throughout the novel are multivocal, pointing toward the character and narrator simultaneously, toward discourse and story.[2] Similarly, "stared at by the greenish dead eye of the TV tube" suggests Oedipa's feeling herself the object of the TV's emptiness and perhaps the emptiness of her life at that moment, but it does so in terms starkly different from those she herself would use (9).

Others might parse these double voicings differently, but I am not concerned here with establishing my reading as definitive; rather, students can be asked to consider the concept of double voicing as a way of distinguishing diegetic functions in the narrator's voice and thereby becoming more attentive to the subtleties and pleasures of the text.[3]

Tracing the novels' polyvocality can lead the class to recognize the social dimension of language. One passage among many that can be used to good effect is the narrator's account of Mucho's job as used car salesman (12–14). As one student wrote, "I read about Mucho and his jobs like three times because the voice of the narrator was confusing, even a bit alienating to me. I was sure that this must be something important and I was theme hunting."[4] One contributing factor in student alienation from passages like this one may be Pynchon's practice of speaking for people who are frequently invisible to readers. Classroom discussions might drive the point home by asking for more recent equivalents of Mucho's used car customers—homeless city dwellers, patients in emergency rooms, Wal-Mart shoppers—bringing social class more explicitly into play and reducing the distance between the language of the novel and social figures they recognize from everyday life, through contact or various media outlets.

## Heteroglossia

Pynchon's fiction also displays double or multiple voicings within a single phrase. An example from *Gravity's Rainbow:* "Welcome Mister Slothrop Welcome To Our Structure We Hope You Will Enjoy Your Visit Here" (194). The sentence simultaneously enacts voices of at least the following: Them, the unseen forces of control over Slothrop (and by extension us); Slothrop, projecting his own scared-elated response to the rendezvous with Katje; narrative conventions such as that of lending printed words a different intonation by capitalizing them (or in other passages, placing them in quotation marks or italics); and the novel's narrator, responsible for rendering aspects of the characters' consciousness but not through their dialogue. (This multiple voicing corresponds roughly to the New Critical use of irony or paradox but is placed more emphatically in a social context.) As with the vocal traces in polyvocality, examining the overtones in heteroglossia can enrich students' understanding of the text's complexity, as well as the social dimensions of language, including their own.

According to Bakhtin, not only are units of text composed of voices drawn from several contexts, but *any* utterance points at once to two or more categories of discourse. Any double-voiced utterance involves a struggle, as the speaker draws terms used by others and puts them to her or his own uses ("Discourse" 275–85). The previous contexts for the utterance speak through the new utterance. In the opening paragraph of *Lot 49*, Oedipa finds that she has been named "executor, or she supposed executrix," of Pierce's will (9). Parts of this paragraph point toward unitary language: the use of a specific term for the role Oedipa believes at the outset that she is to play in dealing with Pierce's affairs (legal discourse, like other professional jargons, insists on precise terms); the afterthought that changes the gender of the term, an impulse grounded in a different sort of unitary language, which expects precision of another sort—gender-specific terms. Other aspects point to heteroglossia and away from unitary language: First, the afterthought itself. Oedipa is not qualified for legal matters (a point she makes in talking the matter over with Mucho later), and in encountering the term *executor* she brings what may be a bookish concern with getting the details right into her discourse. Second, the conflict between the worldviews implied by the terms. The change to *-trix* in effect makes legal language subject to the language of precise usage and tells us that Oedipa is vaguely aware of gender distinction, perhaps even of a latent feminism in her disposition. Third, "she supposed": Oedipa doesn't reside in a world of black-and-white distinctions but in what will soon become more and more radical shifts between discourse communities, yet her recognition of the precise legal term (for a female executor) is consistent with her interrogation of other discourses she encounters—compare her response to Koteks's explanation of Maxwell's demon, "Sorting isn't work?" (86). Not least, the phrase cited above is not in Oedipa's own voice but reported by the novel's narrator. As such it contains both the inflection of Oedipa's reported internal monologue and that of the overall narrator, sympathetic to but distinct from his character's represented consciousness (*skaz*).[5]

The labor of pointing to these various elements in the double voicing may seem extreme, since practically every phrase in the novel offers something comparable. In fact, a key argument of Bakhtin's is that every utterance participates simultaneously in multiply voiced contexts. This multiplicity can be seen as enriching the text rather than complicating its reading. Instructors might want to demonstrate a few such readings, illustrate their importance to reading the novel as a social tapestry, and then leave other examples for students to complete.

## Carnival, Grotesque Realism

The concepts of carnival and grotesque realism found in Bakhtin's work are less directly involved with polyvocality but can also be useful in analyzing Pynchon's novels. Bakhtinian carnival is a somewhat utopian, licensed period during which social classes may mix freely, suspending or inverting established hierarchies in a spirit of play. Activities ordinarily taboo are carried out with abandon, taboo words and phrases are spoken with gusto, and the freedom of this disorder allows for a way around too-rigid categories. Carnival can be traced as a subversive impulse far beyond literal feast days: it is present in any circumstances in which "the low" transgress rules established by social superiors. Contemporary equivalents may be found in *The Daily Show*, *South Park*, or in films by Michael Moore, which appropriate and repurpose texts by those in political power.

Carnival as a concept aptly describes the diverse masquerades and eruptions into song, along with the physical humor, bad jokes, and puns, characteristic of Pynchon's novels. Allied with carnival is the description and celebration of bodily functions. As in Rabelais, Pynchon's characters eat, drink, excrete, and fornicate to excess. Students' responses to these aspects of the texts range from agreeing with the Pulitzer board that called *Gravity's Rainbow* "turgid" and in parts "obscene" (qtd. in Kihss) to feeling liberated by a literary text that includes a trip down the toilet, a nasal hard-on, the *Anubis* orgy, the Saint James adenoid, mock battles with huge rubber penises, and other imaginative but offensive breaks with decorum.

## Authoritative Discourse and Internal Persuasion

Less often emphasized in accounts of Bakhtin's writing is the dialogue between voices representing power (unitary discourse, centripetal force) and those of ordinary members of society (heterogeneous discourses, centrifugal forces). As individuals, we internalize the discourse of authority by restating its positions in our own words, thereby positioning ourselves as ideological subjects. In doing so, Bakhtin argues in "Discourse in the Novel," subjects actively buy into hegemony, instead of simply accepting dictates under compulsion (342–49).

Examples of historical impulses toward unitary discourse include Aristotelian poetics or Cartesian neoclassicism, which attempt to systematize and regularize discourse and thought; resistance to these impulses comes from multiple directions. Pynchon's work presents fictional equivalents: in *Gravity's Rainbow*, "They" remain remote and uncharacterizable, while Their representatives, such as Pointsman, act as (fallible) agents. "Proverbs for Paranoids, 1: You may never get to touch the Master, but you can tickle his creatures" (237). Authority is further symbolized by the Rocket: "Vectors in the night underground, all trying to flee a center, a force, which appears to be the Rocket"

(318). As with the Schwarzkommando, resistance is occasionally heroic, mostly farcical, and scattered—but likely to break out unpredictably.

Internal persuasion may be played out in the classroom variously, with the author, the instructor, or literary tradition as authoritative. Whenever possible, students should be invited to consider how they construct and change interpretations, drawing on Pynchon's texts as a resource.

## *Pedagogical Applications*

Classrooms are places where dialogue is enacted in different forms, ranging from the most monologic (lecture, pseudodiscussions dominated by the instructor, and formal assignment) through written forms having more rapid feedback (shorter papers, informal papers, asynchronous and synchronous online texts) to dialogic classroom discussion among peer groups or the entire class. The best examples of ways to make use of Bakhtinian concepts in reading Pynchon's work will be found in specific local contexts.

Students in a recent class of mine responded to the variegated surface and interpretive openness of Pynchon's novel in one of two or three ways. A few registered their confusion but chose to wait for the instructor to clarify matters. Some assigned the confusion to Oedipa, to the sixties, or to the author (Pynchon must have been taking drugs). The most satisfactory responses associated readers' confusion with themes in the novel: in dealing with the novel's strange characterization and unresolved plot, we experience something like Oedipa's paranoia, trying to sort true plot from false leads, ourselves awaiting the crying of lot 49 as we construct our own interpretations of reality.

Readers of *Lot 49* commonly see names as important interpretive data. Several posts to the class's forum offered ideas about *Lot 49*'s names, either in the form of lists of the most comic instances or attempts to find thematic significance. The double-voicing of Pynchon character names is impossible to ignore, even on first encounter. Early on, readers become caught up in sifting names for puns and comic references (Manny Di Presso, Genghis Cohen, Mike Fallopian, Dr. Hilarius, Stanley Koteks) or for thematic significance (Oedipa Maas, Pierce Inverarity) and then begin to look for comic or thematic significance in the less obvious ones (Randolph Driblette, Metzger, John Nefastis).

Students often come to us convinced that there is a vast gulf between their discourse and that of the texts we ask them to interpret. To counter this belief, we need to train ourselves to slow down and attend more carefully to the multiple voices in many utterances. If we can learn to use Pynchon's fiction as emblematic of the ongoing interactions between social and cultural contexts, we may help them to bridge this perceived gulf.

NOTES

[1] In what follows, *voice* should be regarded as a synecdoche, standing for various aspects of real and represented persons. (Their status as real or represented is not unimportant but may be deferred to concentrate on the mixed nature of discourse.) In addition to dialect or verbal style, *voice* can represent *consciousness*, *identity*, *role*, even *discourse community*. (Bakhtin sometimes uses two terms for roughly the same concepts, as with *polyvocality* and *heteroglossia*.) *Voice*'s shiftiness illustrates that key terms do not necessarily have fixed boundaries, either in literary texts or in discussions drawing on literary theory.

[2] *Diegesis* refers to those aspects of a novel that apply to the plot function as opposed to the storytelling (cf. *dramaturgical* for plays). Michel Riffaterre gives a full critical exposition of the term in *Fictional Truth*.

[3] The resurgence of interest in Bakhtin since the publication of his work in English in the 1980s is a confirmation of Michel Foucault's contention that "the author" is more significantly a textual effect than a biographical person. Many of the early texts treated as emanating from Bakhtin were published in collaboration with or under the names of others such as Valentin Voloshinov and Pavel Medvedev. With respect to the texts written during Stalin's lifetime, treating them all as written by Bakhtin may obscure the likely degree of collaboration in their creation.

[4] Student text is used by permission.

[5] *Skaz* is a term used by Russian formalists to denote "a special type of narrative structured as emanating from a person distanced from the author (whether concretely named or presumed), and one who possesses a distinct manner of discourse" (qtd. in Cornwell). American examples might include *Adventures of Huckleberry Finn*, whose narrator's voice is sharply distinguished from Mark Twain's.

# Hypertextualizing *The Crying of Lot 49*

*Todd Rohman*

The initial approaches I used in teaching *Lot 49* were typically lecture centered and tended toward the parochial. I saw myself as a type of literary SUV, blazing new referential trails in narrative spaces where I assumed students dared not go. In preparation for class meetings, I relied heavily on my personal reading of the novel, highlighting those aspects that I found most compelling, and those which supported my take—that the novel centrally explores Oedipa's (and, by implication, our own) struggle to maintain a stable identity in the face of vertiginous layers of information and commodities that dominate contemporary American life. Along the way, I would freshen and expand my knowledge of Pynchon's historical and cultural references with the intention of sharing these with my students as we met to analyze the novel. Inevitably, many students (deeply versed in New Critical approaches to interpreting the narrative) would stick closely to intratextual concerns (character, plot, symbol) while nodding with mild interest at the extratextual references my lectures or discussion points sought to illuminate. I noticed that despite my efforts to demonstrate ways the novel functioned as an open text, one rich with allusive connections, a communicative gap seemed to form between issues generated solely within the narrative structure (which my students perceived to be their domain) and the multitude of historical, cultural, mythological, technological, political, literary, and artistic allusions that circulate outside *Lot 49*'s margins (perceived by them to be my domain). Occasionally, I would turn students loose with a copy of J. Kerry Grant's companion to the novel, but I found that assigning this work early in their reading repeated the thunder-stealing effect my lectures sometimes might have had on their developing insights.[1] If *Lot 49* has been so meticulously digested in a wide range of published works, some students seemed to think, where would they find new ground to explore?

In each new learning context (I principally teach junior, senior, and master's level English majors, though I have also taught the work to nonmajors and to doctoral students abroad) I find that an effective pedagogical strategy lies in approaching the novel with a simple question: if a friend sees you in the local coffee shop reading *The Crying of Lot 49* and asks you what the book is about, what do you tell them? What ensues is a discussion of the features that make the text unconventional. Students soon discover (often on their own) that *Lot 49* is, by turns, a detective story, a work of science fiction, a mystery, a bildungsroman, an urban myth, a psychological treatise, a social satire, an artifact of pop-cultural kitsch. Some contend that the novel fits squarely into one category, while many submit that the work skips across multiple forms and genres. Some students begin to question the usefulness of boundaries and margins imposed by literary categories and are intrigued by the open possibilities of the text.

Though many of my upper-level students may have read Fredric Jameson or Jean-François Lyotard, even those without this background come to recognize features of *Lot 49* as postmodern, among them the text's tendency to resist categorization and generate what Brian McHale terms "ontological hesitation" (*Constructing* 208). While the foregrounding of structure is not as aggressively apparent in *Lot 49* as in other reputedly postmodern texts I teach, such as William S. Burroughs's *Naked Lunch* or works by Kathy Acker, who fragment and rupture linearity at every turn, many students find the task of explicitly concentrating their analyses on how a story is told an alien process.[2]

*Lot 49* is such a rigorous, problematic, and finally productive text for classroom analysis because the novel rebukes attempts to shelve it comfortably into a literary category, forcing readers to contend with issues of structure to arrive at a meaningful interpretation of content. This challenge resonates in the narrative itself, in which we find a protagonist searching for (or generating her own) plot and a quest that imbricates increasingly dense informational patterns. In a sense, Oedipa's adventure is a study in how to "read" complex experience, a struggle against a "sense of buffering, insulation," or confinement in a self-imposed "Rapunzel-like role" (20).

To harness this range of inclinations and to make group study of the novel as productive and stimulating as possible, I recommend tapping our most recent, powerful, and accessible metaphor of nonlinear form in narrative design—hypertext and the Internet—since it provides students with a constructive model for addressing the open nature of *Lot 49*. In a discussion of hypertext structure, J. Yellowlees Douglas recounts a modern critical history that considers

> closure as the single entity that confers cohesion and significance on narratives in a way that strongly suggests that the experience . . . numbers among the principal pleasures of reading narratives . . . showing us how closure both prompts and encourages us to read. (161)

She goes on to suggest that this pleasure taken in closure is even true for a novel like *Lot 49*, granting that while

> [m]any twentieth-century print narratives . . . have rendered problematic the traditional definition of closure . . . their physical endings ensure that their readers can hold no further expectations that something else will happen in the narrative, or that they will need to revise their concept of the narrative as a whole as a result of some as yet unexperienced narrative episode.

Such texts, Douglas contends, still carry the function of "promising readers that they will soon be able to see their inferences about the narrative action either affirmed or disproved when they finish reading" (164). In other words, *Lot 49*, though resistant to and pressing the boundaries of closure, is nevertheless haunted by its print-bound conclusiveness. While it is true that *Lot 49* does not generate new versions of itself in a fashion identical to Michael Joyce's hypertext novel *Afternoon* (the focus of Douglas's study), *Lot 49* certainly expresses what Douglas describes as "narrative structure [that] enables us to delve through layer upon layer of singular versions of narrative events" in a manner more similar to hypertext navigation than to traditional reading (172).

In the classroom, *Lot 49* offers students the unique opportunity to perform a hypertext-style reading of print narrative. To facilitate this approach, consider assigning students the role of human search engines, each closely reading the text with any number of "search terms" in place. This activity brings multiple perspectives on the novel into dialogue in the classroom, guarantees that each student contributes constructively to the text, and also helps them avoid the common problem of feeling overwhelmed by *Lot 49*'s encyclopedic scope. Whereas one student may be in charge of links to visual art, another may focus on technical data, another on Pynchon's provocative use of names, and so on. An instructor familiar with the novel can come up with a list of many more and may even classify them (art, music, history, conspiracies, cinema, television, science, etc.). While some search terms may lead to "dead links"—"Driblette" may not get one as far as "Inverarity"—this approach narrows the research field without necessarily limiting its critical possibilities.[3] Perhaps most important in this process, as students meet and exchange their private findings collectively the classroom becomes a richly interconnected critical space, a productive region of uncertainty where new associations emerge as each link is developed and discussed. From these interactions, students begin to see the broad range of topics available to them for further critique and analysis and gain a greater sense of intellectual ownership over some chosen territory in the novel—activities that echo Pierce Inverarity's charge to "keep it bouncing" (178).

What makes the novel unique is that, unlike other highly referential texts (let's say works by James Joyce or other high modernists), such linkage, referencing, and densely interwoven meaning production goes beyond enriching the narrative moment or lending depth of significance to a given character (as Stephen Dedalus's classical namesake does) and becomes inherently what *The Crying of Lot 49* is about. Given the limited time frame in which most of us attempt to address the novel's political, cultural, or historical concerns and the broad array of topics available to students, sometimes I simply assign such links. Another option is to encourage students to randomly select them, even before they've cracked the book. Once students focus their analyses on manageable regions of inquiry, they find their sense of indeterminacy in the novel more energizing than daunting. And, significantly, they've not been handed interpretations of the text.

A student who initially narrowed her search to etymological concerns writes in her response journal:

> Throughout my reading I found myself probing and delving for meaning. . . . The solutions, I thought, would be embedded in words like

> *Yoyodyne*, which I unsuccessfully parsed into *yoyo* and *dyne*, looked up separately and then reconnected, hunting for semantic codes with secret implications.

This student acknowledges her discovery of a new way of reading that offers more interpretive possibility: "I combed dictionaries for *Trystero*, *Tryst-ero*, *Try-stero*, *Trys-tero*, and *Tristero*," concluding that "*Lot 49* is a living source that grows or diminishes in direct proportion to the knowledge each reader brings to its pages . . . because every nuance is an open invitation to speculate and project." These impressions suggest that linked readings can help shift student focus from generalization or totalizing gestures toward an expanding matrix of textual continuity. Hypertextualizing grants flexibility to close reading, giving space to shuttle among micro- and macro-level details in the novel with relative ease—even with a sense of critical adventure.

Another student "linking" to the novel's suggestive use of naming characterizes Oedipa's interpretive quest as a complex act of reading. The reader's interpretive moves, this student contends, mirror Oedipa's gestures. Such responses acknowledge that the pursuit of these textual details can be as productive a practice as more conventionally tracking each plot development. Any of the terms she discovers may serve as a useful point of critical entry into the novel's interconnected layers.

Another student chooses to focus her attention on this correlation between *Lot 49* and hypertextual reading, submitting this perspective in one of her response essays:

> [T]here is a tendency towards multiperspectivism and inconclusiveness that was especially acute in Pynchon's *The Crying of Lot 49* . . . which features a woman, Oedipa Maas, in a constant search for a meaning that seems more and more elusive. . . . It is particularly obvious in those [texts] that resort to the strategy of the hypertext since meaning depends on the reader's choices and on the decisions he makes.

Each of these responses shows a hypertextual approach to *Lot 49* directing a student's analysis productively toward metapractices of reading and criticism. Many students, given the opportunity, need little encouragement to pursue hypertextualizing the novel.

The amount of time most of our students spend online renders the metaphor of hypertext a familiar context for critical analysis. Joseph Janangelo addresses the impulse a growing number of students have to read and write in new ways in "Joseph Cornell and the Artistry of Composing Persuasive Hypertexts," in which he discusses the ways such a digital inclination might be informed. He writes, "[I]t interests me that some students are beginning to compose beyond print paradigms—even if they must simulate hypertextual format to do so" (26). Considering the unexpected phenomenon of hypertext-inspired student submissions, he reflects, "[I]t makes me wonder if the use of hypertext programs at the K–12 levels is leading students to compose with an understanding that linear argumentation is not the only credible form that academic writing can take" (275). *Lot 49* implicitly urges readers to construct (that is, select, prioritize, and confer meaning on) its narrative as they move through it, so hypertextualizing offers a model for reading that many students may have already internalized.

A recent student submission, which adhered in every respect to the specifications listed in my syllabus, nevertheless found room to innovate. For a research analysis paper required in my Contemporary American Literature course, a student chose to submit her work on multicolored paper that she ran through a shredder and sealed into a quirky malt beverage bottle. Her gesture is multiform, a literal "cut-up" method in which each portion of her text is equally (in)accessible and a demonstration of work that both has value and is waste. Its containment in the transparent veneer of disposable, excessively niched advertising (do we really need Hooch *Ice*?) humorously undermines the authenticity of her submission (as just another item of mass production, readily consumed and forgotten) and demands a new method of reading, critique, and evaluation, should one make such an attempt. The unique form of her submission marks the difficulty of distinguishing signal from noise, the challenge of navigating discordant, simultaneous flows of information in a range of cultural contexts. This creative student was energized by the possibility of generating a nonlinear critical reaction, suggesting that the bottle, like Pynchon's text, appears deceptively contained, yet is open to broad speculation and inquiry and indeterminacy. Orienting herself through discussions of hypertextual narrative, she illustrates that print-based forms can be literally closed but not necessarily stable or conclusive. While some readers privilege the "unsatisfying" conclusion of the novel ("The auctioneer cleared his throat. Oedipa settled back, to await the crying of lot 49" [183]) and hastily pronounce the whole journey pointless or just a trick, glossing over some of the more tantalizing narrative possibilities, this unique submission subverts the impulse to make swift assessments of *Lot 49* that could hinder fuller exploration of the text.

By contemplating alternative models to linearity and closure in their reading and analyses, some students contend that one can follow multiple versions of Oedipa through the links of her experiences—experiences that help penetrate margins and boundaries imposing on her identity. Once students recognize that Oedipa may be the author of her own quest, that some of her "discoveries" may in fact be projections generated in the hope of unraveling the legacy of Pierce Inverarity, they begin to connect her journey through a host of secret societies and systems functioning outside the margins of official culture with their own labyrinthine pursuits.

Oedipa evolves from the ennui of her Californian, suburban, Tupperware-party existence, seeing her executrix role as an escape from the confines of a "captive maiden" narrative, a life off of the Monopoly board, and a locus for generating new fictions, new identities, and establishing new interpretive frames (21). New readers, like Oedipa, may come to see a relation between embracing a possibility of "revelation . . . trembl[ing] just past the threshold" and their own experience with open reading (24).

Instead of seeking determinate solutions, students discover through hypertextual reading that the real pleasure of the novel lies in following Oedipa as she tries to "fix" her experiences and order her reality, chasing post horns in an ever-shifting paradigm. Through her own linked searches, Oedipa "stumble[s]" into "a network by which X number of Americans are truly communicating." Oedipa weighs the malleable nature of her perceptions, telling herself, "[Y]ou are hallucinating it. Or a plot has been mounted against you. . . . Or you are fantasying some such plot, in which case you are a nut, Oedipa, out of your skull," and in this epistemological uproar concludes that "[t]hose, now that she was looking at them, she saw to be the alternatives" (170–71). On noticing the novel's hypertextual possibilities, a recent graduate became intrigued by the way Oedipa meets characters who are separate yet linked in unexpected ways. These unexpected relations through language and group dynamics became the focus of both her research and discussion contributions. Encouraging such interpretive reactions helps students focus on the key issues of connection and dialogue between complex interpenetrating systems, arrived at through the consideration of alternative models of storytelling, identity construction, and textual production.

We can attest, as does Michael Joyce, that "Literary hypertexts" garner much "critical and media attention, challenging notions of textual closure, authorship, and reader response" (28). But despite this impression that the "technological age" or "information age" seems to be self-generating, "it is *we* who fashion it, *we* who discover and recover it, *we* who shape it, *we* who literally give it form" (119). Those of us who introduce *Lot 49* to our students may find the evolving metaphor of hypertext a useful tool to help students reexamine their expectations of closure, discuss formal innovations and indeterminacy, and address the multiple, open potentialities of Pynchon's work.

## NOTES

[1] I hasten to add how useful Grant's *A Companion to* The Crying of Lot 49 is for scholars further along in their critical inquiries. The work attempts, in the author's words, "to loosen some of the novel's interpretive tangles by reproducing critical commentary and offering commentary of [Grant's] own" (xvi).

[2] Ihab Hassan's "Toward a Concept of Postmodernism" offers a schematic that usefully articulates a "postmodern tendency" if not an outright definition of the term. As it draws its descriptors from "rhetoric, linguistics, literary theory, philosophy, anthropology, psychoanalysis, political science, even theology," postmodernism serves as a resource for comparing aspects of the novel with a wide range of work in the arts not typically but usefully explored in literary contexts (283).

[3] How is it possible to narrow one's field of vision to such a specific area without limiting the potential critical yield of the novel? Oedipa's hierophantic moment gazing down on the landscape of San Narciso is a useful illustration. Her view suggests to her an order and complexity previously evoked by examining the circuit card of a transistor radio. There is an aspect of fractal scaling or self-similarity in her view of the city that links her macro- and microperspectives. Students will find their more narrowly defined "link" searches just as illuminating, likely even more illuminating, than attempting to attack a whole dense forest of allusions at once.

# Teaching *Gravity's Rainbow*: Correlation in Life and Reading

*Alan Nadel*

For a number of years I taught *Gravity's Rainbow* as the last book in my graduate course Post–World War II American Fiction. The course usually included a dozen books, with a separate, short writing assignment on each. The students were required to do any three of these short assignments and then a long research paper. In the short assignments, I usually identified a brief passage from the assigned novel, raised a long list of specific questions about the passage, and asked students to answer some of those questions in the process of relating a careful analysis of the language to thematic, stylistic, or generic issues concerning the book as a whole. Devising an assignment of that sort for *Gravity's Rainbow,* however, became problematic in ways that foregrounded some of the issues important to reading Pynchon and to understanding the questions of emplotment and identification that his work impels.

Reading fiction depends on forms of identification: readers must identify the shapes of letters, their organization into words, and the codes of grammar that produce utterances from those words. They must also identify the objects and concepts signified by that process. This act of identifying and decoding a text does not differ, in the most general way, from the acts of identification and interpretation necessary to navigate the social and physical world. One must correlate, through a process of paradigmatic and syntagmatic substitutions, perceptions and their general forms. Such a routine process enables one to identify and sort the signs meaningful to crossing a street or entering a building through the door.

This process replicates itself at the level of literary criticism as well, in that all literary criticism, it can be argued, can be seen as an attempt to establish some form of correlation—between themes, details, structures, characters, and so forth—either within the text (as prescribed most intensely by New Criticism) or between the text and themes, details, structures found elsewhere, be it in the author's biography or the Freudian canon, in the work of Marx or the cultural context, to name a few. The students in my course, primarily aspiring scientists and engineers, have little difficulty with the concept of correlation, a central activity of statistical analysis. It makes sense to them that comprehension of text and context depends on acts of correlation. Although it is axiomatic to scientific method that correlation does not prove causality, human notions of causality, as Karl Pearson pointed out in his groundbreaking *The Grammar of Science*, nevertheless depend on correlation. If "causality" means that under identical conditions acts produce identical results, Pearson explained, we can rarely establish the requirements to assert a causal relation because conditions are rarely, if ever, absolutely identical.

Reasonable predictions thus depend on how significantly conditions, acts, and results correlate with one another.

This correlation can be plotted on a graph as the correlation between vertical and horizontal axes and can be calculated mathematically on a scale of zero to one, in which "one" indicates a hundred percent correlation between changes along each axis, and "zero" indicates the absence of any meaningful correlation. Since in life and in reading, as in mathematics, the ability to identify any object or action depends on recognizing its correlation to known constants, ambiguity arises from correlations that fall in the middle range between zero and one.

Students needn't have backgrounds in science or mathematics, however, to appreciate the thematic and narrative significance of correlation to Pynchon's novels. This range between zero and one, after all, is one of the "excluded middles" Oedipa deplores in *The Crying of Lot 49* (181) and the territory belonging to a major character of *Gravity's Rainbow*, the statistician Roger Mexico. Like Roger Mexico, Pynchon's reader is caught in the middle,

> in the domain of zero to one, not-something to something [while] Pointsman can only possess the zero and one. . . . Like his master I. P. Pavlov before him, [Pointsman] imagines the cortex of the brain as a mosaic of tiny on/off elements. . . . But to Mexico belongs the domain *between* zero and one—the middle Pointsman has excluded from his persuasion—the probabilities. (55)

In this way, at least, Mexico is Pynchon's surrogate reader. As Peter Cooper explains, in Pynchon's work

> the disquieting or even sinister uncertainty experienced by the characters extends to envelop the reader. The reader then tries to corroborate his sense of reality, or at least to orient himself within the fictional world, by finding some meaningful pattern in events. (175)

In this sense, Mexico is the professional embodiment of the reader, to the extent that Mexico is obliged to make tentative sense of a world in which causality will remain, by definition, a mystery.

Having established the centrality of correlation to both the novel and the reader, students may be asked to identify the various ways that Pynchon builds the idea and practice of correlation into questions of identification and emplotment raised by *Gravity's Rainbow*. In particular, discussion may be focused on the figure of Tyrone Slothrop, around whom all the tenets of the plot converge. He is, after all, the descendant of Constant and Variable Slothrop and as such is the heir to relentless plots, as *plotting* is the term we use to graph—that is, write—the relation of a constant to a variable. Fittingly, Pynchon introduces us to these ancestors through a meditation on their graveyard plots in the "Congregational churchyard back home in Mingeborough, Massachusetts" (26). The meditation focuses on the mystery surrounding the debt (i.e., death) that life owes to nature: is it a sacred debt or secular, the hand of God or the random implications of a natural world? This tension between constancy and variation follows from the process of identifying the axes and plotting the trajectories they make possible.

Teachers may ask whether or not the novel's language of axis and correlation constitutes another of Pynchon's riffs on the elementary terms of statistical analysis. The geopolitical Axis and the axes of the table of correlation inevitably create readerly suspicions of a rich Pynchonesque connection between the particulars of the Allies' war with the Axis powers and Pynchon's more general concerns with inscrutable otherness. Fathoming the Axis is the purpose of the White Visitation, and identifying the Axis (rocket) trajectories, from the outset of the novel, is the task that sends Slothrop through the ruins where the rockets have landed, looking for clues, trying to find a pattern—that is, a plot. Not surprisingly, in the absence of constants, the secular plot turns for Slothrop into a sacred text in which his actions are correlated in the form of divine narrative: "Ruins he goes daily to look in are each a sermon on vanity. . . . Slothrop's Progress: London the secular city instructs him: turn every corner and he can find himself inside a parable" (25). Is Slothrop the author of this parable or the reader, the creator of the narrative or the Creator's audience?

Students can be invited to discuss Slothrop's plotting, on a graph that is either color-keyed or randomly colored, of his myriad sexual encounters throughout bombed London. Just as the colors may correlate the encounters with a constant scale or merely be the manifestation of random coincidence, so too Slothrop's plotted sexual encounters, which correlate perfectly with the sites where the rockets subsequently land, may reveal the constants that predict the Axis's targets. By the same token, they may be random coincidences. The range of this possibility—that Slothrop can reveal everything or nothing about the Axis—makes Slothrop the object of relentless plotting by an array of characters, each of whom is attempting to define Slothrop's trajectory within a different set of axioms, defined by their set of disciplinary boundaries and assumptions.

The meaning of Slothrop's plotted graph thus correlates strongly with the promotion of disciplinary interests. Slothrop provides the possibility, in other words, of proving one discipline a source of truth. The novel dramatizes this as a battle between Pointsman, the cause-and-effect man, and Mexico, the statistician.

These competing disciplinary forces—in some ways no less vehement than the clashes of (political? social? economic? genetic?) philosophy between Axis and Allies—generate ancillary plots and conspiracies among those ostensibly allied in their desire to define Slothrop: in other words, to grasp the true identity of a character whose numerous "guises or roles," as David Seed notes, "take on such prominence that they smother identity" (162). In *Gravity's Rainbow*, therefore, the acting out of the plots—the attempts to define Slothrop within a certain matrix of cause-and-effect—transforms the plot of a graph into the plot of a fiction. At the same time, since each attempt to define Slothrop depends on an informing narrative, each failure to identify him reveals that the narrative is fictional.

To say then that the attempts to plot Slothrop fail because they do not distinguish constants from variables is to echo Joseph Slade's insight that in *Gravity's Rainbow* "concepts of determinism have been eroded by indeterminacy" (197). One might say the axis of the graph loses its axiomatic status, and without any constant axes the variables are impossible to plot. Indeed, the purported constant of Slothrop's conquests and their location is undermined later in the novel when Speed and Perdoo, on orders from Pointsman, can't find any of the women (Duyfhuizen, "Starry-Eyed Semiotics"). As the ostensive constants (e.g., war, Christianity, pre-Christian religion, physics, behavioral psychology, Freudian psychology, biochemistry, economics, history) become matters of convention, merely the agreement or shared assumptions of self-interested parties, all the novel's plotting reduces to conspiracies: attempts to represent the arbitrary as natural, the random as predictable. But if "correlation characterizes the relationship between variables" (F. Williams 121), then as the constants turn into variables and the variables proliferate, the potential for correlation approaches zero. The resulting inverse correlation indeed demonstrates Pynchon has constructed a world in which information takes one further from, rather than closer to, the possibility of truth. Pynchon's "fictional worlds," Molly Hite reminds us,

> are pluralistic—governed not by a rigid, absolute, universal Idea of Order, but by multiple, partial, overlapping, and often conflicting *ideas* of order. And these worlds are familiar, even when they are most bizarre and surreal, because they evoke a multi-layered reality in which multiple means of putting things together manage to co-exist without resolving into a single, definitive system of organization. (*Ideas* 10)

In one of the novel's fragments, the reader is even teased into guessing what a series of town names have in common—to discover the underlying order of their selection—only to be rebuffed: "Well, you're *wrong*, champ" (*Gravity's Rainbow* 695).

Because ideas of order also underlie reader identification and character identity, teachers may ask students to consider how Pynchon's fictional world also confounds the reader's capacity for identification. If one necessary act of reading is identifying (words, sentences, references, events), another is "identifying with"—that is, constructing a set of correlations between character and reader. Here too the correlations reside not at the poles but in the middle, for a correlation of one would mean that character and reader were completely indistinguishable from each other. By the same token, a correlation of zero would make the character totally unrecognizable as a character. In the end, this zero correlation is exactly what happens to Slothrop. Just as other characters in

*Gravity's Rainbow* become less and less able to locate Slothrop geographically, the reader becomes less and less able to fix him axiomatically, to identify him or to identify with him. In a state of zero correlation, as we have noted, people, objects, acts lose all identity. Slothrop's gradual dissolution, in one of the novel's most hilarious episodes, is described in just these terms, as a narrowing of his "temporal bandwidth" (509).

At the same time, discussion should then seek to situate Slothrop's dissolution within the larger thematic purposes of the novel. The failure of this novelistic convention (that main characters will persist or remain stable) correlates with the implication that one legacy of World War II may be the shattering of constants, to be replaced with self-contained systems, each operating according to its own arbitrary rules of self-regulation (and self-interest). Because the uncanny correlation of Slothrop's sexual encounters to the rocket's destinations, which motivates the novel's relentless plotting, reveals not a systematic explanation but a proliferation of explanatory systems, Slothrop precludes the possibility of a plottable trajectory, becoming instead a multiplicity of coincident events, set free of all axes. To the extent that Slothrop is the central character of *Gravity's Rainbow*, then, the novel can be seen as examining the destabilization of culture, psyche, identity, history, and governance—what Jean-François Lyotard has identified as the postmodern condition of knowledge (*Postmodern Condition*).

This destabilization, through which constants and variables continually exchange roles, operates in the novel on the stylistic plane as well as the cognitive, for the style of the novel similarly evokes shifting voices, points of view, perspectives, and frames of allusion that destabilize the reading by confounding the possibility of a constant authorial authority through which to contextualize the variants. In the absence of constants, the novel's pervasive preoccupation with linkage further intensifies the instability, foregrounding, as Schaub notes, "the difficulty of knowing from the *inside* whether or not a set of events constitutes a designed plot or is merely coincidental" (*Pynchon* 105).

In this context, the idea of selecting for the students—as I do with many other novels—a stylistically or thematically representative passage seemed to suggest a constancy or typicality to the representation in *Gravity's Rainbow* in opposition to the points I make about the book. I am, after all, trying to get my students to realize that information, *Gravity's Rainbow* implies, becomes legible only through systems of interpretation and that interpretation originates not in the object of scrutiny but in the method of the scrutinizer. Any methodology, I argue, depends on privileging one type of interpretation over another. Like a good scholar of the postmodern, I make this case rather consistently throughout the course, and finally I invoke *Gravity's Rainbow* as the piece of privileged information to support my methodology. Since, according to my own claims, if I were to choose a specific passage in the text as representative, I would already be structuring the interpretation of the whole, I have my students choose the passages on the premise that, in trying to do so, they will discover how much that decision predetermines their interpretations. Perhaps this is, however, a needless lesson; the lesson that interpretation does not reside in a text but in a system of privilege may no longer be much of a revelation.

A more complex point, and one much harder to make, is that their own identities, including the way they locate themselves in history, depend on correlation and interpretation. At this point, in other words, I invite them to apply what they have learned about reading, in reading *Gravity's Rainbow,* to their lives. As historical subjects, I suggest, they are both the readers of history and the objects to which history refers. Their sense of their identities—as people of the twentieth century, as Americans, as children of the 1970s and 1980s—relies, analogously, on creating systems of interpretation by privileging specific bits of information. I want them thus to see how their interpretive problems resemble those of *Gravity's Rainbow*, how, even when not writing literature papers (especially when not writing them), they have to negotiate the world by privileging arbitrary, if pragmatic, systems of correlation. I want them to see that, in making their quotidian claims to be real people with real histories, they define themselves in terms of systems of understanding they cannot identify. I try, in other words, not only to help them identify with what, for most of them, is the most bizarre, estranging book they have ever read but also to help them see their attempts at identification as definitive of their cultural cognition and everyday perception.

This is, of course, an absurd aim. Who, for even one moment, would think of himself or herself as Slothrop, much less admit it in writing? The assignment is necessarily, therefore, a compromise, one that (almost) arbitrarily selects topics in hope of demonstrating that correlation creates interpretation and that *Gravity's Rainbow* can be correlated with central concerns of students' lives. To help the class make such correlations, I ask them to select a passage of two hundred to three hundred words from part 3 of *Gravity's Rainbow* that contains shifts in or juxtapositions of narrative voices, points of view, realms of diction, or frames of reference (contextual or metaphorical or both), and then I pose a series of questions: What is the effect of these shifts? What presumptions does the reader have to make to render the passage intelligible? In other parts of the novel that use similar voices, are the voices juxtaposed in the same way or differently? Are there different characters in other parts of the novel that replicate the language, perceptions, or situations of those in this passage? Do the echoes and repetitions help provide a method for constructing the presumptions necessary for reading, or do the echoes and repetitions undermine the process? How? Does the novel: (a) contain, (b) create, (c) destroy, or (d) resurrect information systems? There follows the writing task:

> Consider these questions and write a paper on one of the following topics, using *Gravity's Rainbow* and especially your selected passage from it, as your only source: the nature of love; the search for meaning in an insincere world; the difficulty of finding a rewarding career.

Over the years this assignment has produced a number of respectable papers that demonstrate the students' sensitivity to language and to the problematics of correlation and identification produced by various narrative instabilities. One paper I received seemed not only to get the point but also to enhance the level of analysis, first by contextualizing the reading of *Gravity's Rainbow* within the student's difficulties in finding a career and then by inverting the process, so that Enzian's search in the novel became the context for the student's autobiographical concerns. My student wondered how, for example, he could know when a job became a career and what scale was definitive in measuring its rewards. In the light of the terminology that I have been developing, he wondered in what ways the operative terms that compose the cliché "rewarding career" consisted of dependent or independent variables. For the student, therefore, making sense of *Gravity's Rainbow* was

> like trying to decide if you really, really do have a rewarding career. It all depends upon how you look at it—or, from the perspective of the book, what axes you use to plot the data. It all depends on what narrative you fit the information into . . . on what information system you use."[1]

Through a brilliant interweaving of the context and the contextualized, the paper exposed some of the ways that *Gravity's Rainbow* frustrates interpretation by destabilizing the reader's capacity for identification. In its place, the paper made clear, Pynchon supplied the reader with the means to identify with the process of making meaning:

> [O]ne of the main points of *Gravity's Rainbow* is that if we want or need to make sense of something, all we need to do is believe it's possible, and our paranoid little minds will make the connections. . . . But the flip side of that coin, another main motif of *Gravity's Rainbow*, is that once we start to get a lot of information, we start to make connections that don't make sense, or only make sense from a different perspective. And before long, we have more perspectives than we can put together into a coherent whole. . . . (Jukiri and Nadel 85)

In the two-page excerpt from *Gravity's Rainbow* discussed in the paper, Enzian attempts, unsuccessfully, to situate himself in a coherent narrative, one accommodating the intersection of personal and public history that delimits his life experiences. In the terms I have laid out, he is looking for a set of constants that will allow him to plot the public and the private, the personal and the historical. He is, in other words, attempting to understand the emplotment of his own life in the same way that the reader (and the novel's plethora of surrogate readers) is impelled to comprehend the emplotment of Slothrop.

Unlike the characters in the novel, however, the reader may reasonably expect some help from the author, that figure whose explanatory power is endemic to the history of fictional narrative. But Pynchon's world is one of entropy—that is, one characterized by the diffusion rather than the exertion of power, and that diffusion extends from the details of *Gravity's Rainbow* to the novel's framing authorial authority. Thus, Pynchon makes clear, the author is a theological notion, with the emphasis on "notion": a belief or inclination, a hypothetical source of validity. This notional author becomes part of the thematics in the excerpt discussed in the student's paper, as Enzian seems to treat Weissmann as a Christ figure, "The Deliverer, returned and walking among the people, just the way the old stories promised . . ." (325; ellips. in orig.). The paper points out, however, that Enzian too might be considered a Christ figure, as might Slothrop or even Mexico. "The point here," the paper states, "is that almost anyone can be Christ just as almost any career can be a 'rewarding' career. . . . It depends on whom and what you privilege" (88).

Identifying Christ, therefore, is no different from constructing any other form of correlation. Finding the internal correspondence of themes, images, and details, plotting the correlation between them, identifying patterns in the plotting is a way of making meaning, as much in theological study as in literary criticism and career management.[2]

In understanding exactly how Pynchon undermines access to constants, students thus gain some understanding not only of Pynchon's engagement with the entropy of information systems but also of the ways in which disparate, often competing modes of literary criticism can produce viable understandings of texts. Finally, in seeing interpretation and analysis as a process rather than a goal, students may become more attuned to the textual aspects of culture, as well as to the constructed narrative by which they live their lives.

## NOTES

[1] The full text of Stephen Jukiri's essay appears in *Pynchon Notes* (Jukiri and Nadel).

[2] Among Pynchon critics, Katherine Hume does the best job of finding and explicating coherent patterns in the novel.

# Pynchon, Kant, Lyotard, and the Sublime

*Zofia Kolbuszewska*

> This sadness . . . for those things which men do to one another . . . is sublime. . . .
>
> —Immanuel Kant

> [L]et us be witnesses to the unpresentable.
>
> —Jean-François Lyotard

*The Crying of Lot 49* begins with the news that Oedipa Maas has become the executrix of Pierce Inverarity's will, which interrupts her boring suburban existence and starts her on a quest that originates in her unsuccessful attempts to make sense of an ever-elusive, threatening Tristero looming behind Inverarity's estate. Early in the novel the protagonist recalls a moment of terror she experienced on seeing a picture by Remedios Varo of girls embroidering a "kind of tapestry which spilled out the slit windows and into a void, seeking hopelessly to fill the void" (12). Oedipa starts crying, overwhelmed with anxiety and fear at the thought of nothingness.

Since the eighteenth century the sublime has often been considered an antidote to rapidly spreading boredom, whose intensity has been symptomatic of the most basic of modern anxieties: the anxiety of nothingness, or absence. The sublime is a kind of "homeopathic therapy" by means of the stronger but momentary anxiety involved in astonishment and terror (Weiskel 18). Indeed, Oedipa's quest can be interpreted as an encounter with the sublime that effects a "terror therapy," whose abrupt thwarting by the open ending seems designed as an aesthetic shock therapy for the reader.

I suggest reading the novel in the light of the concept of the sublime as understood by Immanuel Kant and reconsidered by Jean-François Lyotard. The idea of reading *Lot 49* in terms of Kantian and Lyotardian sublime occurred to me a few years ago owing to a lucky sequence of student questions. During a discussion a student shared her insight that to her Oedipa's position with respect to the Nefastis machine resembles that occupied by the God of deists. Another student asked whether despite the abrupt ending it might still be possible to determine the moral and ontological status of Tristero, and still another questioned the psychological credibility of Oedipa's exhaustion. Somebody else posited that Oedipa's lack of familiarity with the situation of the disinherited must testify to her moral blindness, which provoked someone else to counter that her encounter with the sailor and the revelation of mortality she experiences testify to her moral sensitivity.

These queries and observations made me think of the structure of Kantian sublime because the concept simultaneously engages such questions as the problem of the ontological status of the world (reconsidered in Kant's system as an epistemological issue), the problem of a realm beyond the sensible world and its traumatic revelation in the sublime experience, and the problem of human moral sensibility. The essential appeal of the sublime is the promise of transcending the human in the direction of the inscrutable beyond, often represented as a flight toward dizzying heights or a downward fall into an infinite abyss. The aesthetic interest and difficulty of the sublime rest precisely in the problem of its (re)presentation. Whereas for Kant the Mosaic law interdiction on making a graven image is most sublime (*Judgment* 115; sec. 29), an influx of creative power in the Romantic sublime is often presented by elision and then metonymically diffused over space or time (Weiskel 29). Modernism sought formal means to present the unrepresentable, while postmodern sublime consists in presenting the unpresentable in the very presentation. Finally, the ethical interest of the sublime lies in its power to reveal to subjects not only the internal contradictions of their mind but also their predisposition to moral feeling. According to Kant, "[T]he sublime is that, the mere ability to think which shows a faculty of the mind surpassing every standard of sense" (*Judgment* 89; sec. 25). Thus the sublime can be seen as linking incommensurate discourses and understood in terms of a metaphor or Lyotard's "differend."

Although in section 59 of the *Critique of Judgment* Kant states that beauty is the symbol of the morally good (196, 198; sec. 59), it is the experience of the sublime rather than that of the beautiful that reveals the human to him- or herself as subject to moral law (109; sec. 29). The philosopher observes that in the sublime judgment, unlike in that of the beautiful, the imagination is constantly referred to reason on "a subjective presupposition . . . viz. The presupposition of the moral feeling [in human beings]" (106; sec. 29). Sublime feeling cannot thus be identified with moral feeling. However, Kant emphasizes that only predisposition to moral feeling makes the subject susceptible to the sublime: "a feeling for the sublime in nature cannot well be thought without combining therewith a mental disposition which is akin to the moral" (109; sec. 29). This moral predisposition governed by practical reason operates in the sublime in the interest of moral ends and contains the disturbing power of imagination by stopping its progress beyond proper limits, to infinity (*Judgment* 89, 108–09; secs. 25, 29; *Practical Reason* 42; sec. 48). It thus follows that instead of granting any concrete knowledge, the clash with the finitude of imagination and the subsequent revelation of the supersensible in the sublime experience reveal to the subject the might of the moral law that enjoins him or her to exercise freedom by acting morally (*Judgment* 111–12; sec. 29)—that is, in accordance with the moral law inherent in practical reason, which is the fundamental law of a supersensible nature (*Practical Reason* 38; sec. 43).

Kant distinguishes two types of the sublime. In the dynamic sublime, imagination raises the human being above nature's power and elevates human dignity above the world of nature. In contrast, in the experience of the mathematical sublime, imagination collapses, defeated by reason when attempting to present boundlessness or absolute magnitude.

Conversely, Lyotard's discussion of the conflict of reason and imagination in the sublime in terms of "the differend" manifests a distrust of reason (*Lessons* 125). The philosopher defines the differend as a conflict between two heterogeneous phrases or genres that "cannot be equitably resolved for lack of the rule of judgment applicable to both arguments" (*Differend* xi).

The differend instantiates the situation when something unspeakable that must be articulated cannot yet be put into phrases. "This state includes silence." Literature, philosophy, and—Lyotard adds—perhaps politics are called to bear witness to differends by finding idioms for them. He suggests that the traumatic experience of a (Holocaust) victim is sublime in the sense that the victim's experience can only be felt in a silence that defies rational thought (13–14).

The philosopher claims that the sublime can be understood as an extreme case of the beautiful where imagination runs wild in its proliferation of forms. In the postmodern sublime it is the excess of form rather than the inability of the imagination that is at issue (*Lessons* 75). Lyotard challenges the primacy of reason as the highest authority and questions its ability to contain the disturbing power of imagination in the sublime.

Before commencing the classroom discussion of Pynchon's novels in the light of Kantian and Lyotardian sublime, the teacher might consider preparing a packet of materials to be handed out in class: definitions and brief explanations of such terms and concepts as boredom and melancholy, the categorical imperative, discourse, entropy and Maxwell's demon, *epistemological*, metaphor, *ontological*, and the sublime; passages from Kant's *Critique of Judgment* (perhaps a list of the quotations discussed in this essay or, better, copies of entire sections of Kant's Third Critique with the quotations highlighted)—*Judgment*, secs. 23, 25–29, and 86; *Practical Reason*, secs. 43 and 48; and the quotations from Lyotard presented in this essay (either in the context of the texts they are culled from or on their own). I also recommend showing the students a reproduction of Remedios Varo's painting depicting girls embroidering the mantle of the earth. If time allows for brief presentations by students, I suggest asking them to prepare a general overview of Kant and Lyotard, to be given before discussion of *The Crying of Lot 49* commences.

The start of Oedipa's survey of Inverarity's estate in San Narciso is marked by an "odd, religious instant" (24), when the sight of a sprawl of houses viewed from a slope forces on her memory the image of a printed circuit. Subsequently, revelations and signs proliferate that in a paranoid way appear to refer to an enigmatic and mysterious organization, Tristero. This phenomenon elicits feelings in Oedipa that resemble the reaction of the mind facing the task of presenting to itself "what is great beyond all comparison," something "absolutely great," which Kant calls "sublime" (*Judgment* 86; sec. 25). Toward the end of the quest it seems that it is America that is "coded in Inverarity's testament" (*Lot 49* 180). The nebulous network of networks Oedipa faces presents itself to her as something that extends in all directions and dimensions, something formless and boundless, beyond her grasp. It can therefore be regarded as mathematically sublime in the Kantian sense: "the sublime . . . is to be found in a formless object, so far as in it or by occasion of it boundlessness is represented, and yet its totality is also present to thought" (Kant, *Judgment* 82; sec. 23). Accordingly, when ascribing the disappearance of her men in its dark machinations, Oedipa thinks of Tristero as a limitless menace.

Oedipa is overwhelmed by acronyms, signs depicting muted horns, stamps, and different endings of Wharfinger's play, all pointing to the cryptic Tristero. This saturation of Oedipa's perception can also be construed in Lyotardian terms as the feeling of the sublime prompted by the imagination gone wild in proliferating forms (*Lessons* 75). The signs are emblematic of various incommensurate and incompatible discourses that in projecting conflicting visions of America give rise to a differend that the prevailing paranoia links into one great and powerful net of the sublime Tristero. At this point the teacher may draw the students' attention to the fact that the differend yielded by the various discourses Oedipa encounters signals different possible interpretations of the moral status of Tristero: as the individualistic and egotistic American tradition of success, as a force enjoining a feeling of solidarity with the victimized and marginalized, or, paradoxically, as an ambiguous phenomenon that embraces both of these possibilities.

Oedipa's senses and imagination are overpowered, which leads to a feeling of exhaustion and dejection. According to Kant, the feeling of the sublime "is produced by the feeling of a momentary checking of the vital powers and a consequent stronger outflow of them, so that it seems regarded as emotion" (*Judgment* 83; sec. 23). Oedipa's energy has been drained: " 'It's over,' she said, 'they've saturated me. From here on I'll close them out' " (177). Kant describes the state of indisputable frustration felt by Oedipa thus: "For there is here a feeling of the inadequacy of . . . imagination for presenting the ideas of a whole, wherein the Imagination reaches its maximum, and, in striving to surpass it, sinks back into itself . . ." (*Judgment* 91; sec. 26). Oedipa is haunted by the thought of the void and the abyss. Indeed, Kant points out that "[t]he transcendent . . . is for the imagination like an abyss in which it fears to lose itself" (*Judgment* 97; sec. 27). Oedipa feels like a "fluttering curtain in a very high window, moving up to then out over the abyss," and later she again has a "vertiginous sense of fluttering out over an abyss" (152–53, 156). Sitting at night, hardly able to "breathe in a vacuum," she realizes that "this, oh God, [is] the void" (171). The narration ends abruptly, in an auction room, short of the sublime moment of revelation, leaving the protagonist in pain rather than granting her the satisfaction of "a pleasure that arises only indirectly" in the sublime experience, an experience that, as Kant stresses, is a mixture of pain and pleasure (Kant, *Judgment* 83; sec. 23).

Nefastis's machine functions in the novel as a parodic thematization of the sublime experience. The apparatus can be seen as a model of the mind, which in a mysterious way—through an operation carried out by a demon—links two incommensurate discourses, as happens in the sublime experience. Designed to operate in material reality, the machine is a literalization of a metaphor that connects notions of entropy borrowed from different disciplines and therefore mockingly demonstrates the outcome of a misguided attempt to settle a differend by a rule of judgment applicable only to one argument.

To her chagrin, Oedipa fails to put Nefastis's machine in motion, thereby apparently proving her insensitivity. The experiment's lack of success emphasizes the impossibility of conceiving of a settled differend (Lyotard, *Differend* xi, 5–6) or a literal sublime (Weiskel 4), in which the incommensurability of the sensible and supersensible discourses is reduced to the material, sensible pole. Indeed, in Nefastis's experiment information is considered to belong to the thermodynamic realm, while Oedipa's position in relation to the machine is that of Kant's supreme Being, whose presence legislates human morality (*Judgment* 295; sec. 86). In Kantian terms, Oedipa should thus be located outside sensible nature. The experiment fails because she, like the apparatus, is a part of the sensible world. On the other hand, according to Kant, the final purpose of the human being—namely, to act morally as a free agent—can be actualized only in nature and in accordance with its laws (32–33; sec. 9).

The teacher might explain at this point that what the failure of the experiment shows is that moral purpose emerges from the incommensurability, a gap between the supersensible and the sensible, and the supersensible legislation of morality is as indispensable as its exercise in the sensible world. Appositely, Oedipa's moral sensitivity and compassion are revealed in her encounter with a dying sailor while she is roaming the debris-filled landscape of the America of the disinherited.

Oedipa's awakened moral sensibility prompts her to explore this disinherited America. Her exploration brings her face to face with the conflict between the witness she bears and the authority of the tradition of the "founding father[s]" reflected in Pierce's legacy (26). Here, the teacher can remind the students of the ambiguity of Oedipa's relation to what could turn out to be Tristero-as-the-whole-of-America, or alternatively, the teacher might ask them to describe it themselves.

Oedipa is both repelled and attracted: she does not want to be engulfed, yet she is on the verge of letting herself dissolve in Tristero. The mysterious network appears to loom large as both Kantian sublime and Lyotardian differend, leaving Oedipa torn between the imperative to follow the moral injunctions of America's founding fathers to become rich and successful and the call to bear witness to the victimization of the disinherited who suffer in silence.

Compelling as the American dream of success may be, Oedipa cannot pass over the victimized and disinherited. This suspension is signaled on the plane of form and becomes a reader experience by virtue of the novel's open ending. At this point the teacher might ask students to discuss whether one can see a correspondence between the plot of the novel and Lyotard's view on the postmodern sublime and whether the presentation of the unpresentable can be connected with the sublimity of the victims' plight.

Pynchon's formal solution foregoes any ideological determination of Oedipa's identity and her knowledge of the world; nor does it enable us to establish the ontological status of Tristero or its authority to legislate moral choices. Thus, the Kantian impossibility of presenting the infinite turns into Lyotardian "postmodern" sublime: "The postmodern would be that which . . . puts forward the unpresentable in presentation itself" (Lyotard, "Answering" 81). Pynchon places a void, a tear, in the texture of the novel. The form, the fabric of signifiers, does not veil a void. The veil itself is torn.

In this manner the reader's attention is drawn to the moment of radical disorientation that, in its indeterminacy, enables the relation between the cognizing mind (Oedipa's) and the sensible world (this one) and the moral horizon it offers to take any number of forms, without excluding the possibility, paradoxical from the point of binary logic, that all these forms can hold true simultaneously. The teacher can emphasize the point by putting it differently: the sense of potential conveyed by the open ending of the novel comes from that ending's suggestion that it might be possibile to identify with the legacy of America without endorsing its rejection and victimization of the disinherited.

## NOTE

The epigraphs to this essay are taken from Kant's *The Critique of Judgment* (117; sec. 29) and Lyotard's "Answering the Question: 'What Is Postmodernism?' " (82).

# NOTES ON CONTRIBUTORS

**Hanjo Berressem** is professor of American studies at the University of Cologne. He is the author of *Pynchon's Poetics: Interfacing Theory and Text* (1992), *Lines of Desire: Reading Gombrowicz's Fiction with Lacan* (1998), and with P. Hofmann edited *Chaos-Control / Complexity: Chaos Theory and the Human Sciences* (2002).

**David Cowart** is Louise Fry Scudder Professor at the University of South Carolina, Columbia. He is the author of *Thomas Pynchon: The Art of Allusion* (1980), *Arches and Light: The Fiction of John Gardner* (1983), *History and the Contemporary Novel* (1989), *Literary Symbiosis: The Reconfigured Text in Twentieth-Century Writing* (1993), *Don DeLillo: The Physics of Language* (2002), and *Trailing Clouds: Immigrant Writing in America after 1970* (2006).

**Inger H. Dalsgaard** is associate professor of American studies at the University of Aarhus. The author of numerous articles on British and American literature and culture, from Mary Shelley to Melville to Pynchon, she is currently working on a book on the perceptions of technological progress in American society and literature and a book on American first ladies.

**Amy J. Elias** is associate professor of English at the University of Tennessee, Knoxville. She has published essays on postmodern art and culture, narrative theory, historiography, and novels by international contemporary authors. She is the author of *Sublime Desire: History and Post-1960s Fiction* (2001) and is at work on a book concerning dialogism and contemporary art.

**Norbert Finzsch** is professor of history at the University of Cologne. He is the author and editor of books on United States and German historical topics, including *Identity and Intolerance* (1998), edited with Dietmar Schirmer; *Institutions of Confinement* (1996), edited with Robert Jütte; and *Atlantic Communications* (2004), edited with Ursula Lehmkuhl. His research and teaching interests include the history of sexualities, genders, and racisms and theories of narrative in historiography.

**Michael Harris** is professor of English at Central College. He is the author of articles on Edna O'Brien, Pynchon, Rushdie, Conrad, and Patrick White. His *Outsiders and Insiders: Perspectives of Third World Culture in British and Post-colonial Fiction* (1993) was named a *Choice* Outstanding Academic Book of 1994. His current project is cultural memory in the work of J. M. Coetzee and the saxophonist John Coltrane.

**Luc Herman** is professor of American literature and narrative theory at the University of Antwerp. He has published *Concepts of Realism* (1996); has edited the proceedings of the Antwerp conference on *Gravity's Rainbow* (1998) for the journal *Pynchon Notes*; has cowritten and translated, with Bart Vervaeck, *Handbook of Narrative Analysis* (2005); and, along with John Krafft, has just completed a series of essays on the typescript of Pynchon's *V.* at the Harry Ransom Center in Austin.

**Molly Hite** is professor of English at Cornell University. She is the author of *Ideas of Order in the Novels of Thomas Pynchon* (1983), named a *Choice* Outstanding Book, and *The Other Side of the Story: Structures and Strategies of Contemporary Feminist*

*Narrative* (1992), as well as two novels: *Class Porn* (1987) and *Breach of Immunity* (1992). She is at work on *Weird Woolf: Tonal Cues, Polemical Precedents, and Modernism.*

**Zofia Kolbuszewska** is assistant professor of English at Catholic University of Lublin. She is the author of articles on Pynchon, American postmodernism, American gothic, and ekphrasis in American literature and of *The Poetics of Chronotope in the Novels of Thomas Pynchon* (2000). Her current projects include the sublime and apocryphal mode in Pynchon's works and the image of the gothic child in American literature.

**Deborah L. Madsen** is professor of American literature and culture at the University of Geneva. She is the author of *The Postmodernist Allegories of Thomas Pynchon* (1991), *Rereading Allegory: A Narrative Approach to Genre* (1994), *Allegory in America: From Puritanism to Postmodernism* (1996), *American Exceptionalism* (1998), *Feminist Theory and Literary Practice* (2000), and several books that reflect her growing interest in American multiculturalism: *Maxine Hong Kingston* (2000), *Understanding Contemporary Chicana Literature* (2000), and *Chinese American Literature* (2002). She is president of the Swiss Association for North American Studies.

**Robert L. McLaughlin** is professor of English at Illinois State University. He is author of essays on the work of Thomas Pynchon and of *We'll Always Have the Movies: American Cinema during World War II* (2006), cowritten with Sally E. Parry. He is the editor of *Innovations: An Anthology of Modern and Contemporary Fiction* (1998).

**Alan Nadel** is William T. Bryan Professor of American Literature at the University of Kentucky. He is the author of *Invisible Criticism: Ralph Ellison and the American Canon* (1988), *Containment Culture: American Narratives, Postmodernism, and the Atomic Age* (1995), *Flatlining on the Field of Dreams: Cultural Narratives in the Films of Ronald Reagan's America* (1997), and *Television in Black-and-White America: Race and National Identity* (2005).

**Stacey Olster** is professor of English at the State University of New York, Stony Brook. She is the author of *Reminiscence and Re-Creation in Contemporary American Fiction* (1989) and *The Trash Phenomenon: Contemporary Literature, Popular Culture, and the Making of the American Century* (2003) and editor of *The Cambridge Companion to John Updike* (2006).

**Alison T. J. Preston** is lecturer in English at California Polytechnic State University. She has published an essay on Pynchon in the *Arkansas Review* (1996), a study of using literature to teach multicultural composition in the *CATESOL Journal* (2005), and essays on California in *California History* (2005) and *Cal Poly Land: A Field Guide* (2002). Her research and teaching interests include contemporary literature, second language acquisition, composition pedagogy, and environmental studies.

**Mark Rohland** is an administrator in the College of Liberal Arts at Temple University. He has published on Pynchon in *Pynchon Notes*, written articles and edited books on education policy issues, conducted research on teacher quality in the United States, and taught literature at several colleges.

**Todd Rohman** is associate professor of English at Governors State University. His research and teaching interests include literary theory and criticism, postmodern studies, film, and American Romanticism. His essay on protest as fantasy in DeLillo's *Cosmopolis* appeared in *English Studies Forum* (2005).

**Thomas H. Schaub** is professor of English at the University of Wisconsin, Madison. He has published essays on James Fenimore Cooper, William Carlos Williams, Richard Wright, Ralph Ellison, and Thomas Pynchon. He is the author of *Pynchon: The Voice of Ambiguity* (1981) and *American Fiction in the Cold War* (1991) and is editor of *Contemporary Literature*. His interests include the politics of culture and environmental studies.

**Gary Thompson** is professor of English at Saginaw Valley State University. His essay on Pynchonian pastiche appeared in *Thomas Pynchon: Reading from the Margins* (2003). He is the author of *Rhetoric through Media* (1997) and is researching the connections among performance theory, rhetoric, and electronic media.

**Jerry Varsava** is professor of comparative literature and English and associate dean, Faculty of Graduate Studies and Research at the University of Alberta. He has published articles on Hemingway, DeLillo, Coover, Abish, Pynchon, Wideman, Wolfe, Musil, Handke, Calvino, and Houellebecq. He is the author of *Contingent Meanings: Postmodern Fiction, Mimesis, and the Reader* (1990) and is at work on a monograph, "The Dialectics of Self and Other: The Contemporary American Social Novel."

**Robert N. Watson** is professor of English at the University of California, Los Angeles. He won the 2001 campus-wide Distinguished Teaching Award and the 2006–08 Gold Shield Faculty Prize. His books include *Back to Nature: The Green and the Real in the Late Renaissance* (2006; awarded the Association for the Study of Literature and the Environment prize for the best book of ecocritical scholarship and the Dietz Memorial prize for the year's best book on early modern literature), *The Rest Is Silence* (1994), *Ben Jonson's Parodic Strategy* (1987), and *Shakespeare and the Hazards of Ambition* (1984).

**Steven Weisenburger** is professor of English and Mossiker Chair in the Humanities at Southern Methodist University. He is the author of *Fables of Subversion: Satire and the American Novel, 1930–1980* (1995), A Gravity's Rainbow *Companion: Sources and Contexts for Pynchon's Novel* (rev. ed. 2005), and *Modern Medea: A Family Story of Slavery and Child-Murder from the Old South* (1998).

# SURVEY PARTICIPANTS

Hanjo Berressem, *University of Cologne*
David Cowart, *University of South Carolina, Columbia*
Inger H. Dalsgaard, *University of Aarhus*
Barbara Eckstein, *University of Iowa*
Amy J. Elias, *University of Tennessee, Knoxville*
Norbert Finzsch, *University of Cologne*
Michael Harris, *Central College*
Katherine Hayles, *University of California, Los Angeles*
Luc Herman, *University of Antwerp*
Tessa Hines
Molly Hite, *Cornell University*
Zofia Kolbuszewska, *Catholic University of Lublin*
Stan Kozikowski, *Bryant College*
John M. Krafft, *Miami University, Hamilton*
W. T. Lhamon, Jr., *Florida State University*
Deborah L. Madsen, *University of Geneva*
Ernest Mathijs, *Vrije University, Brussels*
Robert L. McLaughlin, *Illinois State University*
Alan Nadel, *University of Kentucky*
James Neighbors, *Wofford College*
Stacey Olster, *State University of New York, Stony Brook*
Alison T. J. Preston, *California Polytechnic State University*
Tracy J. Prince, *University of British Columbia*
Mark Rohland, *Temple University*
Todd Rohman, *Governors State University*
Lance Schachterle, *Worcester Polytechnic Institute*
Joseph Tabbi, *University of Illinois, Chicago*
Gary Thompson, *Saginaw Valley State University*
Jerry Varsava, *University of Alberta*
Robert N. Watson, *University of California, Los Angeles*
Steven Weisenburger, *Southern Methodist University*

# WORKS CITED


Abbas, Niran, ed. *Thomas Pynchon: Reading from the Margins*. Madison: Fairleigh Dickinson UP, 2003.

Aberbach, Joel D., and Jack L. Walker. *Race in the City*. Boston: Little, 1973.

Achebe, Chinua. "Named for Victoria, Queen of England." *Morning Yet on Creation Day*. Garden City: Anchor, 1976. 95–103.

Adams, Henry. *The Education of Henry Adams*. 1906. Boston: Houghton, 1961.

Aitchison, Cara, Nicola E. Macleod, and Stephen J. Shaw. *Leisure and Tourism Landscapes: Social and Cultural Geographies*. New York: Routledge, 2000.

Appiah, Kwame Anthony. *In My Father's House: Africa in the Philosophy of Culture*. Oxford: Oxford UP, 1992.

Arendt, Hannah. *Eichmann in Jerusalem: A Report on the Banality of Evil*. London: Faber, 1963.

Ashe, Frederick. "Anachronism Intended: *Gravity's Rainbow* in the Sociopolitical Sixties." *Pynchon Notes* 28-29 (1991): 59–75.

Baker, Jeffrey S. "A Democratic Pynchon: Counterculture, Counterforce, and Participatory Democracy." *Pynchon Notes* 32-33 (1993): 99–131.

Bakhtin, Mikhail. *The Dialogic Imagination: Four Essays*. Ed. Michael Holquist. Trans. Caryl Emerson and Holquist. Austin: U of Texas P, 1981.

———. "Discourse in the Novel." Bakhtin, *Dialogic Imagination* 259–422.

———. "Epic and Novel." Bakhtin, *Dialogic Imagination* 3–40.

———. "From the Prehistory of Novelistic Discourse." Bakhtin, *Dialogic Imagination* 41–83.

Baldwin, James. *The Fire Next Time*. 1963. New York: Vintage, 1993.

Barth, John. "The Literature of Exhaustion." *Atlantic Monthly* Aug. 1967: 29–34.

Baudrillard, Jean. "The Precession of Simulacra." *Art and Text* 11 (1983): 3–47. Rpt. in *Art after Modernism: Rethinking Representation*. Ed. Brian Wallis. New York: New Museum of Contemporary Art; Boston: Godine, 1984. 253–81.

Baxter, Charles. "De-faced America: *The Great Gatsby* and *The Crying of Lot 49*." *Pynchon Notes* 7 (1981): 22–37.

Baym, Nina, et al., eds. *The Norton Anthology of American Literature*. Vol. 1. New York: Norton, 1994.

Beidler, Philip. *Scriptures for a Generation: What We Were Reading in the '60s*. Athens: U of Georgia P, 1994.

Bellah, Robert, Robert Madsen, William M. Sullivan, Ann Swidler, and Steven M. Tipton. *Habits of the Heart: Individualism and Commitment in American Life*. 1985. Updated ed. Berkeley: U of California P, 1996.

Benjamin, Walter. *The Arcades Project*. Trans. Howard Eiland and Kevin McLaughlin. Cambridge: Belknap–Harvard UP, 2002.

Bercovitch, Sacvan. *The American Jeremiad*. Madison: U of Wisconsin P, 1978.

Bergh, Patricia. "(De)Constructing the Image: Thomas Pynchon's Postmodern Woman." *Journal of Popular Culture* 30 (1997): 1–12.

Berlin, Isaiah. "Two Concepts of Liberty." *Four Essays on Liberty*. London: Oxford UP, 1969. 118–72.

Berressem, Hanjo. *Pynchon's Poetics: Interfacing Theory and Text.* Urbana: U of Illinois P, 1993.

Bérubé, Michael. *Marginal Forces / Cultural Centers: Tolson, Pynchon, and the Politics of the Canon*. Ithaca: Cornell UP, 1992.

Bhabha, Homi. "The Other Question: Stereotype, Discrimination, and the Discourse of Colonialism." *The Location of Culture*. New York: Routledge, 1994. 66–84.

Black, Joel. "The Hermeneutics of Extinction: Denial and Discovery in Scientific Literature." *Comparative Criticism: A Yearbook* 13 (1991): 147–69.

Blackford, Russell. "Physics and Fantasy: Scientific Mysticism, Kurt Vonnegut, and *Gravity's Rainbow*." *Journal of Popular Culture* 19 (1985): 35–44.

Blaine, Diana York. "Death and *The Crying of Lot 49*." Abbas 51–70.

Bloom, Alexander, and Wini Breines. *"Takin' It to the Streets": A Sixties Reader*. 2nd ed. New York: Oxford UP, 2003.

Bloom, Harold, ed. *Thomas Pynchon's* Gravity's Rainbow. New York: Chelsea, 1986.

Blunt, Alison, and Gillian Rose, eds. *Writing Women and Space: Colonial and Postcolonial Geographies*. New York: Guilford, 1994.

Boltzmann, Ludwig. *Lectures on Gas Theory*. Trans. Stephen G. Brush. New York: Dover, 1995.

Booker, M. Keith. "America and Its Discontents: The Failure of Leftist Politics in Pynchon's *Vineland*." *Literature Interpretation Theory* 4 (1993): 87–99.

Borges, Jorge Luis. *Labyrinths*. New York: New Directions, 1962.

———. "The Library of Babel." Trans. James E. Irby. *HyperDiscordia*. Ed. Joe Formoso. 13 Mar. 2003. 11 July 2007 <http://jubal.westnet.com/hyperdiscordia/library_of_babel.html>.

Breithaupt, Jim. *Physics*. London: Hodder, 2002.

Brown, Norman O. *Life against Death: The Psychoanalytical Meaning of History*. Middletown: Wesleyan UP, 1959.

Browning, Robert. *Childe Roland to the Dark Tower Came*. *Poems of Robert Browning*. Ed. Donald Smalley. Boston: Houghton, 1956. 162–68.

Brückner, Martin. *The Geographic Revolution in Early America: Maps, Literacy, and National Identity*. Chapel Hill: U of North Carolina P, 2006.

Caesar, Terry. "Motherhood and Postmodernism." *American Literary History* 7 (1995): 120–40.

Calvino, Italo. *Invisible Cities.* Trans. William Weaver. New York: Vintage, 1987.

Camus, Albert. *"The Myth of Sisyphus" and Other Essays*. 1942. Trans. Justin O'Brien. New York: Vintage, 1955.

———. *The Stranger*. Trans. Matthew Wood. New York: Vintage, 1989.

Carter, Dale. *The Final Frontier: The Rise and Fall of the American Rocket State*. London: Verso, 1988.

Castles, Stephen, and Alastair Davidson. *Citizenship and Migration: Globalization and the Politics of Belonging*. New York: Routledge, 2000.

Chambers, Erve. *Native Tours: The Anthropology of Travel and Tourism*. Prospect Heights: Waveland, 1999.

Chase, Richard. *The American Novel and Its Tradition*. London: Bell, 1957.

Chatwin, Bruce. *The Songlines*. New York: Penguin, 1999.

Clerc, Charles, ed. *Approaches to* Gravity's Rainbow. Columbus: Ohio State UP, 1983.

———. *Mason & Dixon & Pynchon*. Lanham: UP of America, 2000.

Clifford, James. *Routes: Travel and Translation in the Twentieth Century*. Cambridge: Harvard UP, 1997.

Coe, Justin Scott. "Haunting and Hunting: Bodily Resurrection and the Occupation of History in *Mason & Dixon*." *Reconstruction* 2.1 (2002). 10 Nov. 2006 <http://www.reconstruction.eserver.org/021/Haunting.htm>.

Coetzee, J. M. *Waiting for the Barbarians*. New York: Vintage, 2004.

Conway, Martin. *Collaboration in Belgium: Léon Degrelle and the Rexist Movement, 1940–1944*. New Haven: Yale UP, 1993.

Cooley, Ronald W. "The Hothouse or the Street: Imperialism and Narrative in Pynchon's *V.*" *Modern Fiction Studies* 39 (1993): 307–25.

Cooper, James Fenimore. *The Pioneers*. 1823. New York: Signet, 1980.

Cooper, Peter L. *Signs and Symptoms: Thomas Pynchon and the Contemporary World*. Berkeley: U of California P, 1983.

Cornis-Pope, Marcel. *Narrative Innovation and Cultural Rewriting in the Cold War and After*. New York: Palgrave, 2001.

Cornwell, Neil. "Skaz Narrative." *The Literary Encyclopedia*. 8 June 2005. Literary Dictionary Company. 6 June 2007 <http://www.litencyc.com/php/stopics.php?rec=true@UID=1561>.

Coveney, Peter, and Roger Highfield. *The Arrow of Time: A Voyage through Science to Solve Time's Greatest Mystery*. New York: Fawcett, 1990.

Cowan, James. *Mapmaker's Dream: Meditations of Fra Mauro*. Boston: Shambala, 1996.

Cowart, David. "Pynchon and the Sixties." *Critique: Studies in Contemporary Fiction* 41 (1999): 3–12.

———. *Thomas Pynchon: The Art of Allusion*. Carbondale: Southern Illinois UP, 1980.

Crang, Mike, and N. J. Thrift, eds. *Thinking Space*. New York: Routledge, 2000.

Crownshaw, Richard. "*Gravity's Rainbow*: Pynchon's Holocaust Allegory." Herman, *Approach* 199–212.

Davidson, Cathy. "Oedipa as Androgyne in Thomas Pynchon's *The Crying of Lot 49*." *Contemporary Literature* 18 (1977): 38–50.

DeLillo, Don. *White Noise*. New York: Viking, 1985.

D'haen, Theo. "Postmodern Gothic." *Exhibited by Candlelight: Sources and Developments in the Gothic Tradition*. Ed. Valeria Tinkler-Villani, Peter Davidson, and Jane Stevenson. Amsterdam: Rodopi, 1995. 283–94.

Dorling, Daniel, and David Fairbairn. *Mapping: Ways of Representing the World*. Harlow: Addison, 1997.

Dos Passos, John. *The Big Money*. Vol. 1 of Dos Passos, *U.S.A.*

———. *U.S.A.* 3 vols. 1938. New York: Modern Lib.–Random, n.d.

Douglas, J. Yellowlees. " 'How Do I Stop This Thing?': Closure and Indeterminacy in Interactive Narratives." *Hyper/Text/Theory*. Ed. George Landow. Baltimore: Johns Hopkins UP, 1994, 159–88.

Dudar, Helen. "Pynchon: The Man Who Won't Come to Dinner." *Los Angeles Times* 22 Apr. 1974, calendar section: 6.

Duncan, James, and Derek Gregory, eds. *Writes of Passage: Reading Travel Writing*. New York: Routledge, 1999.

Duncan, Nancy, ed. *Bodyspace: Destabilizing Geographies of Gender and Sexuality*. London: Routledge, 1996.

Duyfhuizen, Bernard. " 'Hushing Sick Transmissions': Disrupting Story in *The Crying of Lot 49*." O'Donnell, *New Essays* 79–95.

———. "Starry-Eyed Semiotics: Learning to Read Slothrop's Map and *Gravity's Rainbow*." *Pynchon Notes* 6 (1981): 5–33.

———. " 'A Suspension Forever at the Hinge of Doubt': The Reader-Trap of Bianca in *Gravity's Rainbow*." *Postmodern Culture: An Electronic Journal of Interdisciplinary Criticism* 2 (1991).

Dworkin, Ronald. *Sovereign Virtue: The Theory and Practice of Equality*. Cambridge: Harvard UP, 2000.

Eco, Umberto. *Travels in Hyperreality*. Trans. William Weaver. San Diego: Harcourt, 1986.

Eliade, Mircea. *The Sacred and the Profane: The Nature of Religion*. New York: Harcourt, 1959.

Elias, Amy J. *Sublime Desire: History and Post-1960s Fiction*. Baltimore: Johns Hopkins UP, 2001.

Eliot, T. S. "Ulysses, Order, and Myth." *Selected Prose of T. S. Eliot*. Ed. Frank Kermode. New York: Harcourt, 1975. 175–78.

Emerson, Ralph Waldo. "Nature." 1836. Baym et al. 993–1021.

Evans, Sara. *Personal Politics: The Roots of Women's Liberation in the Civil Rights Movement and the New Left*. New York: Random, 1980.

*eXistenZ*. Dir. David Cronenberg. DVD. Dimension, 1999.

Fanon, Frantz. *Black Skin, White Masks*. Trans. Charles Marksmann. New York: Grove, 1967.

Fariña, Richard. *Long Time Coming and a Long Time Gone*. New York: Random, 1969.

Feidelson, Charles, Jr. *Symbolism and American Literature*. 1953. Chicago: U of Chicago P, 1959.

Fernie, J. Donald. "Transits, Travels, and Tribulations, II." *American Scientist* 85 (1997): 120–22.

Feynman, Richard. *The Character of Physical Law*. 1965. New York: Modern Lib., 1994.

Fitzgerald, F. Scott. *The Crack-Up*. Ed. Edmund Wilson. New York: New Directions, 1945.

Foreman, David. "Historical Documents Relating to *Mason & Dixon.*" Horvath and Malin 143–66.

Forster, E. M. *Aspects of the Novel*. London: Arnold, 1927.

Foucault, Michel. *Discipline and Punish: The Birth of the Prison*. Trans. Alan Sheridan. New York: Vintage, 1979.

———. *Dits et Écrits*. Paris: Gallimard, 1994.

———. "Foucault étudie la raison d'État." Foucault, *Dits et écrits* 801–05.

———. "Of Other Spaces, Heterotopias." 1967. Trans. Jay Miskowiec. *Foucault. info.* 10 May 2007 <http://foucault.info/documents/heteroTopia/foucault.heteroTopia.en.html>.

———. "Préface à la transgression." Foucault, *Dits et écrits* 233–50.

Fowler, Douglas. *A Reader's Guide to* Gravity's Rainbow. Ann Arbor: Ardis, 1980.

Freud, Sigmund. *Beyond the Pleasure Principle*. Trans. James Strachey. New York: Liveright, 1954.

———. *Civilization and Its Discontents*. Trans. James Strachey. New York: Norton, 1961.

———. *Jokes and Their Relation to the Unconscious*. c. 1905. Ed. and trans. James Strachey. New York: Norton, 1963. Vol. 8 of *The Standard Edition of the Complete Psychological Works of Sigmund Freud.*

———. *Totem and Taboo: Some Points of Agreement between the Mental Lives of Savages and Neurotics*. Trans. James Strachey. New York: Norton, 1962.

Friedan, Betty. *The Feminine Mystique*. New York: Dell, 1963.

Friedman, Alan J. "Science and Technology." Clerc, *Approaches* 69–102.

Friedman, Alan J., and Manfred Puetz. "Science as Metaphor: Thomas Pynchon and *Gravity's Rainbow*." Pearce 69–81.

Frye, Northrop. *Anatomy of Criticism*. Princeton: Princeton UP, 1957.

———. *The Secular Scripture: A Study of the Structure of Romance*. The Charles Eliot Norton Lectures, 1975–76. Cambridge: Harvard UP, 1976.

Fukuyama, Francis. *The End of History and the Last Man*. New York: Avon, 1992.

Galbraith, John Kenneth. *The Affluent Society*. Boston: Houghton, 1958.

Geertz, Clifford. "Deep Play: Notes on the Balinese Cockfight." *The Interpretation of Cultures*. New York: Harper, 1973. 412–53.

Geyh, Paula, Fred G. Leebron, and Andrew Levy, eds. *Postmodern American Fiction: A Norton Anthology*. New York: Norton, 1998.

Gibson, William. *Neuromancer*. New York: Ace, 1994.

Ginsberg, Allen. "Sunflower Sutra." Howl *and Other Poems*. San Francisco: City Lights, 1956. 28–30.

Girvetz, Harry K. *Science, Folklore, and Philosophy*. New York: Harper, 1966.

Gitlin, Todd. *The Sixties: Years of Hope, Days of Rage*. Toronto: Bantam, 1987.

Grant, J. Kerry. *A Companion to* The Crying of Lot 49. Athens: U of Georgia P, 1994.

———. *A Companion to* V. Athens: U of Georgia P, 2001.

Graves, Robert. *The White Goddess: A Historical Grammar of Poetic Myth*. London: Faber, 1948.

Green, Geoffrey, Donald J. Greiner, and Larry McCaffery, eds. *The* Vineland *Papers: Critical Takes on Pynchon's Novel*. Normal: Dalkey Archive, 1994.

Gregory, Derek. *Geographical Imaginations*. Cambridge: Blackwell, 1994.

Guillen, Matthew. "Pynchon's Social Aesthetics: Sixties Activism in Postmodern American Literature." *Revue Française d'Etudes Américaines* 84 (2000): 106–24.

Hajdu, David. *Positively 4th Street: The Lives and Times of Joan Baez, Bob Dylan, Mimi Baez Fariña, and Richard Fariña*. New York: Farrar, 2001.

Harley, J. B. "Maps, Knowledge, and Power." *The Iconography of Landscape: Essays on the Symbolic Representation, Design and Use of Past Environments*. Ed. Denis Cosgrove and Stephen Daniels. Cambridge: Cambridge UP, 1988. 277–312.

Harrington, Michael. *The Other America: Poverty in the United States*. New York: Macmillan, 1962.

Hartnett, Michael. "Thomas Pynchon's Long Island Years." *Confrontation* 30-31 (1985): 44–48.

Harvey, David. *The Condition of Postmodernity: An Enquiry into the Origins of Cultural Change*. Oxford: Blackwell, 1989.

———. *Spaces of Capital: Towards a Critical Geography*. New York: Routledge, 2001.

Hassan, Ihab. "Toward a Concept of Postmodernism." Natoli and Hutcheon 273–86.

Hassan, Waïl. "This Is Not a Novel: *The Crying of Lot 49*." *Pynchon Notes* 32-33 (1993): 86–98.

Hawthorne, Nathaniel. Preface. 1852. *The Blithedale Romance*. Columbus: Ohio State UP, 1965. 1–3. Vol. 3 of *The Centenary Edition of the Works of Nathaniel Hawthorne*.

———. Preface. 1851. *The House of the Seven Gables*. Columbus: Ohio State UP, 1964. 3–5. Vol. 2 of *The Centenary Edition of the Works of Nathaniel Hawthorne*.

———. *The Scarlet Letter*. 1850. *Nathaniel Hawthorne: The Novels*. Columbus: Ohio State UP, 1968. Rpt. New York: Lib. of Amer., 1983.

Hayles, N. Katherine. *Chaos Bound: Orderly Disorder in Contemporary Literature and Science*. Ithaca: Cornell UP, 1990.

———. *The Cosmic Web: Scientific Field Models and Literary Strategies in the Twentieth Century*. Ithaca: Cornell UP, 1984.

———. " 'Who Was Saved?' Families, Snitches, and Recuperation in Pynchon's *Vineland*." *Critique* 32 (1990): 77–92. Rpt. in Green, Greiner, and McCaffery 14–30.

Heat Moon, William Least. *Blue Highways*. Boston: Back Bay, 1999.

Heller, Joseph. *Catch-22*. New York: Dell, 1990.

Henkle, Roger B. "The Morning and Evening Funnies: Comedy in *Gravity's Rainbow*." Clerc, *Approaches* 273–90.

———. "Pynchon's Tapestries on the Western Wall." *Modern Fiction Studies* 17 (1971): 207–20. Rpt. in Mendelson, *Pynchon*.

Herman, Luc, ed. *Approach and Avoid: Essays on* Gravity's Rainbow. Spec. issue of *Pynchon Notes* 42-43 (1998): 9–342.

———. "Enzian's Meditation on Technology in *Gravity's Rainbow*." *Rivista di Studi Anglo-Americani* 8 (1994): 556–62.

———. Introduction. Herman, *Approach* 9–11.

———. "L'ipertesto e *L'arcobalaneo della gravità*." *La dissoluzione onesta: Scritti su Thomas Pynchon*. Ed. Giancarlo Alfano and Mattia Carratello. Naples: Cronopio, 2003. 119–28.

———. "Parody in *Gravity's Rainbow* (1973) by Thomas Pynchon." *European Journal of English Studies* 3 (1999): 206–25.

Hinds, Elizabeth Jane Wall, ed. *The Multiple Worlds of Pynchon's* Mason & Dixon*: Eighteenth-Century Contexts, Postmodern Observations*. Rochester: Camden, 2005.

Hite, Molly. "Feminist Theory and the Politics of *Vineland*." Green, Greiner, and McCaffery 134–52.

———. *Ideas of Order in the Novels of Thomas Pynchon*. Columbus: Ohio State UP, 1983.

Hoffman, Abbie. *The Autobiography of Abbie Hoffman*. Fwd. Norman Mailer. Afterword by Howard Zinn. New York: Putnam, 1980.

———. "Testimony of Abbie Hoffman." *"The Chicago Seven" Trial*. *Famous Trials*. Ed. Douglas O. Linder. 2005. 6 Apr. 2007 <http://www.law.umkc.edu/faculty/projects/ftrials/Chicago7/Hoffman.html>.

Hofstadter, Richard. *The Paranoid Style in American Politics*. Cambridge: Harvard UP, 1996.

Holton, Robert. "In the Rathouse of History with Thomas Pynchon: Rereading V." *Textual Practice* 2 (1988): 324–44.

*The Holy Bible*. Rev. Standard Version. New York: Nelson, 1953.

Horkheimer, Max, and Theodor Adorno. *Dialectic of Enlightenment*. New York: Seabury, 1972.

Horvath, Brooke, and Irving Malin, eds. *Pynchon and* Mason & Dixon. Newark: U of Delaware P; London: Associated UP, 2000.

Hume, Kathryn. *Pynchon's Mythography: An Approach to* Gravity's Rainbow. Carbondale: Southern Illinois UP, 1987.

———. "Pynchon's Mythological Histories." *Thomas Pynchon*. Ed. Harold Bloom. Philadelphia: Chelsea, 2003. 131–44.

Hutcheon, Linda. "Beginning to Theorize Postmodernism." Natoli and Hutcheon 243–72.

———. *A Poetics of Postmodernism: History, Theory, Fiction*. New York: Routledge, 1988.

Iser, Wolfgang. *The Act of Reading: A Theory of Aesthetic Response*. 1976. Baltimore: Johns Hopkins UP, 1978.

Isserman, Maurice. *The Other American: The Life of Michael Harrington*. New York: Public Affairs, 2000.

Ivison, Douglas. "Outhouses of the European Soul: Imperialism in Thomas Pynchon." *Pynchon Notes* 40-41 (1997): 134–43.

Jacobs, Jane. *The Death and Life of Great American Cities*. New York: Vintage, 1992.

Jameson, Fredric. "Postmodernism and Consumer Society." *The Anti-aesthetic: Essays on Postmodern Culture.* Ed. Hal Foster. Port Townsend: Bay, 1983. 111–25.

———. *Postmodernism; or, The Cultural Logic of Late Capitalism.* Durham: Duke UP, 1991.

Janangelo, Joseph. "Joseph Cornell and the Artistry of Composing Persuasive Hypertexts." *College Composition and Communication* 49 (1998): 24–44.

Jasper, Alison. "Thomas Pynchon's Absurd Truths: Puns and Metaphor in *The Crying of Lot 49.*" *Arkansas Review* 5.1-2 (1996): 39–67.

Johnston, John. "Toward the Schizo-Text: Paranoia as Semiotic Regime in *The Crying of Lot 49.*" O'Donnell, *New Essays* 47–78.

Joyce, Michael. *Afternoon: A Story*. Diskette. Watertown: Eastgate, 1987.

Jukiri, Stephen, and Alan Nadel. " 'How Do You Spell Reality?—"O-U-T-A-S-E" '; Or, How I Learned to Stop *Gravity's Rainbow* and Start Worrying." *Pynchon Notes* 26-27 (1990): 81–90.

Kant, Immanuel. *The Critique of Judgment*. Trans. J. H. Bernard. New York: Hafner, 1951.

———. *Critique of Practical Reason*. Trans. Mary Gregor. Cambridge: Cambridge UP, 1997.

Kaplan, Caren. *Questions of Travel: Postmodern Poetics of Displacement*. Durham: Duke UP, 1996.

Kateb, George. *The Inner Ocean: Individualism and Democratic Culture*. Ithaca: Cornell UP, 1992.

Kaufman, Marjorie. "Brunnhilde and the Chemists: Women in *Gravity's Rainbow.*" Levine and Leverenz, *Mindful Pleasures* 197–228.

Keats, John. To George and Thomas Keats. 21 or 27 Dec. 1817. *The Letters of John Keats*. Ed. Hyder E. Rollins. Vol. 1. Cambridge: Harvard UP, 1958. 2 vols.

Kermode, Frank. "Decoding the Trystero." Mendelson, *Pynchon* 162–66.

Kharpertian, Theodore D. *A Hand to Turn the Time: The Menippean Satires of Thomas Pynchon*. Rutherford: Fairleigh Dickinson UP, 1990.

Kihss, Peter. "Pulitzer Jurors; His Third Novel." *New York Times* 8 May 1974: 38.

Kincaid, Jamaica. *A Small Place.* New York: Plume, 1988.

Krafft, John, Bernard Duyfhuizen, and Khachig Tölölyan, eds. *The Index Issue*. Spec. issue of *Pynchon Notes* 36-39 (1995–96): 7–222.

Kristeva, Julia. *Desire in Language: A Semiotic Approach to Literature and Art*. Ed. Leon S. Roudiez. Trans. Thomas Gora, Alice Jardine, and Roudiez. New York: Columbia UP, 1980.

Kunstler, James Howard. *The Geography of Nowhere: The Rise and Decline of America's Man-Made Landscape*. New York: Touchstone-Simon, 1994.

Kymlicka, Will. *Contemporary Political Philosophy: An Introduction*. Oxford: Oxford UP, 1990.

Lacan, Jacques. "The Agency of the Letter in the Unconscious or Reason Since Freud." 1958. *Critical Theory Since 1965*. Ed. Hazard Adams and Leroy Searle. Tallahassee: Florida State UP, 1986. 738–56.

———. *The Seminar of Jacques Lacan, Book II: The Ego in Freud's Theory and in the Technique of Psychoanalysis (1954–55).* Trans. Sylvana Tomaselli. New York: Norton, 1988.

Leccese, Michael, and Kathleen McCormick, eds. *Charter of the New Urbanism.* New York: McGraw, 1999.

LeClair, Tom. *In the Loop: Don DeLillo and the Systems Novel*. Urbana: U of Illinois P, 1987.

Lefebvre, Henri. *The Production of Space*. Trans. Donald Nicholson-Smith. London: Blackwell, 1991.

Lennon, John, and Paul McCartney. "Revolution." *The Beatles* [*The White Album*]. Apple, 1968.

Levine, George, and David Leverenz, eds. *Essays on Thomas Pynchon*. Spec. issue of *Twentieth Century Literature* 21.2(1975): iii–v, 151–252.

———, eds. *Mindful Pleasures: Essays on Thomas Pynchon*. Boston: Little, 1976.

Lhamon, W. T., Jr. "Pentecost, Promiscuity, and Pynchon's *V.*" Levine and Leverenz, *Mindful Pleasures* 69–86.

Lodge, David. *After Bakhtin: Essays on Fiction and Criticism*. New York: Routledge, 1990.

Low, Setha. *The Anthropology of Space and Place: Locating Culture*. London: Blackwell, 2003.

Lyotard, Jean-François. "Answering the Question: 'What Is Postmodernism?' " Trans. Régis Durand. Lyotard, *Postmodern Condition* 71–82.

———. *The Differend: Phrases in Dispute*. Trans. Georges Van Den Abbeele. Minneapolis: U of Minnesota P, 1988.

———. *Lessons on the Analytic of the Sublime*. Trans. Elizabeth Rottenberg. Stanford: Stanford UP, 1994.

———. *The Postmodern Condition: A Report on Knowledge*. Trans. Geoff Bennington and Brian Massumi. Fwd. Fredric Jameson. 1984. Manchester: Manchester UP, 1991.

MacCannell, Dean, and Lucy R. Lippard. *The Tourist: A New Theory of the Leisure Class*. Berkeley: U of California P, 1999.

MacIntyre, Alasdair. *After Virtue*. Notre Dame: U of Notre Dame P, 1981.

Mackey, Louis. "Paranoia, Pynchon, and Preterition." *Sub-stance* 30 (1981): 16–30.

Madsen, Deborah L. *The Postmodernist Allegories of Thomas Pynchon*. New York: St. Martin's, 1991.

Malik, Kenan. *The Meaning of Race: Race, History, and Culture in Western Society*. New York: New York UP, 1996.

Mangel, Anne. "Maxwell's Demon, Entropy, Information: *The Crying of Lot 49*." Levine and Leverenz, *Mindful Pleasures* 87–100.

Mangen, Anne. "Thomas Pynchon's Writing Space; *Gravity's Rainbow* as Pseudo-Hypertext." *Blissful Bewilderment: Studies in the Fiction of Thomas Pynchon*. Ed. Mangen and Rolf Gaasland. Oslo: Novus, 2002. 139–62.

Marcuse, Herbert. *Eros and Civilization: A Philosophical Inquiry into Freud*. Boston: Beacon, 1966.

———. *One-Dimensional Man: Studies in the Ideology of Advanced Industrial Society*. Boston: Beacon, 1964.

Marine, Gene. "I've Got Nothing against the Colored, Understand." *Ramparts* Nov. 1966: 13–18.

*The Matrix*. Dir. Andy Wachowski and Larry Wachowski. Warner, 1999.

Mattessich, Stefan. *Lines of Flight: Discursive Time and Countercultural Desire in the Work of Thomas Pynchon*. Durham: Duke UP, 2002.

McCarthy, Cormac. *The Road*. New York: Vintage, 2007.

McDaid, John, and Stewart Moulthrop. " 'Not Yet Blindingly One': *Gravity's Rainbow* and the Hypertextualists." *Pynchon Notes* 32-33 (1993): 132–51.

McDowell, Linda. *Gender, Identity, and Place: Understanding Feminist Geographies*. Minneapolis: U of Minnesota P, 1999.

McHale, Brian. *Constructing Postmodernism*. London: Routledge, 1992.

———. *Postmodernist Fiction*. New York: Methuen, 1987.

———. "Thomas Pynchon: A Portrait of the Artist as a Missing Person." *Cencrastus* 5 (1981): 2–3.

McHoul, Alec, and David Wills. *Writing Pynchon: Strategies in Fictional Analysis*. Urbana: U of Illinois P, 1990.

McHugh, Patrick. "Cultural Politics, Postmodernism, and White Guys: Affect in *Gravity's Rainbow*." *College Literature* 28.2 (2001): 1–28.

McLuhan, Marshall. *The Gutenberg Galaxy*. Toronto: U of Toronto P, 1962.

———. *Understanding Media: The Extensions of Man*. New York: McGraw, 1964.

Mead, Clifford. *Thomas Pynchon: A Bibliography of Primary and Secondary Materials*. Elmwood Park: Dalkey Archive, 1989.

Melley, Timothy. *Empire of Conspiracy: The Culture of Paranoia in Postwar America*. Ithaca: Cornell UP, 2000.

Melville, Herman. *Moby Dick; or, The Whale*. 1851. Oxford: Oxford UP, 1929.

Menand, Louis. "Entropology." Rev. of *Mason & Dixon*. *New York Review of Books* 12 June 1997: 22–25.

Mendelson, Edward. "Encyclopedic Narrative: From Dante to Pynchon." *MLN* 91 (1976): 1267–75.

———. "Gravity's Encyclopedia." Levine and Leverenz, *Mindful Pleasures* 161–95.

———, ed. *Pynchon: A Collection of Critical Essays*. Twentieth Century Views. Englewood Cliffs: Prentice, 1978.

———. "The Sacred, the Profane, and *The Crying of Lot 49*." Mendelson, *Pynchon* 112–46.

Milesi, Laurent. "Postmodern Ana-Apocalyptics: Pynchon's V-Effect and the End (of Our Century)." Herman, *Approach* 213–43.

Miller, James. *Democracy Is in the Streets: From Port Huron to the Siege of Chicago*. 1987. New York: Touchstone, 1988.

Millhauser, Steven. *Martin Dressler: The Tale of an American Dreamer*. New York: Vintage, 1997.

Mills, C[harles] Wright. *The Power Elite*. London: Oxford UP, 1956.

Mohanram, Radhika. *Black Body: Women, Colonialism, and Space*. Minneapolis: U of Minnesota P, 1999.

Moore, Thomas. *The Style of Connectedness:* Gravity's Rainbow *and Thomas Pynchon*. Columbia: U of Missouri P, 1987.

Morrison, Toni. *Playing in the Dark: Whiteness and the Literary Imagination*. Cambridge: Harvard UP, 1992.

Mumford, Lewis. *The City in History: Its Origins, Its Transformations, and Its Prospects*. New York: Harvest, 1968.

Muste, John. "Singing Back the Silence: *Gravity's Rainbow* and the War Novel." *Modern Fiction Studies* 30 (1984): 5–23.

Nadeau, Robert. *Readings from the New Book on Nature: Physics and Metaphysics in the Modern Novel*. Amherst: U of Massachusetts P, 1981.

Nadel, Alan. *Containment Culture: American Narrative, Postmodernism, and the Atomic Age*. Durham: Duke UP, 1995.

Nash, Roderick. *Wilderness and the American Mind*. New Haven: Yale UP, 1967.

Natoli, Joseph, and Linda Hutcheon, eds. *A Postmodern Reader*. Albany: State U of New York P, 1993.

Ngũgĩ wa Thiong'o. "Moving the Centre: Towards a Pluralism of Cultures." *Moving the Centre: Struggles for Cultural Freedoms*. Portsmouth: Heinemann, 1993. 2–11.

*North by Northwest*. Dir. Alfred Hitchcock. MGM, 1959.

Nozick, Robert. *Anarchy, State, and Utopia*. New York: Basic, 1974.

O'Donnell, Patrick. Introduction. O'Donnell, *New Essays* 1–20.

———. *New Essays on* The Crying of Lot 49. Cambridge: Cambridge UP, 1991.

Oliver, Anna. "The Use of Maps in Contemporary Art." Master's thesis. Cardiff School of Art and Design, 2003. 10 May 2007 <http://www.annao.pwp.blueyonder.co.uk/text_dissertation.htm>.

Olsen, Lance. "Pynchon's New Nature: The Uncertainty Principle and Indeterminacy in *The Crying of Lot 49*." *Canadian Review of American Studies* 14 (1983): 153–63.

Olster, Stacey. "When You're a (Nin)Jette, You're a (Nin)Jette All the Way—or Are You? Female Filmmaking in *Vineland*." Green, Greiner, and McCaffery 119–34.

Osterhaus, Frank. "A Bibliography of Pynchon Scholarship in Japan." *Pynchon Notes* 44-45 (1999): 195–204.

Palmeri, Frank. "Neither Literally nor as Metaphor: Pynchon's *The Crying of Lot 49* and the Structure of Scientific Revolutions." *ELH* 54 (1987): 979–99.

Patell, Cyrus R. K. *Negative Liberties: Morrison, Pynchon, and the Problem of Liberal Ideology*. Durham: Duke UP, 2001.

Pearce, Richard, ed. *Critical Essays on Thomas Pynchon*. Boston: Hall, 1988.

Pearson, Karl. *The Grammar of Science*. Final ed. 1911. New York: Meridian Lib., 1957.

Peirce, Charles Sanders. *The Philosophy of Peirce*. Ed. Justus Buchler. London: Routledge, 2000.

Pérez-Llantada Auría, Carmen. "Questing for Social Justice: The Role of Woman in Thomas Pynchon's Narrative." *Estudios de la mujer en el ambito de los países de habla inglesa*. Ed. Margarita Ardanaz et al. Madrid: U Complutense de Madrid, 1994. 275–87.

Petillon, Pierre-Yves. “A Re-cognition of Her Errand into the Wilderness.” O’Donnell, *New Essays* 127–70.

Plato. *The Republic*. Trans. Francis MacDonald Cornford. New York: Oxford UP, 1978.

Poirier, Richard. “The Importance of Thomas Pynchon.” Levine and Leverenz, *Mindful Pleasures* 15–29.

Porush, David. *The Soft Machine: Cybernetic Fiction*. New York: Methuen, 1985.

Pratt, Mary Louise. “Travel Narrative and Imperialist Vision.” *Understanding Narrative*. Ed. James Phelan and Peter J. Rabinowitz. Columbus: Ohio State UP, 1994. 199–221.

Purdy, Strother. “*Gravity’s Rainbow* and the Culture of Childhood.” *Pynchon Notes* 22-23 (1988): 7–23.

Pynchon, Thomas. *Against the Day*. New York: Penguin, 2006.

———. *The Crying of Lot 49*. Philadelphia: Lippincott, 1966.

———. “Entropy.” *Kenyon Review* 22 (1960): 277–92.

———. *Gravity’s Rainbow*. New York: Viking, 1973.

———. “The Heart’s Eternal Vow.” *New York Times Book Review* 10 Apr. 1988: 1+.

———. Introduction. *Been Down So Long It Looks Like Up to Me*. By Richard Fariña. New York: Random, 1983. v–xiv.

———. Introduction. *1984*. By George Orwell. London: Penguin, 2003. v–xxv.

———. “Is It O.K. to Be a Luddite?” *New York Times Book Review* 28 Oct. 1984: 1+.

———. “A Journey into the Mind of Watts.” *New York Times Magazine* 12 June 1966: 34+.

———. *Mason & Dixon*. New York: Henry Holt, 1997.

———. “Mortality and Mercy in Vienna.” *Epoch* 9 (1959): 195–213.

———. “Nearer, My Couch, to Thee.” *New York Times Book Review* 6 June 1993: 3+.

———. “Pynchon’s Reading for *Gravity’s Rainbow*.” Letter to Thomas F. Hirsch. Seed 240–43.

———. “The Secret Integration.” Pynchon, *Slow Learner* 139–93.

———. *Slow Learner*. Boston: Little, 1984.

———. “Under the Rose.” Pynchon, *Slow Learner* 99–137.

———. *V*. Philadelphia: Lippincott, 1963.

———. *Vineland*. Boston: Little, 1990.

Quilligan, Maureen. *The Language of Allegory: Defining the Genre*. Ithaca: Cornell UP, 1979.

Rand, Ayn. 1957. *Atlas Shrugged*. New York: Signet, 1996.

Rand, Ayn, et al. *Capitalism: The Unknown Ideal*. New York: New Amer. Lib., 1966.

Rawls, John. *A Theory of Justice*. Cambridge: Harvard UP, 1971.

Riffaterre, Michael. *Fictional Truth*. Baltimore: Johns Hopkins UP, 1990.

Rojek, Chris, and John Urry. *Touring Cultures: Transformations of Travel and Theory*. London: Routledge, 1997.

Rosenblith, Walter. Afterword. Wiener, *Human Use* 265–81.

Rosenblum, Nancy L. "Pluralism and Self-Defense." *Liberalism and the Moral Life*. Ed. Rosenblum. Cambridge: Harvard UP, 1989. 207–26.

Ross, Andrew. *The Celebration Chronicles: Life, Liberty, and the Pursuit of Property Values in Disney's New Town*. New York: Ballantine, 1999.

Russell, Charles. "The Context of the Concept." Natoli and Hutcheon 287–98.

Said, Edward. *Culture and Imperialism*. New York: Random, 1993.

———. *Orientalism*. New York: Vintage, 1979.

Sale, Kirkpatrick. *SDS*. 1973. New York: Vintage, 1974.

Sandel, Michael. *Liberalism and the Limits of Justice*. Cambridge: Cambridge UP, 1982.

Savage, Mike, Gaynor Bagnall, and Brian Longhurst. *Globalization and Belonging*. London: Sage, 2005.

Schachterle, Lance. "Thomas Pynchon and the Civil Wars of Technology." *Literature and Technology*. Ed. Mark Greenberg and Schachterle. Bethlehem: Lehigh UP, 1992. 253–74.

Schaub, Thomas H. "The Environmental Pynchon: *Gravity's Rainbow* and the Ecological Context." *Pynchon Notes* 42-43 (1998): 59–72.

———. *Pynchon: The Voice of Ambiguity*. Urbana: U of Illinois P, 1981.

Schulz, Max F. *Black Humor Fiction of the Sixties*. Athens: Ohio UP, 1973.

Seed, David. *The Fictional Labyrinths of Thomas Pynchon*. Iowa City: U of Iowa P, 1988.

Seidel, Michael. "The Satiric Plots of *Gravity's Rainbow*." Mendelson, *Pynchon* 193–212.

Shannon, Claude E. "The Mathematical Theory of Communication." *The Mathematical Theory of Communication*. By Shannon and Warren Weaver. Urbana: U of Illinois P, 1949. 3–91.

Sigvardson, Joakim. *Immanence and Transcendence in Thomas Pynchon's* Mason & Dixon*: A Phenomenological Study*. Stockholm: Almquist, 2002.

*SimCities and @Culture*. Cyberculture. Course project page. Spring 2005. *Humanities division, Swarthmore Coll*. 10 May 2007 <http://www.swarthmore.edu/Humanities/ssimon1/cyberculture/simcitypres/index.htm>.

Simonelli, Frederick J. *American Fuehrer: George Lincoln Rockwell and the American Nazi Party*. Urbana: U of Illinois P, 1999.

Slade, Joseph. *Thomas Pynchon*. New York: Lang, 1990.

Slemon, Stephen. "Magic Realism as Post-colonial Discourse." *Canadian Literature* 116 (1988): 9–25.

Smith, Henry Nash. *Virgin Land: The American West as Symbol and Myth*. Cambridge: Harvard UP, 1950.

Smith, Marcus, and Khachig Tölölyan. "The New Jeremiad: *Gravity's Rainbow*." Pearce 169–86.

Smith, Neil. *The New Urban Frontier: Gentrification and the Revanchist City*. New York: Routledge, 1996.

Snow, C. P. *The Two Cultures and the Scientific Revolution*. Cambridge: Cambridge UP, 1959.

Sorkin, Michael. *Variations on a Theme Park: The New American City and the End of Public Space*. New York: Hill, 1992.

Spiegelman, Art. *In the Shadow of No Towers*. New York: Pantheon, 2004.

Stephenson, Neal. *Snow Crash*. New York: Spectra, 2000.

Strehle, Susan. *Fiction in the Quantum Universe*. Chapel Hill: U of North Carolina P, 1992.

Student Nonviolent Coordinating Committee. *We Want Black Power*. 1967. *The Times Were a Changin': The Sixties Reader*. Ed. Irwin Unger and Debi Unger. New York: Three Rivers, 1998. 144–48.

Tabbi, Joseph. *Postmodern Sublime: Technology and American Writing from Mailer to Cyberpunk*. Ithaca: Cornell UP, 1995.

Tanner, Tony. "Caries and Cabals." Levine and Leverenz 49–67.

———. *City of Words: American Fiction, 1950–1970*. New York: Harper, 1971.

———. *Thomas Pynchon*. London: Methuen, 1982.

*The Thirty-Nine Steps*. Dir. Alfred Hitchcock. Gaumont-British, 1935.

Thompson, James Westfall. *A History of Historical Writing*. Vol. 2: *The Eighteenth and Nineteenth Centuries*. New York: Macmillan, 1942.

Tindall, George B., and David E. Shi. *America: A Narrative History*. Brief 2nd ed. New York: Norton, 1989.

Tölölyan, Khachig. "War as Background in *Gravity's Rainbow*." Clerc, *Approaches* 31–67.

*The Truman Show*. Dir. Peter Weir. Paramount, 2005.

Tuan, Yi-Fu. *Space and Place: The Perspectives of Experience*. Minneapolis: U of Minnesota P, 1981.

Turner, Frederick Jackson. *The Frontier in American History*. New York: Henry Holt, 1921.

Varsava, Jerry A. "The Dialectics of Self and Community in Toni Morrison and Thomas Pynchon." Rev. of *Negative Liberties: Morrison, Pynchon, and the Problem of Liberal Ideology*, by Cyrus P. K. Patell. *Contemporary Literature* 43 (2002): 794–803.

———. "Thomas Pynchon and Postmodern Liberalism." *Canadian Review of American Studies* 25.3 (1995): 63–100.

*Wag the Dog*. Dir. Barry Levinson. Videocasseette. New Line Home Video, 1998.

Walker, Alice. *Meridian*. New York: Harcourt, 1976.

Watson, Robert N. "Who Bids for Tristero? The Conversion of Pynchon's Oedipa Maas." *Southern Humanities Review* 17 (1983): 59–75.

Weisenburger, Steven. *A* Gravity's Rainbow *Companion: Sources and Contexts for Pynchon's Novel*. Athens: U of Georgia P, 1988.

———. "Thomas Pynchon at Twenty-Two: A Recovered Autobiographical Sketch." *American Literature: A Journal of Literary History, Criticism, and Bibliography* 62 (1990): 692–97.

Weiskel, Thomas. *The Romantic Sublime: Studies in the Structure and Psychology of Transcendence*. Baltimore: Johns Hopkins UP, 1976.

White, Hayden. "The Burden of History." *History and Theory* 5 (1966): 111–34.

———. *The Content of the Form: Narrative Discourse and Historical Representation*. Baltimore: Johns Hopkins UP, 1987.

———. *Metahistory: The Historical Imagination in Nineteenth-Century Europe*. Baltimore: Johns Hopkins UP, 1973.

Whitfield, Stephen. *The Culture of the Cold War*. Baltimore: Johns Hopkins UP, 1991.

Whitman, Walt. "Democratic Vistas." *Walt Whitman*. Selected and with notes by Mark Van Doren. New York: Viking, 1945. 385–469.

Wiener, Norbert. *Cybernetics; or, Control and Communication in the Animal and the Machine*. New York: Wiley, 1948.

———. *The Human Use of Human Beings: Cybernetics and Society*. New York: Discus-Avon, 1967.

Wiener, Philip Paul. *Dictionary of the History of Ideas*. New York: Scribner, 1973.

Wilde, Alan. *Horizons of Assent: Modernism, Postmodernism, and the Ironic Imagination*. Baltimore: Johns Hopkins UP, 1981.

Williams, Frederick. *Reasoning with Statistics*. 2nd ed. New York: Holt, Rinehart, 1979.

Williams, Raymond. *The City and the Country*. Oxford: Oxford UP, 1973.

Williams, William Carlos. "The universality of things." *Imaginations*. Ed. Webster Schott. New York: New Directions, 1970. 118.

Willis, Jim, ed. *Images of Germany in the American Media*. Westport: Praeger, 1999.

Winston, Matthew. "The Quest for Pynchon." *Twentieth Century Literature* 21 (1975): 278–87.

Wittgenstein, Ludwig. *Tractatus Logico-Philosophicus*. Trans. D. F. Pears and B. F. McGuinness. London, 1961.

Wolfley, Lawrence C. "Repression's Rainbow: The Presence of Norman O. Brown in Pynchon's Big Novel." *PMLA* 92 (1977): 873–89. Rpt. in Pearce 99–123.

Young, James Dean, ed. *Critique: Studies in Modern Fiction* 16.2 (1974): 30–90.

Young, Robert J. C. *Colonial Desire: Hybridity in Theory, Culture and Race*. London: Routledge, 1995.

# INDEX OF NAMES

Abbas, Niran, 7
Aberbach, Joel D., 19
Achebe, Chinua, 99, 102
Acker, Kathy, 40, 149
Adams, Henry, 68–69, 92, 93
Adorno, Theodor, 126, 127
Aitchison, Cara, 133
Althusser, Louis, 98
Appiah, Kwame Anthony, 99
Arendt, Hannah, 87
Arrabal, Fernando, 38
Ashe, Frederick, 8

Bachofen, Johann Jakob, 92
Bagnall, Gaynor, 133
Baker, Jeffrey S., 8
Bakhtin, Mikhail, 115–16, 141, 142–46, 147n1, 147n3
Baldwin, James, 19
Baltimore, George Calvert, Lord, 137
Barrio, Raymond, x
Barth, John, x, 98n1, 114
Baudrillard, Jean, 133, 139
Baxter, Charles, 8
Beckett, Samuel, 81
Beidler, Philip, 8
Bellah, Robert, 63, 64, 65
Bellow, Saul, ix, 47
Benjamin, Walter, 113n6, 132, 139
Bentham, Jeremy, 133, 134
Bercovitch, Sacvan, 7
Bergh, Patricia, 8
Berlin, Isaiah, 64, 65
Berressem, Hanjo, xii, 6
Bertalanffy, Ludwig von, 66
Bérubé, Michael, 5, 6, 39, 102
Bhabha, Homi, 99
Bible, 15, 16
Black, Joel, 9
Blackford, Russell, 9
Blaine, Diana York, 51
Bloom, Alexander, 8
Bloom, Harold, 7
Blunt, Alison, 132
Bohr, Niels, 74
Boltzmann, Ludwig, 74
Booker, M. Keith, 8
Borges, Jorge Luis, 132, 133, 139
Born, Max, 74
Bourdieu, Pierre, 98
Bradley, James, 136
Breines, Wini, 8
Breithaupt, Jim, 67
Brooks, Mel, 83
Brown, Norman O., 7, 41, 102
Browning, Robert, 16
Brückner, Martin, 133
Burckhardt, Jacob, 92
Burroughs, William S., 149

Caesar, Terry, 8
Calvino, Italo, 132, 133
Camus, Albert, 77
Capote, Truman, x
Carson, Rachel, 61
Carter, Dale, 9
Castles, Stephen, 133
Chambers, Erve, 132, 139
Chase, Richard, 25–26
Chatwin, Bruce, 132
Chavez, Cesar, 61
Clausius, Rudolph, 73
Clerc, Charles, 6, 7, 136, 139
Clifford, James, 133, 139
Clive, Robert, 136
Coe, Justin, 137, 139
Coetzee, J. M., 132, 139
Conrad, Joseph, 54
Conway, Martin, 113n2
Cooley, Ronald, 8
Cooper, James Fenimore, 25, 27, 29–30
Cooper, Peter, 6, 155
Coover, Robert, ix, 98n1
Corey, Irwin, 5
Cornis-Pope, Marcel, 50
Cornwell, Neil, 147n5
Coveney, Peter, 67
Cowan, James, 132, 133, 139
Cowart, David, xii, 4, 6, 8
Crang, Mike, 133
Cromer, Evelyn Baring, 88
Crownshaw, Richard, 110, 113n6

Dalsgaard, Inger H., xii
D'Annunzio, Gabriele, 97
Darwin, Charles Galton, 34, 74
Davidson, Alistair, 133
Davidson, Cathy, 8
Davis, Angela, 40
Daw, Larry, 10
Degrelle, Léon, 107, 108
Deleuze, Gilles, 39
DeLillo, Don, ix, 49, 66
Derrida, Jacques, 39
D'haen, Theo, 137, 139
Dickens, Charles, 25, 51

Didion, Joan, x
Disraeli, Benjamin, 38
Dixon, Jeremiah, 121
Doctorow, E. L., 98n1
Dorling, Daniel, 133
Dos Passos, John, 38, 71
Douglas, J. Yellowlees, 149–50
Dudar, Helen, 5
Duncan, James, 133
Duncan, Nancy, 139
Duyfhuizen, Bernard, 6–7, 10, 158
Dworkin, Ronald, 64

Eco, Umberto, 98n1, 133, 139
Einstein, Albert, 34, 67, 74
Eliade, Mircea, 31, 36
Elias, Amy J., xii, 139
Eliot, George, 25
Eliot, T. S., 80, 92
Ellison, Ralph, ix
Emerson, Ralph Waldo, 27, 28
Emerson, William, 136
Evans, Sara, 19
Exner, Franz, 74

Fairbairns, David, 133
Fanon, Frantz, 55, 57, 99
Fariña, Richard, 4, 5
Feidelson, Charles, 27
Feingold, Mimi, 19
Fernie, J. Donald, 136, 139
Feynman, Richard, 67
Finzsch, Norbert, xii
Fitzgerald, F. Scott, 98
Ford, Henry, 86
Foreman, David, 136
Forster, E. M., 25
Foucault, Michel, 39, 118, 124, 127, 133, 139, 147n3
Fowler, Douglas, 10
Fowles, John, 98n1
Freud, Sigmund, 14, 34, 38, 42–43, 44, 78, 98
Friedan, Betty, 20, 31, 37, 61
Friedman, Alan J., 7, 67
Frye, Northrop, 27, 92
Fukuyama, Francis, 62

Galbraith, Kenneth, 36, 41–42
García Márquez, Gabriel, 4
Geertz, Clifford, 99
Geyh, Paula, 10
Gibson, William, 66, 72
Ginsberg, Allen, xi, 39
Girvetz, Harry K., 75
Gitlin, Todd, 9
Gould, Jay, 38, 59
Gramsci, Antonio, 98
Grant, Cary, 21
Grant, J. Kerry, 10, 59, 148, 153n1
Graves, Robert, 92–93
Green, Geoffrey, 7, 10
Gregory, Derek, 133, 139
Greiner, Donald, 7, 10
Guattari, Felix, 39
Guillen, Matthew, 8

Hajdu, David, 5
Hardy, Thomas, 25
Harley, J. B., 133, 139
Harrington, Michael, 18, 31, 37–38, 55–56
Harris, Michael, xii
Harrison, Jane, 92
Hartnett, Michael, 5
Harvey, David, 132, 133, 139
Hassan, Ihab, 153n2
Hassan, Waïl, 30
Hawthorne, Nathaniel, 25, 26, 27, 28–29, 30n1
Hayles, N. Katherine, 9, 46, 67, 119
Heat Moon, William Least, 132
Hegel, Georg Wilhelm Friedrich, 42, 62
Heidegger, Martin, 40
Heisenberg, Werner, 74, 75
Heller, Joseph, 79, 82
Henkle, Roger, 7, 46, 82n2
Herman, Luc, xii, 7, 109, 113n1, 113n3, 113n7
Highfield, Roger, 67
Hinds, Elizabeth Jane Wall, 7
Hirsch, Thomas F., 4, 6, 34, 101, 108
Hitchcock, Alfred, 14, 21
Hite, Molly, xi, 6, 7, 8, 39, 102, 158
Hitler, Adolf, 86
Hoffman, Abbie, 39, 40, 41, 118
Hofstadter, Richard, 133, 139
Holton, Robert, 102
Holzer, Werner, 84
Hoover, Herbert, 86
Horkheimer, Max, 127
Horvath, Brooke, 7, 139
Hume, Kathryn, 6, 102, 162n2
Hutcheon, Linda, x, 10, 91, 98, 118, 119

Ionesco, Eugene, 81
Iser, Wolfgang, 108
Isserman, Maurice, 38
Ivison, Douglas, 99, 104

Jacobs, Jane, 132
James, E. O., 92
Jameson, Fredric, x, 9–10, 53, 132, 133, 134, 139, 149
Janangelo, Joseph, 151
Jasper, Alison, 82n1

Johnson, Lyndon, 16, 38, 61
Johnston, John, 52
Jones, James, ix
Joyce, James, 51, 92, 150
Joyce, Michael, 150, 153
Jukiri, Stephen, 161, 162n1

Kaplan, Caren, 133, 139
Kant, Immanuel, xiii, 163–64, 165, 166, 167, 168n
Kateb, George, 64
Kaufman, Marjorie, 8
Keats, John, 98
Kermode, Frank, 7
Kerouac, Jack, ix
Kesey, Ken, ix, 118
Kharpertian, Theodore D., 26
Kihss, Peter, 145
Kincaid, Jamaica, 132, 133, 134, 139
King, Martin Luther, 54
Kingston, Maxine Hong, x
Klein, Melanie, 42
Kolbuszewska, Zofia, xiii
Krafft, John, 10
Krassner, Paul, 40
Kristeva, Julia, 39, 42
Kubrick, Stanley, 81
Kuntsler, James Howard, 132
Kymlicka, Will, 65n2

Lacan, Jacques, 39, 42
Leccese, Michael, 133
LeClair, Thomas, 9, 66
Leebron, Fred G., 10
Lefebvre, Henri, 132, 133, 139
Lennon, John, 22
Leverenz, David, 6, 7, 8
Levine, George, 6, 7, 8
Levy, Andrew, 10
Lhamon, W. T., 7
Lippard, Lucy, 133
Lodge, David, 142
Longhurst, Brian, 133
Low, Seth, 132
Lyotard, Jean-François, xiii, 119, 149, 159, 163–65, 167–68, 168n

MacCannell, Dean, 133, 139
MacIntyre, Alasdair, 63, 65
Mackey, Louis, 113n5
Macleod, Nicola, 133
Madsen, Deborah L., xi, 6, 9, 26
Madsen, Robert, 63, 65
Mailer, Norman, ix, x
Malik, Kenan, 55
Malin, Irving, 7, 139
Mangel, Anne, 7, 9, 31, 32, 67
Mangen, Anne, 113n3
Manson, Charles, 24
Marcuse, Herbert, xi, 22, 40–45
Marx, Karl, 42, 155
Maskelyne, Nevil, 136
Mason, Charles, 121
Mattesich, Stefan, 39
Maxwell, Clerk, 23, 31, 32
McCaffery, Larry, 7, 10
McCarthy, Cormac, 132, 139
McCartney, Paul, 22
McCormick, Kathleen, 133
McCray, Joel, 106
McDaid, John, 113n3
McDowell, Linda, 132
McHale, Brian 5, 6, 10, 149
McHoul, Alec, 6, 39
McHugh, Patrick, 58n1
McLaughlin, Robert, xii
McLuhan, Marshall, 31, 34–36, 70
Mead, Clifford, 10
Medvedev, Pavel, 147n3
Melley, Timothy, 133
Melville, Herman, 25, 27, 28, 29
Menand, Louis, 99
Mendelson, Edward, 7, 9, 26, 36–37, 47, 50–51
Michelet, Jules, 92
Milesi, Laurent, 113n4
Miller, James, 118
Millhauser, Steven, 132, 139
Mills, C. Wright, 118
Mineo, Sal, 68
Mohanram, Radhika, 132
Momaday, N. Scott, x
Moore, Michael, 145
Moore, Thomas, 6
Morrison, Toni, 52
Motley, John Lothrop, 38
Moulthrop, Stewart, 113n3
Mulligan, Gerry, 68
Mumford, Lewis, 132
Muste, John, 106

Nabokov, Vladimir, 81
Nadeau, Robert, 9, 67
Nadel, Alan, xiii, 9, 161, 162n1
Nash, Roderick, 133
Nelson, Ricky, 68
Neumann, Erich, 92
Newton, Isaac, 34, 67, 69
Ngũgĩ wa Thiong'o, 99, 102, 104
Nozick, Robert, 60, 65

O'Donnell, Patrick, 5, 7
O'Hara, Maureen, 106
Oliver, Anna, 133, 139
Olsen, Lance, 9
Olsen, Sarah Jane, 18
Olster, Stacey, xii, 8

Orwell, George, 4, 99, 119
Osterhaus, Frank, 10
Ovid, 38

Padgett, Penny, 10
Palmeri, Frank, 9
Patell, Cyrus R. K., 64
Pavlov, Ivan, 34
Pearce, Richard, 7
Pearson, Karl, 155
Peirce, Charles Sanders, 74
Penn, William, 137
Pérez-Llantada Auría, Carmen, 8
Petillon, Pierre-Yves, 38
Piercy, Marge, ix
Plato, 62
Poirier, Richard, x, 7
Porush, David, 9
Powers, Richard, ix
Pratt, Mary Louise, 132, 133, 139
Preston, Alison T. J., xii
Puetz, Manfred, 7
Purdy, Strother, 46
Putnam, Robert, 63

Quilligan, Maureen, 26

Rabelais, François, 145
Ram Dass, Baba, 24
Rand, Ayn, 60, 65
Ranke, Leopold von, 92
Rathenau, Walter, 44
Rawls, John, 64, 65
Reagan, Ronald, 3
Reed, Ishmael, x
Riffaterre, Michel, 147n2
Rimbaud, Arthur, 97
Rockwell, George Lincoln, 53–54
Rohland, Mark, xi
Rohman, Todd, xii
Rojek, Chris, 132, 139
Rose, Gillian, 132
Rosenblum, Nancy, 61
Ross, Andrew, 132
Rubin, Jerry, 40
Ruch, Allen, 10
Rushdie, Salman, 99
Russell, Charles, 114

Said, Edward, 98, 99, 102
Sale, Kirkpatrick, 118
Salinger, J. D., ix
Sandel, Michael, 63
Savage, Mike, 133
Savio, Mario, 24
Schachterle, Lance, 9
Schaub, Thomas H., 6, 45, 102, 159
Schmidt, Peter, 138n1
Schrödinger, Erwin, 74
Schultz, Max F., 82
Seed, David, 4, 6, 99, 157
Seidel, Michael, 9
Sell, Otto, 138n1
Shakespeare, William, 80, 98
Shannon, Claude E., 71
Shaw, Stephen, 133
Shi, David E., 59
Sigvardson, Joakim, 6
Simonelli, Frederick J., 54
Singer, Isaac Bashevis, 5
Slade, Joseph, 6, 31, 158
Slemon, Stephen, 137, 140
Smith, Henry Nash, 133
Smith, Marcus, 7, 26
Smith, Neil, 132
Snow, C. P., 66, 72
Sophocles, 98
Sorkin, Michael, 132
Spiegelman, Art, 132, 133, 140
Stalin, Joseph, 147n3
Steinbeck, John, 38
Stembridge, Jane, 19
Stephenson, Neal, ix, 140
Stravinsky, Igor, 68, 96
Strehle, Susan, 67
Styron, William, x
Sullivan, William M., 63, 65
Swidler, Ann, 63, 65

Tabbi, Joseph, 9
Tanner, Tony 6, 7, 9
Thompson, Gary, xii
Thompson, Hunter, x
Thompson, James Westfall, 124
Thrift, N. J., 133
Tindall, George B., 59
Tipton, Steven M., 63, 65
Tocqueville, Alexis de, 92
Tölölyan, Khachig, 7, 10, 26, 40, 106
Tolstoy, Leo, 51
Tse-tung, Mao, 22
Tuan, Yi-Fu, 132, 133, 140
Turner, Frederick Jackson, 133
Twain, Mark, 147n5

Urry, John, 132, 139

Varo, Remedios, 38, 71, 79, 163, 165
Varsava, Jerry, xii, 8, 64, 65n1
Voloshinov, Valentin, 147n3
Vonnegut, Kurt, Jr., 81
von Trotha, Lothar, ix, 94, 100–01

Walker, Alice, 19
Walker, Jack L., 19
Wallace, David Foster, ix
Ware, Tim, 10, 135, 138n1
Watson, Robert N., xi, 14
Webster, John, 80
Weisenburger, Steven, xii, 5, 10, 106, 107, 110
Weiskel, Thomas, 163, 164, 167
Wellman, William, 106, 113n1
Weyl, Hermann, 75
White, Hayden, x, 92, 98, 118, 124
Whitfield, George, 137
Whitfield, Stephen, 9
Whitman, Walt, 122
Wiener, Norbert, x, 31–33, 67
Wiener, Philip Paul, 74, 75
Wilde, Alan, 55
Williams, Frederick, 158
Williams, Raymond, 133
Williams, William Carlos, xi
Willis, Jim, 84
Wills, David, 6, 39
Winnicott, D. W., 42
Winston, Matthew, 5
Wittgenstein, Ludwig, 35
Wolfe, James, 137
Wolfe, Tom, x
Wolfley, Lawrence, 7, 41
Woolf, Virginia, 92

Young, James Dean, 6
Young, Robert J. C., 57